GAPS IN INTERNATIONAL ENVIRONMENTAL LAW: TOWARD A GLOBAL PACT FOR THE ENVIRONMENT

by
Maria Antonia Tigre

This book was prepared at the request of the International Council on Environmental Law (ICEL).

ENVIRONMENTAL LAW INSTITUTE
Washington, D.C.

1730 M Street NW, Washington, DC 20036

Cover design by Evan Odoms.

Published January 2020.

Printed in the United States of America
ISBN 978-1-58576-219-4

Contents

About the Author

Maria Antonia Tigre (S.JD. Candidate, LL.M., Elisabeth Haub School of Law at Pace University, J.D., Pontifícia Universidade Católica of Rio de Janeiro) is the Deputy Director for Latin America for the Global Network for the Study of Human Rights and the Environment (GNHRE) and a member of the IUCN World Commission on Environmental Law. She is the author and co-author of several publications on themes related to Latin American, regional, and international environmental law. Her current research specifically focuses on issues concerning environmental rights and the reshaping of the existing framework of international environmental law. Originally from Brazil, she also researches environmental protection of the Amazon ecosystem, with an emphasis on regional cooperation. Her first book, *Regional Cooperation in Amazonia: A Comparative Environmental Law Analysis*, was published in 2017. Ms. Tigre has previously worked in the private sector and at nonprofit organizations. She was a visiting scholar at Widener Law School and Maurice A. Dean Law School at Hofstra University.

Acknowledgements

To Nick,
May we bring your generation not only hope
But also answers.

This book was written during the hot summer of 2019 in New York City, as the Open-Ended Working Group met behind closed doors at the United Nations to decide on the future of the Global Pact for the Environment. Following the negotiations that unfolded, the idea of this book advanced based on one goal: to make a record of the steps toward a Global Pact and contribute to the negotiations moving forward. The process so far was far from linear, and supporters of the Global Pact were often discouraged, thinking the proposal would die off along tireless debates on the need for a new framework agreement on environmental principles. However, thanks to the commitment of the co-chairs of the working group, Francisco Duarte Lopes and Amal Mudallali, the initiative took yet another step towards becoming a reality. The recent resolution adopted by the General Assembly in 2019 calls for a political declaration to be adopted by 2022, at the 50th anniversary of the Stockholm Declaration and the 30th anniversary of the Rio Declaration.

Several people were essential in making sure this book was written and published timely as a companion for the next steps in the negotiation of a Global Pact. First and foremost, I am grateful to Prof. Nicholas Robinson, who supported me in every step of this process. As my thesis supervisor, he not only helped me choose the topic of my dissertation but advised me every step of the way, making sure my research was current and useful to other scholars, diplomats, and policymakers. His support was also essential in getting this research published by ELI Press. I am grateful to ELI Press for agreeing to publish this book in such a small timeframe. It was fortunate that the publication was also done in time to commemorate its 50th anniversary, and it is truly an honor to be a small part of the great work ELI has done over the past decades. In particular, I thank Scott Fulton, Jay Pendergrass, and Rachel Jean-Baptiste. I would also like to thank the International Council on Environmental Law (ICEL), represented by Victor Tafur and Prof. Nicholas Robinson, for publishing this book jointly with ELI and for its commitment to this idea.

I was fortunate to modestly contribute to the development of the Global Pact since its launch in 2017. Several people were essential in this initiative and kindly accepted my participation along the way. I am grateful to Yann Aguila, who championed this initiative, was available for interviews to help me gain better clarity on its inception, gave me access to early documents, and contributed his thoughts on the Global Pact's future in this publication. I am also extremely grateful to Teresa Parejo, who became an inspiration and friend along this journey. As one of the early champions of the Global Pact, she always included me in the discussions and invited me to think creatively about where the Pact was headed. She organized incredible events on the Global Pact at the Columbia Center on Sustainable Investment, which significantly advanced discussions on its merits, and were a great source of information for this book. Finally, I am grateful to Victor Tafur, who much supported this project as the UN Representative from ICEL, and was always available to exchange ideas about the Global Pact, the Nairobi discussions, and this book specifically.

As I finish writing this book, my son, Nicholas, turns one year old. The challenges of being an academic triple once one becomes a mother. My support system was essential to continue working while juggling the multiple functions I now have. On a personal level, there are a few people I would like to extend my gratitude. I am eternally grateful to my husband Marcelo, who has always been very supportive of my academic career but was even more so during the last year. Thank you for providing me the structure to keep going, and stepping in when it feels like too much. To Eli, who cared for my son and my house whenever I couldn't and did so like these were her own, I am beyond grateful. To my mother, always, always by my side. To my family, especially Nick, Rodrigo, Ciça, and Maneco. And, finally, to my Peanut friends, for bearing with me, always and forever.

List of Documents

List of Figures

Foreword

Scott Fulton and Nicholas A. Robinson

Maria Antonia Tigre provides a deep dive into the challenges that characterize international environmental law today. Her study describes contemporary negotiations about how, and even whether, to clarify and strengthen the norms that guide actions affecting the environment. The debates described here are about the future, but they rest on the foundation of the past five decades during which environmental law was created.

Fifty years ago, both the Environmental Law Institute (ELI) and the International Council on Environmental Law (ICEL) were established. That the field of environmental law did not then exist is significant. The founders of ELI and ICEL had both foresight and the courage of their convictions. In 1997, ELI honored ICEL's founders, Wolfgang and Françoise Burhenne-Guilmin, for their leadership in the Environmental Law Programme of the International Union for the Conservation of Nature (IUCN) and in building ICEL, which had been established in New Delhi to support IUCN's endeavors at creating and expanding environmental law internationally. Both ELI and ICEL are members of IUCN. ICEL honored one of ELI's inspirations, Russell Train, with its Elizabeth Haub Award for Environmental Law in 1980. Suffice it to say that since 1969, ELI and ICEL have been instrumental in building the legal principles and methods for, as ELI puts it, "making law work for people, places and the planet."[1]

ICEL commissioned this study, especially for the diplomats and jurists who are examining how to strengthen international environmental law. This book offers pathways to gain understanding of the competing trajectories about law and the environment. Questions abound: How extensively should government regulate conduct that affects the environment? Can burdens of applying proposed new laws be added when existing laws remain to be fully implemented? What is the just balance between aspirational policies and norms versus binding rules and regulations? What do the basic juridical principles of care for the Earth mean in each different legal system? Who should decide these questions? These and other issues permeate the dialogue among nations described in this study.

---

1. *See* ELI's "Strategic Vision," *at* https://www.eli.org/strategic-vision.

The outcome of the debates is uncertain, but it is certain that the debates will continue and grow in urgency as problems worsen. Land degradation, sea-level rise, intensifying storm events, biodiversity collapse, exhaustion of nature resources, and persistent pollution increasingly erode the economy of nations. For instance, in 2019, the World Health Organization finds that air pollution remains the greatest risk to human health worldwide.[2] To present this book in 2019 is timely and in the best traditions of both ICEL and ELI as institutions dedicated to advancing what we and the UN now call "the environmental rule of law."[3]

We have confidence in the positive outcome of the debates about law and the environment because of what we have experienced since 1969. We are excited to publish this book. The debate over the proposed "Global Pact for the Environment" offers insights into the challenges environmental law faces in the next fifty years. The Global Pact seeks to codify a set of norms. The right to the environment is now commonly found in constitutions around the world, the idea being that "[e]very person has the right to life in an ecologically sound environment adequate for their health, well-being, dignity, culture and fulfilment, and every State or institution, every person, natural or legal, public or private, has the duty to contribute at their own legal to the conservation, protection, restoration and evolution of Earths' ecosystems."[4]

While the right to the environment, and other principles, are increasingly recognized in national laws and several international agreements, international lawyers still contest this legal obligation. The contending beliefs about national self-interests inhibit arriving at a quick consensus about any next generation of environmental norms. The same questioning is found in different views on how to address gaps in the legal framework for managing global environmental issues. Such debates about environment rights and duties will mark the next fifty years of deliberations. Arguments about how environmental law should guide sustainable development will generate a new consensus on law reflecting the substantive, agreed aims of the United Nations Sustainable Development Goals.[5] The basis for this positive prognosis is found in the accomplishments that nations have attained during the past five decades.

2. WHO, *at* https://www.who.int/emergencies/ten-threats-to-global-health-in-2019.
3. ELI authored the first Global Report on the Environmental Rule of Law Report (January 2019) released by the United Nations Environment. The Report is available online at: https://www.eli.org/sites/default/files/docs/erol/EnvironmentalRuleofLaw_%20FirstGlobalReport.pdf.
4. Adapted from Principles 1 and 2 of the proposed Global Pact for the Environment, in a Motion submitted by ICEL to the IUCN World Conservation Congress, scheduled for June 2020 in Marseille, France. See www.iucncongress2020.org. The right to the environment is recognized in more than 100 nations. David Boyd, The Environmental Rights Revolution (University of British Columbia Press, 2012).
5. *See* https://www.un.org/sustainabledevelopment/sustainable-development-goals/.

In 1987, the United Nations World Commission on Environment and Development published its historic report, *Our Common Future*,[6] which is also known as the Brundtland Commission Report, after its chairwoman, Norwegian Prime Minister Gro Harlem Brundtland. Still timely today, this report summed up our persistent environmental problems well: "The Earth is one, but the world is not." The hydrologic cycle, carbon cycle, other planetary geophysical cycles and the world's oceans link the ecosystems and human settlements on every continent, and yet local and national laws govern only their own country's territory, and adjacent coastal waters. There are precious few laws to manage human impacts on Earth's natural systems. Since environmental laws vary greatly from country to country, inconsistent statutes in one nation can, when it comes to planetary problems, often nullify the effectiveness of laws in another. One government can carefully protect the habitat of a migratory species, while another nation sustains rapid loss of its habitat. Pollution is controlled in one region but increases with weak or non-existent controls in another country. Transboundary pollution is indeed growing globally. It is no wonder that the UN's latest "Global Environmental Outlook" reports a rapid deterioration of the environment in all regions.[7]

The Brundtland Commission embraced a recommendation made earlier by the International Union for the Conservation of Nature (IUCN),[8] which had called for governments to pursue what IUCN called sustainable development. The World Commission's definition caught the attention of policymakers everywhere: "Sustainable development is development that meets the needs of the present without compromising the ability of future generations to meet their own needs."

Following the United Nations Conference on the Human Environment held in Stockholm in 1972, nations began to enact laws to abate air and water pollution and to better protect flora and fauna. The Stockholm Conference led the United Nations to establish its Environment Programme, UNEP, which assisted nations as they developed their first legal provisions for environmental protection. By 1987, most nations boasted having enacted their first generation of environmental protection laws, but the statutes were uneven in scope and most countries lacked adequate experts to implement them fully. Pollution persisted and often increased. Biodiversity losses esca-

6. World Commission on Environment and Development ("Bruntlund Commission"), Our Common Future (Oxford University Press, 1987), available online at https://www.sustainabledevelopment2015.org/AdvocacyToolkit/index.php/earth-summit-history/historical-documents/92-our-common-future.

7. UN Environment, Sixth Environmental Outlook, GEO-6, (2019), *at* https://www.unenvironment.org/resources/global-environment-outlook-6.

8. IUCN/WWF/UNEP, *Caring for the Earth*, *at* https://portals.iucn.org/library/efiles/documents/CFE-003.pdf.

lated. Governments realized that more effective governance was needed. These concerns led nations in 1992 to convene in Rio de Janeiro, Brazil, the largest summit meeting ever held: the UN Conference on Environment & Development (UNCED), dubbed the "Earth Summit."

At UNCED, the world's governments produced two remarkable documents: (a) ***Agenda 21***, a blueprint agreed by consensus, consisting of 800 pages of proposals that all countries agreed would promote environmentally sustainable development, and (b) the ***Rio Declaration,*** a set of agreed principles that each government embraced as the foundational norms for sound environmental stewardship.

Between 1992 and 2019, nearly every country has sought to implement the sensible recommendations of *Agenda 21*, and increasingly observes the norms of the Rio Declaration, as their capabilities permit. For example, virtually all nations have enacted environmental impact assessment laws, as prescribed in Rio Principle 17, and have laws affording public access to environmental information, as provided in Rio Principle 10. Sustainable best practices have been restated by the International Standards Organization (ISO),[9] and many companies and governments have adapted and adopted the ISO methods. These practices, laws and principles have proven that they can meaningfully contribute to the protection of the environment and sustainable socio-economic development. However, while they are all necessary, they alone are not sufficient.

The first generation of environmental statutes, treaties, and principles demonstrably have not yet been sufficient to stem the global environmental degradation. The Millennium Ecosystem Assessment[10] found that fully one-half of the Earth's ecosystems are impaired, and the Intergovernmental Panel on Climate Change's Special Report "Global Warming 1.5° C" (2018)[11] warned of devastating consequences from alteration to the carbon cycle and weather patterns in all regions. The Intergovernmental Science-Policy Platform on Biodiversity and Ecosystem Services (IPBES) in 2018 reports that soil erosion and land degradation is at acute levels that threaten the livelihoods of 3.2 billion people.[12] Some further, more effective, environmental norms evidently are needed.

9. For example, ISO Standards 9,000, 14,000 and 16,000. *See* https://www.techstreet.com/info/iso?sid=msn&utm_source=bing&utm_medium=cpc&msclkid=e8ff5633cdf718a45d0d0b553a38a874&format=html.
10. https://www.researchgate.net/publication/297563785_Millennium_Ecosystem_Assessment_Ecosystems_and_human_well-being_synthesis.
11. https://www.ipcc.ch/sr15.
12. *See* https://www.ipbes.net/news/media-release-biodiversity-nature's-contributions-continue-%C2%A0dangerous-decline-scientists-warn; and *Nature* (28 March 2018), *at* https://www.nature.

How might nations scale up and enhance their environmental laws more effectively to contain escalating environmental deterioration? France's President Emmanuel Macron proposed "The Global Pact for the Environment" as a new set of "rules of the road" to align all nations behind practices that might safeguard the planet for future generations. Supported by many environmental legal experts, Macron recommended in 2017 to the United Nations General Assembly that nations adopt a new *Global Pact for the Environment.* Debates began. In May of 2018, the General Assembly asked the UN Secretary General to prepare a report on the current state of international environmental law. Entitled, "Gaps in International Environmental Law and Environment-Related Instruments: Towards A Global Pact on the Environment," (A/73/419), the report appeared on November 30th, as the General Assembly had required. This report was widely evaluated because it was the first report on the status of international environmental law ever prepared by the UN Secretary General.[13] The United Nations General Assembly endorsed intergovernmental consultations in advance of 2022 by consensus, when it accepted the outcome of its Working Group deliberations held in Nairobi in the first half of 2019.[14]

Both the proposed Global Pact for the Environment and the Secretary General's Report have become the focus of significant diplomatic debate. Maria Antonia Tigre provides, in this book, the chronology of these debates and access to its sources. It is an essential reference for anyone who cares about the future of the environment and of environmental law.

The current and next phases of deliberations about the gaps in international environmental law will reveal that much remains to be done to attain or restore "sustainability" in socio-economic development. It takes years of negotiation to prepare new multilateral environmental agreements (MEAs), and many of those that we now have are barely implemented. Countries are likely to agree upon a set of "soft law" principles, as they did the 1992 Rio Principles, more quickly than they will negotiate the several new MEAs

---

com/articles/d41586-018-03891-1.

13. *See, e.g.*, The Environmental Law Institute (ELI), webinar on "The Global Pact and the Future of Environmental Governance," *at* https://www.eli.org/vibrant-environment-blog/global-pact-and-future-environmental-governance; and Stewart M. Patrick, "A Global Pact for the Environment," *World Politics Review* (22 April 2019) available through the Council on Foreign Relations, *at* https://www.cfr.org/article/global-pact-environment; and the Note on the Secretary General's Report (10 December 2018), by the International Council of Environmental Law (ICEL), *available at* https://www.iucn.org/sites/dev/files/noteforunsgenvllawrptdec2018_final.pdf; The ICEL Note and Secretary General's Report were the subject of a Side Event on the "Global Pact for the Environment: Strengthening the Implementation of International Environmental Law," 10 December 2018, archived at https://globalpactenvironment.org/en/event/un-side-event-strengthening-the-implementation-of-international-environmental-law-commentaries-on-the-sgs-report/.
14. *See* UN Doc. Res. 73/333 (5 September 2019).

needed to fill gaps that threaten Earth's environment, e.g., plastic wastes washed into the oceans, or "acid rain" from air pollution across Asia and the Southern hemisphere, or coping with larger wild fires everywhere. International laws are lacking on these and other "gaps." Rather than waiting years for nations to embrace a comprehensive set of gap-filling treaties, the international community needs to empower governments at all levels to tackle environmental challenges as they appear. Such guidance was the métier of the 1992 Rio Declaration, and its success. Might a declaration of principles like those offered in the draft Global Pact for the Environment build on that experience and success?

If all nations know that they have agreed upon the same basic principles, history suggests that the likelihood that they will conduct themselves in accordance with those norms will increase greatly.[15] As has occurred under the guidance of the 1992 Rio Declaration, gradually, in all regions, laws and behaviors should shift in the direction of the stabilizing and conserving ecological and other environmental benefits for society contemplated by those principles. As nations consider how to commemorate the 1972 Stockholm Declaration, and the 1992 Rio Declaration, a launch by the General Assembly of preparation of a new Declaration, with the goal of adoption in the 50th anniversary year of 2022, would be punctuation of a powerful sort. Doing so could serve to stabilize patterns for the human environment's sustainable development, and reassure socio-economic relations in all regions. It could also establish the environmental norms guiding all nations for the next two decades.

The Earth ***is*** one, but the world remains fragmented. Managing to live in Earth's dynamic and complex environment requires new skills and techniques. Cognitive technologies, such as Artificial Intelligence and Block Chain technologies,[16] offer new methods for managing environmental quality, and breakthroughs in sensing technology promise to dramatically enhance assessment of environmental conditions.[17] The next generation of environmental norms will need to consider how to engage the emerging cognitive and sensing technologies to ramp up environmental conservation in a way that is more fully responsive to escalating threats and at a scale that is capable of containing and reversing their impacts. There is promise here for re-establishing the foundations for sustaining human relationships with

15. Louis Henkin, How Nations Behave: Law and Policy (Columbia University Press, 1979).
16. *See, e.g.*, Primavera De Filippi and Aaron Wright, Blockchain and the Law (Harvard University Press, 2018).
17. See the International Telecommunications Union's annual conference, "AIforGood," *at* https://aiforgood.itu.int/.

nature. We do not pretend to know how this will come to be, but pursuit of a new set of environmental norms stands to stimulate the international cooperation needed for this resilient future state to emerge.

The debates explored in this book set the stage for determining whether or not nations can agree on a new set of principles, like those of the proposed Global Pact. Maria Antonia Tigre's book equips each reader with the knowledge to enter confidently into these ongoing debates toward the further evolution of international environmental law.

Scott Fulton
President, Environmental Law Institute
Member of the International Council of Environmental Law

Nicholas A. Robinson
Executive Governor,
International Council of Environmental Law
Member of the Board of the Environmental Law Institute

November 2019

Introduction

I. The Deteriorating State of Our Environment

At the fourth session of the United Nations Environment Assembly (UNEA), held in Nairobi in March 2019, the UN Environment warned policymakers that the world is not on track to achieve the environmental dimension of the Sustainable Development Goals (SDGS), and other internationally agreed environmental goals by 2030, or to deliver long-term sustainability by 2050.[1] The overall condition of the global environment has continued to deteriorate, despite environmental policy efforts across countries and regions.[2] Unsustainable production and consumption patterns and climate change have degraded the Earth's ecosystems, endangering the ecological foundations of society and hindering policy efforts.[3] With the global population reaching 7.5 billion in 2018, and median projections estimating nearly 10 billion by 2050, this scenario is likely to worsen.[4] Urgent action and strengthened international cooperation are needed to reverse those negative trends and restore the planetary and human health.

Since 1880, the global average surface temperature has increased by between approximately 0.8°C and 1.2°C.[5] Current efforts remain inadequate to halt a rise of 4°C in ambient Earth temperature above the 19th century.[6] Recent studies indicate that humans may be causing an increase of as much as 5°C.[7] A major species extinction is unfolding, which scientists have characterized as the sixth mass extinction.[8] Without complete data that provides a full picture of the challenges we are facing, the current extinction rate could be more than 100 times higher than normal,[9] which could be considered a "biological annihilation."[10] Although governance efforts are progressing, greater efforts are required to achieve international objectives,

1. United Nations Environment Assembly of the United Nations Environment Programme, GEO-6 Key Messages, UNEP/EA.4/INF.18, para. 4 (Feb. 12, 2019).
2. UNEP, Global Environment Outlook (GEO-6): Summary for Policymakers 4 (2019).
5. *Id.* at 7.
6. Intergovernmental Panel on Climate Change, Global Warming 1.5° Celsius (Special Report 15, October 2018), accessible at https://www.ipcc.ch/sr15/.
7. Paul Voosen, *New Climate Models Forecast a Warming Surge*, 364 Science 222 (2019).
8. GEO-6, *supra* note 2, at 8.
9. Gerardo Ceballos, et al., *Accelerated Modern Human-Induced Species Losses: Entering the Sixth Mass Extinction*, 1 Science Advances (2015).
10. Gerardo Ceballos, et al., *Population Losses and the Sixth Mass Extinction*, 114 Proc. Nat'l Acad. Sci. U.S. Am. E6089 (2017).

such as the Aichi Biodiversity Targets within the United Nations Convention on Biological Diversity's Strategic Plan for Biodiversity 2011–2020, and the SDGS.[11]

Ocean warming and acidity,[12] rising sea levels,[13] mass coral bleaching,[14] unsustainable exploitation of living marine resources,[15] and marine plastic litter, including microplastics, threatens the health of our marine and coastal ecosystems. Land degradation, desertification,[16] deforestation,[17] and over-exploitation of natural resources provide an increasing threat for human well-being.[18] Population growth, urbanization, water pollution and unsustainable development induce pressure on water resources across the world, which is further exacerbated by climate change.[19]

II. The Anthropocene and Planetary Boundaries

These combined trends provide strong evidence that humankind is now rivaling Nature in its impact on the functioning of the Earth system.[20] The growing impact of human activity on earth and the atmosphere emphasize the role of mankind in geology and ecology.[21] Humans have so irretrievably altered the Earth in the past centuries that the Anthropocene, a new geological epoch, has begun.[22] The term Anthropocene suggests that the Earth is now moving out of its current geological epoch, the Holocene. The Holocene represents an epoch in which the environment has been unusually stable.[23] Changes occurred naturally and according to the Earth's regulatory capacity. This shift from a period of stability has occurred largely because

11. GEO-6, *supra* note 2, at 9.
12. Lijing Cheng, Kevin E. Trenberth, Peter Jacobs, Yongxin Zhang & John Fasullo, *Hurricane Harvey Links to Ocean Heat Content and Climate Change Adaptation*, Earth's Future 1 (2018); United Nations, The First Global Integrated Marine Assessment: World Ocean Assessment I (Cambridge University Press, 2017).
13. United Nations, *supra* note 12, at 14.
14. GEO-6, *supra* note 2, at 10.
15. United Nations, *supra* note 12, at 11.
16. GEO-6, *supra* note 2, at 12.
17. *Id.* at 12.
18. UNEA, *supra* note 1, at para. 10.
19. GEO-6, *supra* note 2, at 12.
20. Will Steffen, et al., *The Anthropocene: Conceptual and Historical Perspectives*, 369 Philosophical Transactions of the Royal Society 842; 843 (2011). *See also* Paul J. Crutzen, *Geology of Mankind*, 415 Nature 23 (2002).
21. Paul J. Crutzen & Eugene F. Stoermer, *The "Anthropocene,"* 41 Global Change Newsletter 17 (2000).
22. Simon L. Lewis & Mark A. Maslin, *Defining the Anthropocene*, 519 Nature 171 (2015). Jan Zalasiewicz, et al., *The Working Group on the Anthropocene: Summary of Evidence and Interim Recommendations*, 19 Anthropocene 55 (2017).
23. Johan Rockström, et al., *A Safe Operating Space for Humanity*, 461 Nature 472 (2009).

of human activity, since humankind has become a global geological force in its own right.[24]

To meet the challenge of maintaining the Holocene state, scholars at the Stockholm Resilience Centre have proposed a framework of planetary boundaries which defines borders in which human activities can take place without the risk of transgressing the Earth system's ecological thresholds.[25] The team, led by Rockström, identified the following nine Earth system biophysical processes that determine the planet's ability to auto-regulate and therefore maintain its Holocene-like conditions: climate change, stratospheric ozone depletion, land system change, global freshwater use, rate of biodiversity loss,[26] ocean acidification, interference with phosphorus and nitrogen cycles,[27] atmospheric aerosol loading and chemical pollution.[28] These are interdependent, meaning that exceeding the boundaries of one lead to the a change of transgression in another. Four of these boundaries have already entered the uncertainty zone: climate change, land system change, biosphere integrity and biogeochemical flows.[29]

The scientific data makes it clear that the state of the world is deteriorating. In a few instances, we have reached a tipping point. Governments have responded by enacting environmental laws and policies, always trying to catch up with the new environmental problem faced. The same occurs at the international level, in which the international community negotiates new treaties to address global problems. From a policy perspective, UNEP was created to provide a global framework for environmental protection. Still, the world is in trouble. Clearly, the current response is insufficient. The Anthropocene calls for transformative law to respond to the socio-ecological crisis and promote human stewardship of natural systems.[30] Achieving internationally agreed environmental goals on pollution control, clean-up and efficiency improvements is crucial, yet insufficient to achieve the SDGS. A more holistic answer is required. Urgent cross-sectoral policy actions are needed to address the challenges of sustainable development.[31] Transformative change

---

24. Steffen, et al., *supra* note 20, at 843.
25. Rockström, et al., *supra* note 23, at 472. The nine "planetary boundaries" represent thresholds in major planetary processes used to help define a "safe operating space for humanity."
26. Later revised to include genetic and functional diversity and renamed biosphere integrity.
27. Later renamed biogeochemical flows.
28. Rockström, et al., *supra* note 23, at 473.
29. Will Steffen, et al., *Planetary Boundaries: Guiding Human Development on a Changing Planet*, 347 Science 1259855-1 (2015).
30. Nicholas A. Robinson, *Keynote: Sustaining Society in the Anthropocene Epoch*, 41 Denv. J. Int'l L. & Pol'y 467 (2013).
31. United Nations Environment Programme, Meeting of the Bureau of the UN Environment Assembly, Finding the Right Theme for the 2020 UN Environment Assembly, para. 14 (17 June 2019), http://

is needed to enable and combine long-term strategic and integrated policy-making while building bottom-up social, cultural, institutional and technological innovation.[32] Robust international cooperation is one of the key features of effective environmental policies for sustainable development.[33]

III. The Necessity of New Law

Changes in the Earth system mark a distinct new geological period in the Earth's history. The Earth is moving into an unstable state as a result of the global human imprint on the biosphere. Humanity has become a geological agent in much the same way as a volcano or meteor, able to change the Earth and its systems.[34] As Robinson explains, determining the existence of the Anthropocene "is a scientific one, not a socio-economic or cultural determination, yet its greatest implications may lie in the realm of the social sciences."[35] Anthropocene has become a popular lens through which to consider the pure scientific, and increasingly the social aspects of past, present and future global environmental change.[36] We need to prepare politically, legally, socially and economically for the adaptation to those global environmental changes that can no longer be avoided.[37]

The Anthropocene calls for re-imaginations of the role of environmental law, its components and aspects. As Kotzé puts it, the law "cannot continue to comfortably rest on foundations that evolved under the harmonious Holocene, because under the type of biospheric conditions in the Anthropocene, 'Holocene law' will arguably be unable to establish and maintain the type of societal ordering it typically would have sought to achieve under 'normal' Holocene conditions."[38] The Anthropocene pushes for a new cognitive framework, providing an opportunity to question and re-imagine the legal interventions that are best able to respond to the current global socio-ecological crisis. This space was previously preserved for fragmented, issue-specific and narrow legal enquiries that were adequate for a less alarmist expressions

wedocs.unep.org/bitstream/handle/20.500.11822/28387/Note%20on%20theme%20for%20discussion%20by%20the%20Environment%20Assembly%20Bureau.pdf?sequence=15&isAllowed=y.

32. *Id.* para. 15.
33. *Id.* para. 16.
34. Mike Hodson & Simon Marvin, *Urbanism in the Anthropocene: Ecological Urbanism or Premium Ecological Enclaves?*, 14 City 298 (2010).
35. Nicholas A. Robinson, *Fundamental Principles of Law for the Anthropocene?*, 44 Envtl. Pol'y & Law 13 (2014). 13.
36. Louis J. Kotzé, Global Environmental Constitutionalism in the Anthropocene 5 (Hart Publishing Paperback Edition ed. 2016).
37. *Id.* at 6.
38. *Id.* at 6.

of urgency.[39] The Anthropocene calls for transformative law to respond to the socio-ecological crisis and promote human stewardship of natural systems.[40] A globally binding instrument that sets a framework for international environmental law might be just what is needed to navigate through the challenges faced in this new epoch.[41]

IV. Foundation of the Global Pact

When the 1948 Universal Declaration of Human Rights (UDHR)[42] was adopted, the world was a much different place. After the horrors of World War II, nations throughout the globe craved a universal charter that specified individual human rights and freedoms. Environmental concerns were then not a widespread global problem. As environmental consciousness emerged in the 1970s, human rights were already firmly established. As a result, environmental rights were not included among fundamental rights and freedoms in major international human rights agreements,[43] and environmental problems created by humankind exacerbated.

Without a framework that laid the basic ground rules for the development of international environmental law, the field advanced inorganically. It addressed each environmental problem separately, through the careful negotiation of individual agreement. As a result, an abundant web of environmental treaties slowly emerged. Today, over 1,300 multilateral environmental agreements (MEAs) and 2,200 bilateral environmental agreements exist.[44] These encompass a wide range of topics, from biodiversity loss to climate change and desertification, as well as regions, from the Amazon rainforest to Antarctica. However, this framework still lacks a binding treaty harmonizing them, linking the portions that make up international environmental law. Given the obvious correlation between environmental problems, their regulating laws must also be interconnected. Sectoral agreements were essential for multilateralism, and the web of treaties could only be achieved piece

39. *Id.* at 6-7.
40. Robinson, *supra* note 30, at 488.
41. Luisa Leme & Carin Zissis (Producer), *LatAM in Focus: Can International Law Save the Amazon? (Interview with Maria Antonia Tigre)* (AS/COA, 2019), *available at* https://www.as-coa.org/watchlisten/latam-focus-can-international-law-save-amazon.
42. Universal Declaration of Human Rights, G.A. Res. 217A (III), U.N. Doc. A/810 at 71, art. 3 (1948) (UDHR).
43. *See* UDHR; International Covenant on Civil and Political Rights (adopted 16 December 1966, entered into force 23 March 1976) 999 UNTS 171 (ICCPR) and International Covenant on Economic, Social and Cultural Rights (adopted 16 December 1966, entered into force 3 January 1976) 993 UNTS 3 (ICESCR).
44. *See* IEA Database Home, Int'l Envtl. Agreements (IEA) Database Project, https://iea.uoregon.edu (last visited Mar. 27, 2019).

by piece. Nonetheless, this approach has often been criticized for being too fragmented. As highlighted by the UN Secretary-General (UNSG) in the 2018 report on the state of international environmental law, fragmentation leads to many gaps in the field, with challenges left unattended. In an ever-worsening state of the environment, it is time to address fragmentation. The Anthropocene calls for innovative legal solutions that can confront the new environmental challenges emerging each day.

The idea of a comprehensive and legally binding document enshrining fundamental environmental rights and obligations has been exhaustively discussed. A similar universal agreement has been suggested before.[45] These relate to the codification of environmental principles, environmental rights, or the improvement of the governance structure of international environmental law. Several frameworks fell short of a binding treaty, but nevertheless provided a basis for the development of international environmental law. These include the Stockholm Declaration,[46] the World Charter for Nature,[47] and the Rio Declaration.[48] In 1995, the IUCN's World Commission on Environmental Law designed a treaty to serve as an umbrella agreement to "govern the interactions of nations with the Earth's natural systems," based on the absence of a "unifying umbrella agreement to facilitate integrating environment and development."[49] The Draft International Covenant on the Environment and Development (ICED), now in its fifth edition, consolidated environmental principles, much like the Global Pact has done.[50] Through the consolidation of environmental principles, the ICED provides an international "framework for implementing sustainability at all levels of society." In 2016, the IUCN adopted the World Declaration on the Environmental Rule of Law, which similarly promotes the adoption of core principles

---

45. *See, i.e.*, Amedeo Postiglione, an Italian Corte Suprema di Cassazione judge, has argued for a "Universal Convention for the Environment as a Human Right." *See* Amedeo Postiglione, *A More Efficient International Law on the Environment and Setting Up an International Court for the Environment Within the United Nations*, 20 Envtl. L. 321, 322 (1990). A research team in Ukraine, led by Prof. Yuriy Tunytsya, advocated for a World Environment Constitution in 2006. *See* Yuriy Y. Tunytsya & Ihor P. Soloviy, *The World Environmental Constitution as an Instrument of International Environmental Governance*, 10 Interdisc. Envtl. Rev. 85 (2008).
46. Report of the United Nations Conference on the Human Environment, Stockholm 5–16 June 1972, UN Doc. A/CONF.48/14/Rev.1 (1973).
47. UNGA, World Charter for Nature, UN Doc. A/RES/37/7 (28 October 1982).
48. Rio Declaration on Environment and Development in Report of the United Nations Conference on Environment and Development, UN Doc. A/CONF.151/26 (vol I) (12 August 1992) Annex.
49. Nicholas A. Robinson, *IUCN's Proposed Covenant on Environment & Development*, 13 Pace Envtl. L. Rev. 133; 134; 138 (1995).
50. IUCN & ICEL, *Draft International Covenant on Environment and Development* (Fifth Edition, 2015), *available at* https://sustainabledevelopment.un.org/content/documents/2443Covenant_5th_edition.pdf.

and norms as the legal foundation for environmental justice.[51] These documents provide the foundation for the Global Pact. But while they helped promote environmental principles, they also illustrate the limitations of a statement of principles in soft law instruments, highlighting the need for a binding agreement.[52]

In parallel, legal scholars have advocated for the recognition of a human right to a healthy environment. This approach focuses on the adoption of new human rights rather than more broadly supporting the integrity of life's support system and the environment. Spearheaded by French Professor Michel Prieur, the International Center for Comparative Environmental Law (CIDCE) drafted a Covenant on the Right to Environment in 2017.[53] Prof. John Knox's last thematic report as Special Rapporteur on Human Rights and the Environment presented sixteen framework principles, which set out essential obligations of States under human rights law as they relate to the enjoinment of a safe, clean, healthy and sustainable environment.[54] This same trend has been picked up by national and regional courts. In 2018, the Inter-American Court of Human Rights recognized an autonomous right to the environment in a landmark decision, reinforcing this approach and establishing the role of courts in pushing environmental law forward when international and national law is still lacking.[55] While this approach has received broad academic support, several delegates firmly opposed the idea of a third covenant during the Nairobi sessions, arguing that this discussion was beyond the existing mandate and should instead continue within the human rights regime.[56] While the argument is debatable, it shows the lack of diplomatic appetite for such a discussion.

A third approach called for reshaping the institutional framework of international environmental law. Similarly, this has been broadly discussed in

51. IUCN, World Commission on Environmental Law, *World Declaration on the Environmental Rule of Law* (2016), *available at* https://www.iucn.org/sites/dev/files/content/documents/world_declaration_on_the_environmental_rule_of_law_final_2017-3-17.pdf.
52. Yann Aguila & Jorge E. Viñuales, *A Global Pact for the Environment: Conceptual foundations*, 28 Rev. Eur., Comp. & Int'l Envtl. L. 3 (2019).
53. Centre International de Droit Comparé de L'Environnement, *Draft on the International Convention on the Human Right to the Environment, available at* https://cidce.org/ (2017).
54. UN Doc. A/HRC/37/59 (24 January 2018).
55. Inter-American Court of Human Rights, Opinión Consultiva OC-23/17 (Nov. 17, 2017), Solicitada por la República de Colombia, Medio Ambiente y Derechos Humanos, *available at* http://www.aida-americas.org/sites/default/files/oc23_corte_idh.pdf. *See* Maria Antonia Tigre & Natalia Urzola, The 2017 Inter-American Court's Advisory Opinion: Changing the Paradigm for International Environmental Law in the Anthropocene (upcoming).
56. Peter Doran, et al., *Summary of the First Substantive Session of the Ad Hoc Open-Ended Working Group Towards a Global Pact for the Environment: 14-18 January 2019*, Vol. 35 No. 1, International Institute for Sustainable Development (2019), *available at* http://enb.iisd.org/unep/globalpact/oewg1/.

academia, often with a proposal for a new institution such as the World Environment Organization.[57] The recognition that there is still much needed work to be done to reshape the institutional framework was constantly repeated in Nairobi. Explicitly, delegates agreed on the need to address institutional fragmentation and the weak coordination between treaties. However, one of the main outputs of the discussions was the need to reinforce existing institutions such as UNEP and UNEA rather than create new ones, showing the lack of support for this alternative.[58]

The UNSG's Report identified gaps in the scope and content of environmental principles, environmental rights, and environmental governance. The approaches mentioned address these gaps in different ways. While the codification of environmental principles received some pushback by Member States, it received broad support from others. Ultimately, the Global Pact is a response to one of the gaps identified, but it can be part of a multi-pronged solution negotiated at the UN to address gaps in international environmental law.

V. The Global Pact for the Environment

International environmental law developed by steadily responding to environmental problems. Environmental policy-making emerged in a global context at the 1972 Stockholm Conference. Concerns were then limited to conservation and management of natural resources, and it was impossible to predict the severity or variety of problems that would arise. Rather than centralized around a general rule, environmental norms advanced in response to emerging problems, negotiated by way of "specific" regimes considered in relative isolation.[59] When an environmental problem arises, it is identi-

57. Frank Biermann, *The Case for a World Environment Organization*, 42 Environment 22 (2000). Frank Biermann, A World Environment Organization: Solution or Threat for Effective International Environmental Governance? (Routledge Ebook Edition ed. 2005). Adil Najam, *The Case Against a New International Environmental Organization*, 9 Global Governance 367 (2003). John Whalley & Ben Zissimos, *What Could a World Environmental Organization Do?*, 1 Global Envtl. Pol. 29 (2001).
58. Doran, *supra* note 55; Peter Doran, et al., *Summary of the Second Substantive Session of the Ad Hoc Open-Ended Working Group Towards a Global Pact for the Environment*, Vol. 35 No. 2, International Institute for Sustainable Development (2019), *available at* http://enb.iisd.org/unep/globalpact/oewg2/; Peter Doran, et al., *Summary of the Third Substantive Session of the Ad Hoc Open-Ended Working Group Towards a Global Pact for the Environment: 20-22 May 2019*, Vol. 35 No. 3, International Institute for Sustainable Development (2019), *available at* http://enb.iisd.org/download/pdf/enb3503e.pdf.
59. Norichika Kanie, *Governance With Multilateral Environmental Agreements: A Healthy or Ill-Equipped Fragmentation?*, *in* Global Environmental Governance: Perspectives on the Current Debate 70 (Walter Hoffmann & Lydia Swart eds., 2007); Harro van Asselt, *Managing the Fragmentation of International Environmental Law: Forests at the Intersection of the Climate and Biodiversity Regimes*, 44 J. Int'l L. & Pol. 1205; 1208; 1209 (2012).

fied individually as a matter of international legal concern.[60] The approach in international environmental law is inherently reactive. Each agreement addresses a specific challenge and is legally and institutionally distinct from the others. However, the causes and consequences of environmental problems are transboundary and sometimes global in nature. It demands international cooperation, and renders a coordinated approach challenging.[61] The incremental, piecemeal and reactive nature of international environmental law has resulted in a legal framework composed of hundreds of MEAs segregated by topic, sector, and territory.[62]

Fragmentation is inevitable given the "piecemeal, incremental and reactive nature of international environmental law-making."[63] While it is a frequent phenomenon in international law and multilateral decision-making, other fields rely on a binding framework instrument(s) with rules that provide coordination and coherence.[64] International environmental law still lacks such a framework.[65] There is no single overarching normative framework that sets out what might be characterized as rules and principles of general application.[66] The many advantages brought by fragmentation do not necessarily mean that the perceived weaknesses should be left unaddressed. Given the role of environmental principles as building blocks, serving to supplement or complement more specific rules, aiding interpretation, filling gaps, and ultimately unifying the sectoral approach of international environmental law, the UNSG has recommended the adoption of an overarching legal framework of environmental principles. It noted that a comprehensive and unifying international instrument clarifying all the principles of environmental law would contribute to making them more effective and strengthen their implementation.[67]

Since 1972, legal scholars and environmental advocates have encouraged the adoption of a legally binding framework for international environmental law. The idea returns in waves, whenever the political momentum seems favorable to such an agreement. But while several soft law instruments have

60. Bethany L. Hicks, *Treaty Congestion in International Environmental Law: The Need for Greater International Coordination*, 32 U. Rich. L. Rev. 1643; 1646-47 (1999).
61. UN Secretary-General, Gaps in International Environmental Law and Environment-Related Instruments: Towards a Global Pact for the Environment, UN Doc. A/73/419, 43 (30 November 2018).
62. Gerhard Loibl, *International Environmental Regulations—Is a Comprehensive Body of Law Emerging or Is Fragmentation Going to Stay?*, *in* International Law Between Universalism and Fragmentation: Festschrift in Honour of Gerhard Hafner (Isabelle Buffard, et al. eds., 2008).
63. UN Secretary-General, *supra* note 60, at 43.
64. *Id.* at 4. Examples include international human rights law, international trade law, and international law of the seas.
65. *Id.* at 5.
66. *Id.* at 4.
67. *Id.* at 6-5; 43.

been adopted at the United Nations, States have yet to embrace a binding treaty providing guidelines for international environmental law. The most recent initiative to adopt a legally binding agreement on environmental principles is the Global Pact. This initiative had an unorthodox origin. Rather than emerging within the UN, it was brought forward by environmental legal scholars. Dissatisfied with the current state of international environmental law, they envisioned the Global Pact as a solution to improve effectiveness and better prepare the field for the never-ending emerging challenges of the Anthropocene.

After careful drafting by a group of scholars from a wide range of countries, the Global Pact was embraced by the government of France and presented at the United Nations General Assembly (UNGA) in 2017. It was the first time a legally binding instrument codifying environmental principles was proposed by a head of state at the United Nations. In a high-level diplomatic dialogue, States began discussing whether to codify environmental principles as hard law. The response to the proposal was immediately divided, with some Member States favoring the idea, and others pointedly opposing it. Conscious of its unorthodox genesis and of the immediate pushback, the UNGA took a step back and requested a study of the current state of international environmental law prior to proposing any potential solution.

In May 2018, the UNGA adopted a resolution requesting the UN Secretary-General to submit a report identifying possible gaps in international environmental law and environment-related instruments and establish a working group to consider said report and discuss possible options to address gaps. In November 2018, the UNSG published the report, identifying several inefficiencies in international environmental law. These addressed principles, gaps and institutions. It ultimately recommended the adoption of a global pact as one of the solutions to address them. The recommendation was frowned upon by some states, which criticized the UNSG for going beyond its mandate and being biased towards the adoption of a Pact.

Between January and May 2019, the ad-hoc open-ended working group (OEWG) met in Nairobi. Under the guidance of the Co-Chairs, the working group did a global stocktaking of the state of international environmental law, discussing whether there are any gaps, whether these are intentional, and what could be done to address them. Delegates disagreed on some fundamental issues, both in terms of the types of challenges we currently face and how to solve them. It was generally acknowledged, however, that the current framework of international environmental law is insufficient. With a set of guiding questions crafted by the Co-Chairs, discussions were eventually steered towards different solutions to address some of the problems observed by delegates. Ultimately reaching a consensus, the OEWG agreed on a set of 13 recommendations to be submitted to the General Assembly for consideration.

Since there was no mention of a global pact, the recommendations were primarily seen by part of the international community as a failure. Others, however, could acknowledge that these provided a blueprint for the future of environmental law. It included a more flexible timeline to reach an agreement on a new document by 2022, at the 50th anniversary of the Stockholm Convention and the 30th anniversary of the Rio Convention, while keeping the discussion on environmental principles open. It is now up to the UNGA and the Member States to push for the progressive development of international environmental law. On August 2019, the UNGA decided to adopt the recommendations, moving the process forward.

VI. About This Book

This book was written in an effort to inform the upcoming diplomatic discussions on "gaps in international environmental law and environment-related instruments," providing delegates with the necessary background to prepare for the adoption of an agreement in 2022 that effectively promotes environmental protection. The goal of this book is twofold. The first is to leave a record of the development of the discussions on a Global Pact for the Environment, tracking the arguments and positions that came into play. The second is to contribute to the discussion following the adoption of the Recommendations of the ad hoc open-ended working group established by UN General Assembly Resolution A/72/L.51.

The book describes the process in which the Global Pact for the Environment unfolded, discussing its origins and development within the UNGA. It investigates arguments presented in the Nairobi sessions, considering the main issues and discussions brought by delegates. It brings forward the leading causes of inefficiency in international environmental law as presented by States, as well as the menu of options proposed to address them. It concludes with some thoughts towards the future and possible outcomes, including whether a restatement of principles is still on the table. The book largely relies on the updates by the International Institute for Sustainable Development (IISD),[68] which closely followed the substantive sessions of the Ad Hoc Open-Ended Working Group Towards a Global Pact for the Environment,

68. IISD, https://www.iisd.org/.

publishing substantial summaries and analyses of each meeting. This source is complemented by news articles and a few academic articles by leading scholars, which provided insights into the early stages of the discussions. A few other websites by UNEP, the drafters of the GPE and the Elisabeth Haub School of Law at Pace University provided constant updates and resources on the Global Pact. These resources are listed at the end of this book in Annex 1 and 2. Each chapter is accompanied by documents that inform the process, when relevant. These include some of the submissions made by the International Council of Environmental Law (ICEL).

This book is organized as follows. Chapter 1 focuses on the first phase of the development of the Global Pact for the Environment. Phase I, entitled "Genesis of the Global Pact," relates to its beginning, which arose from the efforts of the Club des Juristes (CDJ). Although based on earlier attempts at codifying environmental principles, the idea for this Global Pact was initially proposed in a 2015 report published by the CDJ. As the idea gained traction, a group of experts was convened. Through rounds of discussions, the experts were asked about which principles embodied the foundations of international environmental law, ultimately debating what to include in a Global Pact and how to include them. After the drafting process, a few experts gathered in Paris for a final round of discussion, launching the Global Pact in June 2017. At the end of the chapter, the text of the Global Pact is reproduced, along with a brief commentary by Yann Aguila, who spearheaded this process.

Chapter 2 relates to the second phase of this development, from the proposal of the Global Pact at the 72nd UNGA by President Macron in 2017 to the adoption of a resolution by the UNGA in 2018. The May 2018 resolution called for the elaboration by the UNSG of a report on gaps in international environmental law and gave rise to the open-ended working group discussions on said gaps. Phase II, entitled "Adoption of the Resolution," provides an overview of the initial discussion on the topic, and the reasons why the resolution adopted did not refer to a global pact except in its title. The chapter includes the text of the resolution, along with a brief commentary on its content.

Chapter 3 relates to Phase III, entitled "Fulfilling the Resolution." It covers the first steps set out by the UNGA to fulfill the investigation of gaps in international environmental law. The chapter covers the appointment of the co-chairs of the working group, the financing of its activities, and the organizational session held in September 2018. Additionally, it discusses the report published by the Secretary-General. Finally, the chapter includes the response to the UNSG's report published by ICEL shortly after.

Chapter 4 covers the substantive sessions held by the OEWG in Nairobi. It begins by briefly summarizing each session, without going into much detail about the substantive issues discussed. These issues are then analyzed in Section V, which presents the in-depth discussions of the main topics covered in Nairobi, including, when relevant, references to the arguments raised in the UNSG's report and by academic scholars. It specifically examines (i) what is a gap; (ii) fragmentation of international environmental law; (iii) matters of process; (iv) environmental governance; (v) implementation of international environmental law; (vi) environment-related areas; and (vii) environmental principles. In addition to pointing out the arguments presented by delegates, the chapter provides a brief geopolitical analysis, mapping out in which direction the Member States were leaning towards in terms of the possibility of adopting a new instrument. The chapter then reproduces the Nairobi recommendations as well as ICEL's analysis of the outcome.

Chapter 5 relates to the current stage of the negotiations and provides a potential timeline for 2022. These updates cover developments up to September 2019, when this book went to print. Chapter 6 presents the conclusions, which assess some pathways to fulfill the recommendations, adopting a new instrument by 2022.

Chapter 1: Phase 1: Genesis of the GPE (Nov. 2015 – June 2017)

The Global Pact for the Environment is the most recent proposed solution to address gaps in international environmental law. It developed in a rather unorthodox way, envisioned by academic scholars, who entirely drafted a proposal before its launch at the United Nations. The Pact was conceived by the Club des Juristes (CDJ),[1] a French legal think tank that provides an independent forum for debates and legal proposals. It responded to a report published by the organization during the Paris climate conference, which identified inefficiencies in international environmental law, suggesting ways to address them. A "universal charter" was one of the recommended solutions intended to improve the efficiency of the global legal system. The CDJ gained the support of the French Minister of Foreign Affairs Laurent Fabius, who began pushing forward the idea. A group of experts from around the globe was then assembled, tasked with drafting the charter. After months of consultations, the experts gathered in Paris and launched the Global Pact for the Environment in June 2017.

As an overarching and legally-binding proposed global agreement, the Global Pact could potentially define fundamental environmental rights for humanity. It intends to harmonize international environmental law by defining consolidated and emerging principles currently fragmented in a variety of MEAs, in particular in soft law declarations. The idea is to lay the groundwork for international environmental law by providing fundamental cornerstones through the codification of principles. The codification would unify treaties and provide essential legal answers for substantive gaps in international environmental law. The right to an ecologically sound environment and the obligation of States and other legal persons to take care of the environment form the pillars of the Global Pact.

This chapter focuses on Phase I of the development of the Global Pact, entitled "Genesis of the Global Pact for the Environment," and follows its initial stage traced to the CDJ. Following a chronological order, it is divided as follows. Section I provides an overview of the 2015 Report by the CDJ, and presents the main arguments offered in support of a "uni-

1. Le Club des Juristes, http://www.leclubdesjuristes.com/.

versal environmental charter." Section II focuses on the consultations with a group of international environmental law experts, which gave rise to an earlier draft of the Global Pact. Section III addresses a meeting held in June 2017, in which a smaller group of experts gathered in Paris to hash out the final details of the proposed draft, subsequently launching the proposed agreement at the Sorbonne. Section IV contains a brief commentary on the GPE by Yann Aguila, one of the drafters and supporters of the Global Pact. The draft Global Pact for the Environment, as presented in June 2017, is reprinted at the end of this chapter.

Phase I is depicted in the timeline below.

Figure 1: Phase I Timeline "Genesis of the Global Pact for the Environment" (Nov. 2015 – June 2017):

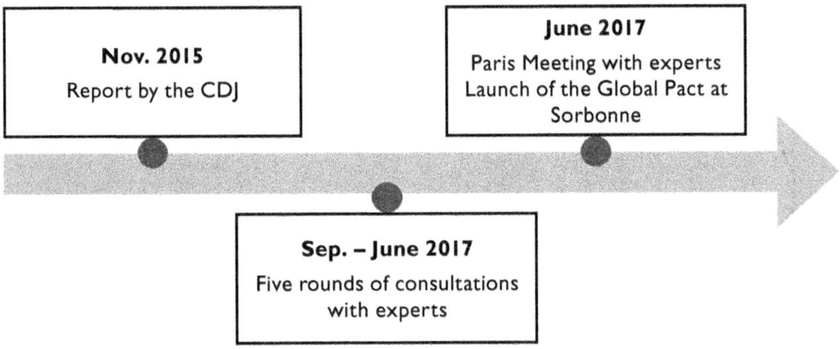

I. November 2015: Report by the Club des Juristes

In November 2015, the Environment Committee of the CDJ released the report "Increasing the Effectiveness of International Environmental Law: Duties of States, Rights of Individuals" on how to strengthen international environmental law.[2] The report was presented in the run up of the Conference of the Parties (COP) in Paris in December 2015, as world leaders were working to reach an agreement on climate change. While the Environment Committee welcomed a climate agreement, they warned that more legal action was needed to safeguard the environment from the current crisis. The report cautions against a "double failure" in international environmental law: failure in its development, and failure in its application.

2. Club des Juristes, Increasing the Effectiveness of International Environmental Law: Duties of States, Rights of Individuals (2015).

The first "failure" relates to the process of adopting MEAs. According to the CDJ, the drafting of environmental treaties is slow, "even paralyzed."[3] As States sometimes object to more stringent commitments, the adoption of non-legally binding agreements is common. Aiming for consensus, rules tend to reflect basic minimum standards, exposing the "common-denominator" problem. For example, the Convention of Biological Diversity (CBD), provides a general and nominal framework for biodiversity conservation,[4] and subsequent meetings of the COP have not culminated in more specific and binding agreements in essential issues such as addressing the extinction of species. Negotiations advance too slowly to respond to the fast and irreversible nature of the declining reserve of biodiversity.[5]

The implementation of international environmental law is also flawed. Enforcement of adopted treaties is frequently weak, due to the absence of compliance mechanisms and effective sanctions. As a result, international environmental law is often unable to produce the results assigned or the behavior it intends to encourage.[6] Prioritizing a cooperative rather than a punitive approach, monitoring of MEAs is largely limited to "non-compliance" procedures, overseen by committees without decision-making authority. Even if sanctions exist, such as those included in the Kyoto Protocol, these have rarely been used.[7] Yann Aguila, one of the drafters of the report and main proponent of the Global Pact, clarifies: "due to a lack of control mechanisms and effective sanctions, states may deliberately choose not to respect the treaties they have signed."[8]

To tackle this "double failure," the report made 21 recommendations[9] based on three pillars: an international environmental court, a world environment organization and a universal charter.[10] The Global Pact for the Environment evolved from Proposal 20, which reads "[a]dopt a Universal Environmental Charter in the form of an international convention with binding legal force."[11] The Universal Environmental Charter (later renamed) involves enshrining the main principles of protecting the planet in a found-

3. *Id.* at 26.
4. Convention on Biological Diversity Convention on Biological Diversity, June 5, 1992, 1760 U.N.T.S. 79.
5. Club des Juristes, *supra* note 2, at 26.
6. *Id.* at 28-29.
7. *Id.* at 29.
8. Yann Aguila, COP 21: "To Arms, Citizens, to Defend Your Rights!" § 2019 (HuffPost 2015).
9. *See* Yann Aguila, *La Adopción de un Pacto Internacional Para la Protección del Medio Ambiente*, 34 Revista Aranzadi de Derecho Ambiental (2016); Yann Aguila, *L'Adozione di un Patto Internazionale per la Protezione dell'Ambiente*, 3 Rivista Giuridica dell'Ambiente 563 (2016).
10. Club des Juristes, *supra* note 2, at 96.
11. *Id.* at 104.

ing text.[12] The report does not go as far as debating the content of the principles. However, the CDJ suggested drafting a text enshrining substantive and procedural rights, as well as the creation of a compliance committee to oversee its applicability. Additionally, the right of recourse would guarantee the enforceability of a charter by national courts, especially by the civil society.

The CDJ questions the legal value of existing principles, which lack binding force and do not constitute a real guarantee of rights.[13] With binding legal force, a Universal Environmental Charter would improve the accessibility and readability of international environmental law, which is made difficult due to its fragmentation across a multitude of MEAs.[14] The charter is intended to clarify founding principles of international law, including the right of each person to a healthy environment, as well as the right of citizens to bring cases to court to force states to respect their international commitments.[15] Additionally, it would provide international environmental law with the necessary cornerstone.[16] Principles could be invoked in court, constituting a real guarantee of rights, supplementing the political and symbolic significance of current principles enshrined in the Stockholm and Rio Declarations, both nonbinding soft law documents.[17] The Committee clarifies:

> "For all these reasons, the Committee believes that a text of universal scope on environmental matters needs to be adopted. This text would be the corner stone of international environmental law. It would lay down the founding principles, from all the sectoral environmental conventions by analysing the variation in, and implementation of, these principles in the specific fields. Furthermore, it could also be envisaged that the Charter would contain a final interpretive clause so that all the sectoral environmental conventions could be interpreted in the light of the major principles which will have been thus enshrined."[18]

The report largely advanced the idea of establishing the influence of civil society in setting the agenda for environmental issues. It invited a reflection on the state of international environmental law, questioning what could be done by different stakeholders to improve it.[19] Through this invitation,

12. *Id.* at 15.
13. *Id.* at 101.
14. *Id.* at 100.
15. Aguila. 2015.
16. Club des Juristes, *supra* note 2, at 96 (Proposal 20).
17. Le Club des Juristes, Report Summary: Increasing the Effectiveness of International Environmental Law—Duties of States, Rights of Individual (2015), *available at* http://www.leclubdesjuristes.com/wp-content/uploads/2015/11/4.-Report-summary_9-pages.pdf.
18. Club des Juristes, *supra* note 2, at 103.
19. Yann Aguila & Patricia Antunes Laydner, *Reforçar a Eficácia do Direito Ambiental do Meio Ambiente: Uma Proposta do Club de Juristes*, 82 Revista de Direito Ambiental (2016).

it reinforced the essential role of non-state actors for environmental governance, advocating for their right to participate in environmental negotiations.[20] The CDJ therefore presented a "called to arms:" in order to make international law more effective, civil society must take ownership of it.[21] The basis for the report explains the unorthodox origins of the Global Pact, as civil society took it upon themselves to ignite the process of adopting of a legally binding treaty on environmental principles. Consequently, the CDJ did precisely what it called for, igniting the drafting process of a Global Pact.

II. September 2016 – June 2017: Consultations With Experts

The idea for a Universal Charter received immediate momentum with the support of Former French Minister of Foreign Affairs Laurent Fabius. Mr. Fabius had presided over the Paris Climate Agreement negotiations and had been recently appointed as President of the French Conseil Constitutionnel.[22] With the ambition to continue being involved in environmental issues at the international level, Mr. Fabius looked for similar proposals, eventually deciding to support the idea of the Global Pact. Yann Aguila, chair of the CDJ's Environment Committee, met with Mr. Fabius and presented a short 2-page memo about what could be a Global Pact and how to make it come true. Mr. Fabius officially showed his support in June 2016.

Following his support, significant legal work was conducted by the CDJ's Environment Committee.[23] Throughout 2016, a documentary basis was assembled to show an example of what a Global Pact could be rather than presenting an abstract idea.[24] French experts and students met to gather information and prepare for the consultations with the experts. In early 2017, the CDJ invited an international network of environmental law experts to draft a blueprint for a Global Pact for the Environment.[25] These were chosen based on a geographic diversity and expertise. The Group of Experts for the Pact (GEP) ultimately included over 100 experts, academics, judges and

---

20. Club des Juristes, *supra* note 2, at Proposal 2.
21. *Id.* at 13.
22. Yann Aguila & Jorge E. Viñuales, *A Global Pact for the Environment: Conceptual Foundations*, *in* A Global Pact for the Environment—Legal Foundations 20 (Yann Aguila & Jorge E. Viñuales eds., 2019). Yann Aguila & Jorge E. Viñuales, *A Global Pact for the Environment: Conceptual Foundations*, 28 Rev. Eur., Comp. & Int'l Envtl. L. 3;7 (2019).
23. Club des Juristes, White Paper: Toward a Global Pact for the Environment 3 (2017).
24. Aguila & Viñuales, *supra* note 22, at 7 (RECIEL).
25. Teresa Parejo Navajas & Nathan Lobel, *Framing the Global Pact for the Environment: Why It Is Needed, What It Aims to Do, How It Proposes to Do It*, 30 Fordham Envtl. L. Rev. 32, 41 (2018).

lawyers, from more than 40 countries.[26] These represented diverse legal systems and ecosystems, allowing them to take into account a variety of legal perspectives of what environmental law entailed.[27] The group provided opinions on different topics through a series of questionnaires. During the first half of 2017, experts responded to five rounds of consultations, starting with broader questions that became more specific as the discussion unfolded.[28] The consultations addressed matters such as the need for an international treaty, its overall structure, content and, more specifically, the formulation of the principles that would feature in the draft agreement.[29]

The exchanges were operationalized by the CDJ's Environment Committee, under the leadership of Yann Aguila.[30] The Environment Committee included 15 experts on environmental law, including academics, judges and lawyers, who served as the operational committee for the project. The Committee oversaw the organizational aspects, the collection and analysis of the experts' input, and the final drafting of the project.[31]. A team of 15 student volunteers helped coordinate the questionnaires and analyze the responses.[32] The group met every 2 or 3 weeks to discuss the architecture of the Pact and the list of principles included, complementing the material gathered with specific research when needed.[33]

A. *First Round of Consultation*

Since the first questionnaire was at the same time the first official approach of experts, it included a general introduction to the project, its background

26. Aguila & Viñuales, *supra* note 22, at 7 (RECIEL). The list of experts is included in Document 2: List of Members of the International Group of Experts for the Pact.
27. Maria Magdalena Kenig-Witkowska, *The Draft Global Pact for the Environment* (2018), *availble at* https://www.documents.clientearth.org/wp-content/uploads/library/2018-10-02-the-draft-global-pact-for-the-environment-ce-en.pdf.
28. World Commission on Environmental Law, *Global Pact for the Environment Introduced to the World*, IUCN-WCEL (2017), *available at* https://www.iucn.org/commissions/world-commission-environmental-law/events-wcel/past-events/global-pact-environment-june-2017. IUCN-WCEL. Aguila & Viñuales, *supra* note 22, at 20. Le Droit Est Essentiel Pour S'Adapter au Monde Nouveau et Pour Adapter ce Monde Nouveau. C'est le But du Pacte Mondial Pour L'Environnement (Entretien Exclusif Avec Laurent Fabius, President du Conseil Constitutionnel), 28 La Semaine Juridique 1354 (July 10, 2017), http://www.tendancedroit.fr/wp-content/uploads/2017/07/entretien.pdf?utm_source=TendanceDroit&utm_medium=ExtraitRevue&utm_campaign=TendanceDroit.
29. Aguila & Viñuales, *supra* note 22, at 20.
30. IUCN-WCEL, *supra* note 28.
31. First Questionnaire Sent to the Group of Experts, The Project for a Global Pact for the Environment, First Consultation of the International Network of Experts, General Introduction and Open-Ended Questions (on file with Yann Aguila).
32. Interview with Yann Aguila, in New York, NY (July 16, 2019).
33. *Id.*

and objective.[34] Based on the premise that principles had been "subject to various wording, based on legislators, and diverse interpretations based on the jurisdictions," the goal of the first round was to "have a better understanding of the dynamics involved in the circulation of the principles enshrined in the Rio Declaration since 1992."[35] The CDJ intended to identify the principles currently subject to a worldwide consensus and to specify their impact. The first round of consultation asked the experts the following open-ended questions:

> "According to you, which principles, already enshrined in various international instruments, and particularly in the Rio Declaration, should take priority?
>
> According to you, are there principles that are not expressly stated in the international instruments, but that form a sufficiently broad consensus and should be legally recognized?
>
> As to the formulation of the Pact, what clarifications need to be integrated to the principles, based on the industry practice since 1992?"

B. *Second Round of Consultation*

Prior to posing the subsequent round of questions, the consultation presented the drafters with initial findings based on the responses from the first questionnaire. The CDJ's Environment Committee found a "double consensus:" drafters agreed on the need for an international agreement enshrining the fundamental principles of environmental law, and on the content of the Pact. The Committee noted "a very broad agreement [that] emerges on most of the principles that should be included in the Global Pact for the Environment." These principles constituted the "core" of the text. While there were different approaches identified, these remained occasional and incidental, and contributions converged on the most important aspects.

The second round of consultation considered the architecture and the drafting approach of the Pact.[36] Based on the findings of the first round, the Committee asked the experts their opinions on a list of principles derived from the Rio Declaration, and subject to broad consensus, as well as on the

34. First Questionnaire, *supra* note 31.
35. *Id.*
36. Second Questionnaire Sent to the Group of Experts, Project on a Global Pact for the Environment, Second Consultation of the International Network of Experts, Architecture and Drafting of the Pact (on file with Yann Aguila).

order these principles should feature in a draft.[37] Secondly, the Committee requested the experts' comments on a set of new principles, which included 1) non-regression and/or progression; 2) *in dubio pro natura*; 3) effective environmental legislation (principle of *effet utile*); and 4) recognition of the role of non-state actors. Thirdly, the Committee asked for suggestions regarding the reorganization, merging or distinction of certain principles. For example, while Principle 10 of the Rio Declaration mentioned public information, public participation and access to justice, some experts had suggested these should be treated as distinct articles. The principle of prevention and the duty to conduct environmental impact assessment could be merged, similarly to the requirement of sustainable development, integration in public policies, and considering patterns of production and consumption.

The fourth question related to the wording and formulation of the principles. Some previous suggestions included using "short, comprehensive and concise wording" and an "open structure" of the principles to allow for more dynamism. As noted by the Committee, "[t]he Pact should be understood as a living instrument: interpretation and implementation of the principles should be undertaken later on by monitoring bodies."[38] Additionally, a general formulation of principles would respect "States' margin of appreciation" and "the necessity of implementing principles in compliance with each national legal context." The questionnaire also left open to discussion whether to use a direct language style with an explicit obligation (e.g., "Each person shall have the right to access information") or formulating the obligation through state intermediaries (e.g., "State Party shall endeavor to ensure that each person has the right to access environmental information").

C. *Third Round of Consultation*

The third round of consultation focused on the potential adoption of follow-up and compliance mechanisms to achieve the goal of strengthening the effectiveness of environmental law.[39] The Committee recognized that a debate on said mechanisms is highly political and would likely be referred to

37. *Id.* The list included the following principles 1) Duty of environment protection; 2) Right to live in a healthy environment; 3) Sustainable development and principle of integration; 4) Interest of future generations/Intergenerational equity; 5) Prevention; 6) Precaution; 7) Liability; 8) Polluter pays; 9) Public information; 10) Public participation; 11) Access to justice in environmental matters; 12) Education and formation; 13) Research and innovation; 14) Duty of law-making; 15) Cooperation; 16) Common but differentiated responsibilities.
38. *Id.*
39. Third Questionnaire Sent to the Group of Experts, Project on a Global Pact for the Environment, Third Consultation of the International Network of Experts, Follow-Up Mechanisms (on file with Yann Aguila).

further diplomatic negotiations. To kickstart the debate, the document sent to experts presented some reflections on the nature of a monitoring mechanism, drafting and institutional choices and examples of existing monitoring mechanisms in MEAs. It invited experts to share their thoughts on options. The first question related to the nature of a compliance mechanism, debating between judicial and non-judicial.[40] Secondly, the Committee asked the experts how they would divide between treaty provisions and subsequent decisions related to the compliance mechanisms.[41] This second question related to the wording, concerning what should be included in the treaty and what should be left to future decisions.[42] This issue leads to a follow-up institutional question: In addition to the follow-up committee, should there be specific bodies to support the Global Pact (such as a COP or an executive secretariat), or does it have to be backed by existing institutions?

D. *Fourth Round of Consultation*

The fourth round of consultation related to the actual wording and content of the various principles to be included in the Global Pact.[43] The Committee noted a convergence on around 80 percent of the topics discussed so far and clarified that this consultation integrated the main elements of this consensus. They asked the suggestions and/or observations of experts on a series of principles, concerning their formulation and content. The document also included brief references and commentaries about each principle, noting some questions that arose during the consultations. For example, the Committee noted a consensus on the right to live in a healthy environment, with 178 States having recognized it. However, questions remained on whether to adopt the "right to a healthy environment," or the "right to live" in a healthy

40. Question 1: Modalities of the monitoring mechanism. What are your suggestions for how to control and monitor the implementation of the Global Pact? More precisely, what would your recommendations be on: the overall objective of the monitoring mechanism; the nature and composition of the body responsible for monitoring (jurisdictional and/or non-jurisdictional); the methods of filing state reports (periodicity); the possibility of communications, especially individual ones; the powers of the monitoring body (support, sanction, incentive, opportunity to set guidelines, etc).
41. Question 2: Institutional choice. Is it necessary to formally create autonomous institutions (COP, secretariat, monitoring committee ...) to monitor the implementation of the Global Pact? Is it necessary to refer to an institution external and pre-existing monitoring of the Covenant? And in the latter case, which one? Could we envisage the combined operation of outside?
42. Question 3: Editor's Choice. Should the provisions of the treaty itself contain all the provisions relating to tracking mechanism? Or should the definition of modalities be referred to subsequent decisions, which could be taken, according to the responses to the question 2, either by a COP or by an external institution and pre-existing?
43. Fourth Questionnaire Sent to the Group of Experts, Project on a Global Pact for the Environment, Fourth Consultation of the International Network of Experts, Wording and Content of the Principles (on file with Yann Aguila).

environment, on a "healthy" or "ecologically sound" environment and/or an environment that "permits a life of dignity and well-being" (Stockholm Declaration) and/or "adequate to his or her health and well-being" (Aarhus Convention), and/or "healthy" and "respectful of biodiversity," for the benefit of "everyone," "any person," or "any human being."[44] The fourth round of consultations invited this type of debate.

E. *Fifth Round of Consultation*

The fifth and final consultation related to a White Paper which describes the origins, the context, and the aim of the Global Pact for the Environment.[45] The Committee also sent around a compendium of different iterations of the principles as included in MEAs and other texts drafted by the civil society.[46] The experts took into account the most representative international environmental law agreements, as well as the implementation practice of States and international institutions.[47]

III. June 2017: Paris Meeting and Launch at the Sorbonne

The individual comments from the contributors enabled the GEP to identify fundamental principles, specify the Pact's content and determine the proper wording of each principle.[48] The GEP intended to prepare a text with clear added value for the development of international environmental law, while also being short, precise and capable of creating consensus among States despite their political, economic and environmental differences.[49] It was necessary to strike a balance between being realistic but also significantly ambitious to warrant the adoption of a new instrument. The draft takes into account the diversity of needs, principles and challenges characterizing the environment.[50] An attempt was made to achieve a balance between rights and obligations, taking into account the special circumstances of developing countries.[51] With respect to the principles and wording chosen, these were based on the most commonly recognized principles and the most often used formulation of such principles.[52] The draft Global Pact was designed to

44. *Id.*
45. IUCN-WCEL, *supra* note 28.
46. Compendium, Project on a Global Pact for the Environment (on file with Yann Aguila).
47. Kenig-Witkowska, *supra* note 27, at 6-7.
48. Aguila & Viñuales, *supra* note 22, at 8 (RECIEL).
49. Club des Juristes, *supra* note 23, at 38.
50. *Id.* at 38.
51. *Id.* at 38.
52. *Id.* at 38.

facilitate implementation of national laws and policies through provisions as general as possible while also having specific legal content.[53]

The CDJ's Environment Committee highlighted that the work to draft a Global Pact was "preparatory," aimed at informing the future reflection of a draft text within the UN. The Global Pact was thus originally designed to be a "working document," complemented by "Comments," which could express the experts' interrogations, debates and hesitations.[54] As a working document, it was meant to be modified and debated. Once an initial version of the document was drafted, thirty experts met for an in-person discussion at the *Conseil Constitutionnel* on June 23rd, 2017.[55] These experts represented the entire network of experts and a diversity of legal systems, and were led by members of the International Union for Conservation of Nature (IUCN) Academy of Environmental Law and the IUCN World Commission on Environmental Law[56] under the presidency of Mr. Fabius.[57] Meeting into the night, the committee discussed the initial draft, drew conclusions, harmonized the principles from a human rights perspective, and finalized the text.[58] The draft consists of a preamble and 26 articles, comprising 20 principles.[59] It encompasses substantive and procedural rights and duties, embodying consolidated and emerging principles of international environmental law.

In the Preamble, the Pact acknowledges the threats to the environment and the need for increased ambition, in particular considering the urgency to tackle climate change, the unprecedented loss of biodiversity and the need to ensure ecosystem resilience. The Preamble reaffirms previous nonbinding declarations as well as the Sustainable Development Goals. The nature of the threats requires State cooperation according to their common but differentiated responsibilities and respective capabilities, in light of their different national circumstances. Additionally, States are motivated to promote sustainable development for present and future generations, considering intragenerational and intergenerational equity, while respecting balance and integrity of the Earth's ecosystems. The Members are conscious of the need to respect human rights and the rights of people in vulnerable situations,

53. Kenig-Witkowska, *supra* note 27, at 6-7.
54. First Questionnaire Sent to the Group of Experts, *supra* note 34.
55. Club des Juristes *supra* note 2, at 8.
56. Doran, et al. 2019. P. 2.
57. Aguila & Viñuales, *supra* note 22, at 20.
58. Club des Juristes, *supra* note 23, 8.
59. Le Club des Juristes, Project Global Pact for the Environment (June 24, 2017), http://www.leclubdesjuristes.com/wp-content/uploads/2017/05/Project-Global-Pact-for-the-Environment.pdf. For an analysis of each principle included in Draft Zero, see Yann Aguila & Jorge E. Viñuales, A Global Pact for the Environment: Legal Foundations (C-EENRG C-EENRG Report 2019-1 ed. 2019). Yann Aguila, et al. (eds.), Principios de Derecho Ambiental y Agenda 2030 (Tirant lo Blanch 2019).

as well as the role of women, and invite non-State actors to participate in environmental protection. They also stress the fundamental importance of science and education for sustainable development. Finally, they affirm the need to adopt a common position and principles that will inspire and guide the efforts of all to protect and preserve the environment.

The Pact is based on two pillars: the right of every person to an ecologically sound environment (Article 1), and the duty of States or international institutions, and every person, to take care of the environment (Article 2.) The duty to integrate environmental protection in national policies and pursue sustainable development is contained in Article 3. Article 4 promotes intergenerational equity, placing a duty on present generations to ensure future generations have the ability to meet their own needs. Articles 5 to 8 refine and consolidate the "older" principles of prevention, precaution, remediation of environmental damages and the polluter-pays. Articles 9, 10 and 11 provide for access to information, public participation and access to environmental justice, while Articles 12 and 13 provide for education and training, as well as research and innovation. Article 14 encourages the role of non-State actors and subnational entities in the implementation of the Pact. Article 15 promotes the duty to adopt and enact effective environmental protections at the national level. Articles 16 and 17 bring the newer principles of resilience and non-regression. Article 18 articulates an organized system that provides for cooperation between nations to facilitate implementation at the international level.[60] Article 19 provides for measures to protect the environment in relation to armed conflicts. Article 20 acknowledges the diversity of national situations, ensuring the common but differentiated responsibilities and respective capabilities, in light of different national circumstances, when appropriate.

Articles 21 and 22 envision the creation of compliance mechanisms through an implementation body and a Secretariat. Article 21 drew on the Aarhus Convention on Access to Information, Public Participation in Decision-Making and Access to Justice in Environmental Matters, a Committee of independent experts will also monitor compliance and facilitate implementation. The design of the Global Pact aims to prevent harm more than to punish it, and to empower non-state actors to strengthen environmental governance at both the national and the international levels.[61] Article 23 provides for signature, ratification, acceptance, approval and accession. Article

60. Maria Antonia Tigre, *Princípio da Cooperação, in* PRINCIPIOS DE DERECHO AMBIENTAL Y AGENDA 2030 (Yann Aguila, et al. eds., 2019).
61. Navajas & Lobel, FORDHAM ENVTL. L. REV. 44 (2018).

24 establishes when the Pact shall enter into force, Article 25 provides for denunciation, and Article 26 for the depositary.

The following day after the meeting of the experts and once agreement had been reached on the Global Pact, a high-profile symposium was held at the *Grand Amphithéatre de la Sorbonne*, in which the draft project was officially presented to the public by Mr. Fabius to French President Emmanuel Macron.[62] The GPE was presented with considerable fanfare and the initiative received ample media coverage.[63] The ceremony featured former UN Secretary-General Ban Ki-moon, former Governor of California Arnold Schwarzenegger, the French Minister of the Environment Nicolas Hulot, the Mayor of Paris Anne Hidalgo, several other political figures, and a wider public of experts, diplomats, students and interested people.[64] The conference closed with a speech from President Macron, who vowed to personally act to push the Pact forward for adoption at the UNGA.[65]

---

62. Le Club des Juristes, Vers un Pacte Mondial Pour l'Environnement: Agir Pour la Planète, Agir par le Droit (June 24, 2017), http://www.leclubdesjuristes.com/wp-content/uploads/2017/05/CDJ_Pacte-mondial-pour-lenvironnement_Programme.pdf.
63. *See, e.g.*, Bid for Environmental Rights Pact to Kick Off in Paris Tomorrow (The Times of India, 23 June 2017); Un Pacte Mondial Pour Protéger l'Environnement (Le Monde, 25 June 2017); Un Projet de Pacte Mondial Pour l'Environnement (Le Figaro, 24 June 2017); Macron Promet de Défendre un "Pacte Mondial Pour l'Environnement" (Reuters, 24 June 2017); Emmanuel Macron Proposera un Pacte Pour l'Environnement à l'ONU (Le Figaro, 24 June 2017), http://www.lefigaro.fr/sciences/2017/06/24/01008-20170624ARTFIG00137-emmanuel-macron-proposera-un-pacte-pour-l-environnement-a-l-onu.php; Macron S'Engage à Défendre le Projet de Pacte Mondial Pour l'Environnement (Le Monde, 24 June 2017), https://www.lemonde.fr/climat/article/2017/06/24/macron-promet-de-porter-le-projet-de-pacte-mondial-pour-l-environnement-devant-l-onu_5150639_1652612.html; Macron, Schwarzenegger Back Global Pact on Environment (France 24, 24 June 2017), https://www.france24.com/en/20170624-macron-launches-global-environment-pact-paris; France's Macron to Back Push for Global Environment Rights Pact (Reuters, 24 June 2017), https://www.reuters.com/article/us-world-climatechange-macron-idUSKBN19F0LG; Emmanuel Macron Teams Up With Arnold Schwarzeneggar to Take Swipe at Donald Trump on Climate Change (Independent, 24 June 2017), https://www.independent.co.uk/news/world/americas/us-politics/trump-macron-arnold-schwarzeneggar-climate-change-make-planet-great-again-a7806491.html.
64. *See* Yann Aguila, *Vers un Pacte Mondial Pour l'Environnement: Acte Fondateur á Paris le 24 Juin 2017* (2017) 25 La Semaine Juridique 718.
65. See Speech delivered by President Emmanuel Macron during the international launch summit of the "Global Pact for the Environment," which took place during the 72nd UN General Assembly, *available at* https://www.diplomatie.gouv.fr/en/french-foreign-policy/united-nations/events/united-nations-general-assembly-sessions/unga-s-72nd-session/article/speech-by-m-emmanuel-macron-president-of-the-republic-summit-on-the-global-pact.

IV. Response to Some Concerns About the Project of a Global Pact for the Environment (Yann Aguila)

Yann AGUILA

President of the Environment Commission of the Club des Juristes

Some concerns have been expressed regarding the project of a Global Pact for the Environment. The present article aims to address these concerns relating, on the one hand, to a risk of regression **(II)** and, on the other hand, to the binding nature of the Pact **(III)**. To address these concerns, however, it is first necessary to briefly recall the origins of the Pact **(I)**.

I/ The project of a Pact finds its origin in a long-standing request from the international legal community

1/ The origin of this project is long-standing. In 1987, the **Brundtland Report** called for the adoption of such treaty, which draft was annexed to the report. In 1995, **the IUCN** (International Union for the Conservation of Nature) presented a similar project named 'International Covenant for the Environment'. As a continuation of these works, the current project was prepared in 2017 by an international group of experts from 40 countries, chaired by Laurent Fabius, former president of the COP21. In October 2018, in a « Call to action » published in various newspapers, **more than a hundred lawyers**, among the most renowned in international law and environmental law, urged States to adopt the Pact.

2/ The Global Pact for the Environment aims to gather the main principles of environment law within a single text with legal value that would form a universal framework of reference. With the momentum created by the adoption of the 2030 Agenda and the Paris Climate Agreement in 2015, the Pact would go beyond the sectorial differences. By not targeting a particular sector (climate, biodiversity, pollution, etc.), the Pact applies to environmental politics as a whole.

3/ The Pact will add value to current international environmental law. The Pact will **strengthen environmental principles and make them more easily available.** Some of them already exist in some States' laws. However, they are scattered in various texts. The Pact will represent a new and very useful legal resource to enshrine rights and duties of citizens and Governments in the environmental field. In each State, the legislator will implement principles of the Pact, by adopting new laws protecting the environment. The Supreme Courts will have a source of inspiration for their jurisprudence, within the Pact principles. The purpose of the Pact is **to harmonize environmental standards on a global scale.**

II/ The risk of normative conflicts or regression is practically zero and, in all circumstances, can be easily prevented

Some are concerned about a risk of weakening existing treaties and normative conflicts with sector-specific agreements.

1/ At the outset, it has to be noted that the purpose of the Global Pact for the Environment is undeniably to ***strengthen*** **the legal framework** and not to weaken it.

2/ A regression risk does not exist: the Pact will create a ***minimum*** set of requirements. However, nothing will prevent States **to go further** in sector-specific international treaties or in domestic laws. In the event that a sector-specific agreement is more demanding, such agreement will prevail. As a comparison, the same articulation applies between **the European Convention on Human Rights and domestic laws**: the ECHR acts as a **minimum** standard but does not prevent States from being more ambitious. Back in the 1950s when the ECHR was adopted, there was no concern about regression.

3/ This type of instrument is a common legal mechanism. It relates to the rule of the primacy of special law over general law (*specialia generalibus derogant*). General law is only intended to apply in cases not covered by special law. Additionally, the Pact will not apply in fields within the scope of sector-specific agreements. The normative conflict is therefore excluded.

4/ Many examples are illustrative in international law:

- **On human rights issues**: both **International Pacts of 1966** (one relating to civil and political rights, the other relating to economic, social and cultural rights) form a minimum set of requirements. They perfectly co-exist with **more precise texts**, such as the 1984 Convention against torture and the 1989 Convention on the Rights of the Child.

- **With regard to the law of the sea**: the major general agreement, so-called the **Montego Bay Convention of 1982**, works in harmony with sector-specific and/or regional texts.

5/ To prevent any risk, it is possible to **add a provision in the Pact** expressly dealing with this matter.

Such provision does not exist in the current project. The Pact could:

- Expressly govern the relationship between the Pact and sector-specific agreements, for example on the basis of Article 237 of the Montego Bay Convention (which provides that *'The provisions of this Part are without prejudice to the specific obligations assumed by States under special conventions and agreements concluded previously'*);

- And/or provide for an interpretation clause aiming to prevent any regression risk (stating, for instance that '*the present Agreement shall not be interpreted as involving a reduction in environment protection*', in the spirit of Article 17 of the ECHR).

III/ Concerns about the binding nature of the Pact are also surmountable

Some are worried about the binding nature of the Pact.

1/ It is very important that the Pact adopts **a legal form**, and is not a purely political statement, as would be a 'declaration' from heads of States and governments.

2/ Indeed, such a declaration already exists with the **Rio Declaration of 1992**. The purpose of the project of a Pact is precisely to grant a legal value to the Rio Declaration. There is no benefit in adopting a new Declaration. Notably, it is this path, from soft law (i.e., a declaration) to hard law (i.e., a treaty), that has been followed for human rights; the **Universal Declaration on Human Rights of 1948**, which was initially restricted to soft law, has been transposed into legal form by the two **International Covenants of 1966** (one relative to political and civil rights, the other to economic, social, and cultural rights).

3/ However, **among legal acts**, there are various possibilities. The distinction between "soft law" and "hard law" may be misleading due to its **divisiveness**: there is in fact a **progressive scale** of binding force that may be present in an international legal instrument. There are many treaties in existence today that are **more or less** binding depending on their substance. For instance, the Paris Agreement is binding due to **its form** (a treaty), but, **in substance**, the more or less precise nature of the obligations and the flexibility of the sanction mechanism may sometimes lead to it being described as a "non-binding" agreement. The same applies with the project of a Pact: because of the general nature of the principles, it offers great flexibility. It provides States with discretion in the implementation of these principles.

A. *Conclusion*

The state of the global environment requires urgent and collective action by all nations. The Global Pact for the Environment is one essential mechanism by which to achieve meaningful action by both state and non-state actors to ensure a sustainable future. The paralysis of the international political community can be overcome by citizen, civil society, and private sector mobilization. The Global Pact can provide the world with a global environmental constitution and the legal tools necessary to achieve a sustainable global society; however, it will require concerted mobilization by individuals. With the Global Pact, there is hope for the planet.

Document 1: Draft Zero of the Global Pact for the Environment (June 2017)

Preamble

The Parties to the present Pact,

Acknowledging the growing threats to the environment and the need to act in an ambitious and concerted manner at the global level to better ensure its protection,

Reaffirming the Declaration of the United Nations Conference on the Human Environment, adopted in Stockholm on 16 June 1972, the World Charter for Nature adopted on 28 October 1982 and the Declaration of the United Nations Conference on Environment and Development, adopted in Rio on 14 June 1992,

Recalling their commitment to the Sustainable Development Goals adopted by the General Assembly of the United Nations on 25 September 2015,

Considering in particular the urgency to tackle climate change and recalling the objectives set by the United Nations Framework Convention on Climate Change adopted in New York on 9 May 1992 and the Paris Agreement of 12December 2015,

Observing that the planet is facing an unprecedented loss of its biodiversity requiring urgent action,

Reaffirming the need to ensure, while using natural resources, that ecosystems are resilient and continue to provide essential services, thereby preserving the diversity of life on Earth, and contribute to human well-being and the eradication of poverty,

Acknowledging that the global nature of threats to the Earth's community of life requires that all States cooperate as closely as possible and participate in an international, effective and appropriate action according to their common but differentiated responsibilities and respective capabilities, in light of their different national circumstances,

Determined to promote a sustainable development that allows each generation to satisfy its needs without compromising the capability of future generation to meet theirs, while respecting the balance and integrity of the Earth's ecosystem,

Emphasizing the vital role of women in sustainable development matters and the need to promote gender equality and the empowerment of women,

Conscious of the need to respect, promote and consider their respective obligations on human rights, the right to health, the rights and knowledge of indigenous peoples, local communities, migrants, children, persons with disabilities and people in vulnerable situation, under their jurisdiction,

Welcoming the vital role of non State actors, including civil society, economic actors, cities, regions and other subnational authorities in the protection of the environment,

Stressing the fundamental importance of science and education for sustainable development,

Mindful of conducting actions guided by intragenerational and intergenerational equity,

Affirming the need to adopt a common position and principles that will inspire and guide the efforts of all to protect and preserve the environment,

Have agreed as follows:

Article 1
Right to an ecologically sound environment
Every person has the right to live in an ecologically sound environment adequate for their health, well-being, dignity, culture and fulfilment.

Article 2
Duty to take care of the environment

Every State or international institution, every person, natural or legal, public or private, has the duty to take care of the environment. To this end, everyone contributes at their own levels to the conservation, protection and restoration of the integrity of the Earth's ecosystem.

Article 3
Integration and sustainable development

Parties shall integrate the requirements of environmental protection into the planning and implementation of their policies and national and international activities, especially in order to promote the fight against climate change, the protection of oceans and the maintenance of biodiversity.

They shall pursue sustainable development. To this end, they shall ensure the promotion of public support policies, patterns of production and consumption both sustainable and respectful of the environment.

Article 4
Intergenerational Equity

Intergenerational equity shall guide decisions that may have an impact on the environment.

Present generations shall ensure that their decisions and actions do not compromise the ability of future generations to meet their own needs.

Article 5
Prevention

The necessary measures shall be taken to prevent environmental harm.

The Parties have the duty to ensure that activities under their jurisdiction or control do not cause damage to the environments of other Parties or in areas beyond the limits of their national jurisdiction.

They shall take the necessary measures to ensure that an environmental impact assessment is conducted prior to any decision made to authorise or engage in a project, an activity, a plan, or a program that is likely to have a significant adverse impact on the environment.

In particular, States shall keep under surveillance the effect of an above-mentioned project, activity, plan, or program which they authorise or engage in, in view of their obligation of due diligence.

Article 6
Precaution

Where there is a risk of serious or irreversible damage, lack of scientific certainty shall not be used as a reason for postponing the adoption of effective and proportionate measures to prevent environmental degradation.

Article 7
Environmental Damages

The necessary measures shall be taken to ensure an adequate remediation of environmental damages.

Parties shall immediately notify other States of any natural disasters or other emergencies that are likely to produce sudden harmful effects on the environment of those States. Parties shall promptly cooperate to help concerned States.

Article 8
Polluter-Pays

Parties shall ensure that prevention, mitigation and remediation costs for pollution, and other environmental disruptions and degradation are, to the greatest possible extent, borne by their originator.

Article 9
Access to information

Every person, without being required to state an interest, has a right of access to environmental information held by public authorities.

Public authorities shall, within the framework of their national legislations, collect and make available to the public relevant environmental information.

Article 10
Public participation

Every person has the right to participate, at an appropriate stage and while options are still open, to the preparation of decisions, measures, plans, programmes, activities, policies and normative instruments of public authorities that may have a significant effect on the environment.

Article 11
Access to environmental justice

Parties shall ensure the right of effective and affordable access to administrative and judicial procedures, including redress and remedies, to challenge acts or omissions of public authorities or private persons which contravene environmental law, taking into consideration the provisions of the present Pact.

Article 12
Education and training

The Parties shall ensure that environmental education, to the greatest possible extent, is taught to members of the younger generation as well as to adults, in order to inspire in everyone a responsible conduct in protecting and improving the environment.

The Parties shall ensure the protection of freedom of expression and information in environmental matters. They support the dissemination by mass media of information of an educational nature on ecosystems and on the need to protect and preserve the environment.

Article 13
Research and innovation

The Parties shall promote, to the best of their ability, the improvement of scientific knowledge of ecosystems and the impact of human activities. They shall cooperate through exchanges of scientific and technological knowledge and by enhancing the development, adaptation, dissemination and transfer of technologies respectful of the environment, including innovative technologies.

Article 14
Role of non-State actors and subnational entities

The Parties shall take the necessary measures to encourage the implementation of this Pact by non-State actors and subnational entities, including civil society, economic actors, cities and regions taking into account their vital role in the protection of the environment.

Article 15
Effectiveness of environmental norms

The Parties have the duty to adopt effective environmental laws, and to ensure their effective and fair implementation and enforcement.

Article 16
Resilience

The Parties shall take necessary measures to maintain and restore the diversity and capacity of ecosystems and human communities to withstand environmental disruptions and degradation and to recover and adapt.

Article 17
Non-regression

The Parties and their sub-national entities refrain from allowing activities or adopting norms that have the effect of reducing the global level of environmental protection guaranteed by current law.

Article 18
Cooperation

In order to conserve, protect and restore the integrity of the Earth's ecosystem and community of life, Parties shall cooperate in good faith and in a spirit of global partnership for the implementation of the provisions of the present Pact.

Article 19
Armed conflicts

States shall take pursuant to their obligations under international law all feasible measures to protect the environment in relation to armed conflicts.

Article 20
Diversity of national situations

The special situation and needs of developing countries, particularly the least developed and those most environmentally vulnerable, shall be given special attention.

Account shall be taken, where appropriate, of the Parties' common but differentiated responsibilities and respective capabilities, in light of different national circumstances.

Article 21
Monitoring of the implementation of the Pact

A compliance mechanism to facilitate implementation of, and to promote compliance with, the provisions of the present Pact is hereby established.

This mechanism consists of a Committee of independent experts and focuses on facilitation. It operates in a transparent, non-adversarial and non-punitive manner. The committee shall pay particular attention to the respective national circumstances and capabilities of the Parties.

One year after the entry into force of the present Pact, the Depositary shall convene a meeting of the Parties which will establish the modalities and procedures by which the Committee shall exercise its functions.

Two years after the Committee takes office, and at a frequency to be determined by the meeting of the Parties, not exceeding four years, each Party shall report to the Committee on its progress in implementing the provisions of the Pact.

Article 22
Secretariat

The Secretariat of the present Pact shall be provided by the Secretary-General of the United Nations [or the Executive Director of the United Nations Environment Program].

The Secretary-General [or the Executive Director of the United Nations Environment Program] convenes in as much as necessary meeting of Parties.

Article 23
Signature, ratification, acceptance, approval, accession

The present Pact shall be open for signature and subject to ratification, acceptance or approval by States and international organizations. It shall be open for signature at the United Nations Headquarters in New York from XXX to XXX and shall be open for accession from the day following the date on which it shall cease to be open for signature. Instruments of ratification, acceptance, approval or accession shall be deposited with the Depositary.

Article 24
Coming into force

The present Pact shall enter into force three months after the date of deposit with the Secretary-General of the United Nations of the XX instrument of ratification, approval, acceptance or accession.

For each State and international organization ratifying, approving, accepting or acceding to the present Pact after the deposit of the XX instrument of ratification or accession, the Pact shall enter into force three months after the date of deposit by that State of its instrument of ratification or accession.

Article 25
Denunciation

On the expiry of a period of three years from the date of entry into force of this Treaty in respect of a Party, that Party may at any time denounce it by written notification to the Depositary. Such denunciation shall take effect on the expiry of a period of one year from the date of receipt by the Depositary of such notification, or on such later date as may be specified in such notification.

Article 26
Depositary

The original of this Treaty, of which the Arabic, Chinese, English, French, Russian and Spanish texts are equally authentic, shall be deposited with the Secretary-General of the United Nations.

Document 2: List of Members of the International Group of Experts for the Pact

PRESIDENT: Laurent FABIUS, President of the Constitutional Council of the French Republic, former President of the COP21, France

ASSISTED BY: Louis SCHWEITZER, Special Advisor, France

SECRETARY-GENERAL: Yann AGUILA, President of the Environment Commission of the Club des juristes, Lawyer at the Paris Bar, Bredin Prat, France

MEMBERS:

Pauline-Marie ABADIE, Associate Professor at the University Paris-Sud, France

Domenico AMIRANTE, Full Professor of Comparative Law and Environmental Law, Director of the PhD School in Human Sciences at University della Campania, Italy

Marisol ANGLES HERNANDEZ, Full-time Researcher at the National Autonomous University (UNAM),Institute for Legal Research, Mexico

Mishig BATSUURI, Presiding Justice of Chamber for Administrative Cases, The Supreme Court of Mongolia

Antonio BENJAMIN, Justice at the High Court of Brazil, Chair of the World Commission on Environment Law of the IUCN, Brazil

Ben BOER, Distinguished Professor, Research Institute of Environmental Law, Wuhan University, People's Republic of China, Emeritus Professor, University of Sydney, Former Deputy Chair of the IUCN World Commission on Environmental Law (2012-2016), Australia

Laurence BOISSON DE CHAZOURNES, Professor at the University of Geneva, Switzerland

Klaus BOSSELMANN, Professor of Law and Founding Director of the New-Zealand Centre for Environmental Law, University of Auckland, Chair of the IUCN World Commission on Environmental Law Ethics Specialist Group, Cjair Ecological Law and Governance Association, New-Zealand

Ioana BOTEZATU, INTERPOL, Romania

Soukaina BOURAOUI, Doctor of Law, Director of Centre of Arab Women for Training & Research (CAWTAR), Tunisia

David BOYD, Professor of Law, Policy, and Sustainability, University of British Columbia, UN Special Rapporteur on Human Rights and the Environment, Canada

Edith BROWN WEISS, Professor Edith Brown Weiss, Francis Cabell Brown Professor of International Law, Georgetown University Law Center, United States

Mingde CAO, Professor at the China University of Political Science and Law (CUPL), China

Joëlle CASANOVA, Director of legal and administrative affairs, Prince Albert II of Monaco Foundation, Monaco

Lord Robert CARNWATH, Justice of the Supreme Court of the United Kingdom

Leila CHIKHAOUI, Professor of Public Law at the University of Tunis, Member of the Tunisian provisional Constitutional court, Tunisia

Bradly J. CONDON, Professor, Instituto Tecnológico Autónomo de México (ITAM), Founding Director, Centre of International Economic Law, Mexico

Carina COSTA DE OLIVEIRA, Professor of International and Environmental Law, University of Brasília, Brazil Coordinator of the Research group on Law, Natural Resources and Sustainability (Gern-UnB), Brazil

Philippe CULLET, Professor of International and Environmental Law, SOAS University of London, Senior Visiting Fellow, Centre for Policy Research, New Delhi, Royaume-Uni

Peter DARAK, President of the Curia of Hungary

Luca D'AMBROSIO, Research Fellow at the Collège de France, PhD in Private Law and Criminal Sciences at the Sorbonne Law School (University Paris I) and the University Naples II, Italy

Carlos DE MIGUEL PERALES, Partner, Uría Menéndez, Professor at the Comillas University (ICADE), Madrid, Spain

Nicolas DE SADELEER, Professor at the St Louis University, Brussels, Jean Monnet Chair, Belgium

Olivier DE SCHUTTER, Professor at the Catholic University of Louvain, Co-Chair at the International Panel of Experts on Sustainable Food Systems (IPES-Food), Member of the UN Committee on Economic, Social and Cultural Rights, Belgium

Dr. Bharat H. DESAI, Professor of International Law, Jawaharlal Nehru Chair in Inter. Environmental Law, Chairman, Center for International Legal Studies, School of International Studies, Jawaharlal Nehru University, India

Leila DEVIA, Professor of Environmental International Law, Universities of Salvador and of Buenos Aires, Director of the Basel Regional Center in South America, Argentina

Charles DI LEVA, Adjunct Professor, George Washington University Law School and American University Law School,Visiting Scholar, Environmental Law Institute, United States

Stéphane DOUMBE-BILLE, Professor at the University Jean-Moulin Lyon, Member of the World Commission on Environmental Law of the IUCN, Member of the International Council for Environmental Law, Cameroun

Geneviève DUFOUR, Professor at the University of Sherbrooke, President of the Quebec International Law Society, President of the Francophone Network for International Law, Canada

Daniel ESTY, Hillhouse Professor of Environmental Law & Policy Yale University, United States

Alexandre FARO, Lawyer at the Paris Bar, Faro & Gozlan, France

Michael FAURE, Professor of Comparative and International Environmental Law, Maastricht University, Professor of Comparative Private Law and Economics at the Rotterdam Institute of Law & Economics (RILE) of the Erasmus University in Rotterdam, The Netherlands

Wahid FERCHICHI, Doctor in Law, Professor of Public Law at the Faculty of Social, Political and Juridical Studies at the University of Carthage (UCAR), Tunis, Tunisia

Rosario FERRARA, Professor at the Libera Università Internazionale degli Studi Sociali Guido Carli (LUISS), Roma, Italy

Elizabeth FISHER, Professor of Environmental Law at Corpus Christi College and the Faculty of Law of Oxford University, United Kingdom

Malcolm FORSTER, Professor, University of Western Ontario, United Kingdom

Francesco FRANCIONI, Professor Emeritus of international Law, European University Institute, Florence, Professor of international law at LUISS University, Rome, Member of the of the Institute of International Law (IIL), Italy

Maria GAVOUNELI, Associate Professor of International Law, Faculty of Law, National & Kapodistrian University of Athens, Greece

Michael GERRARD, Andrew Sabin Professor of Professional Practice, Director of the Sabin Center for Climate Change Law, Columbia Law School, United States

Jan GLAZEWSKI, Professor in the Institute of Marine and Environmental Law at the University of Cape Town, Former Advisor to the former Minister of Environmental Affairs, South Africa

Paule HALLEY, Full Professor at the University of Laval, Holder of the Canada Research Chair in Environmental Law, Quebec, Canada

Parvez HASSAN, Senior Advocate at the Supreme Court of Pakistan, Chairman Emeritus of the IUCN World Commission on Environmental Law, Pakistan

Delphine HEDARY, Former Head of the preparation of the Environmental Charter, Former President of the General Estates for the Modernization of Environmental Law, France

Joel HERNANDEZ, Member of the Inter American Commission on Human Rights, Mexican Representative to the Inter-American Juridical Committee (IAJC) of the Organization of American States (OAS), Legal Adviser of the Ministry of Foreign Affairs, Mexico

Davide JR HILARIO G., Chief Justice of the Philippines (Ret.) Former Permanent Representative to the United Nations in New York

Océni HOUNKPATIN ÀMOUSSA, Jurist in Environmental Law, President of the African Jurists for the Environement Society (AJAPE), Benin

Christian HUGLO, Lawyer at the Paris Bar, Huglo Lepage et Associés, France

Maria IVANOVA, Professor at the University of Massachusetts Boston, Director of the Center for Governance and Sustainability, Bulgaria

Alejandro IZA, Head, IUCN Environmental Law Center, Germany

Marie JACOBSSON, Former Member of the UN International Law Commission and Special Rapporteur, Sweden

Maurice KAMTO, Professor in Public Law at the University Yaounde II, Member of the United Nations International Law Commission, Cameroun

Donald KANIARU, Lawyer, Managing Partner of Kaniaru & Kaniaru Advocates, Nairobi, Former Director of the Division of Environmental Policy Implementation and of the Division of Environmental Conventions at UNEP, Former Chairman of Kenya's National Environment Tribunal, Kenya

Anatoly KAPUSTIN, Professor at the Peoples' Friendship University of Russia, Vice-Director of the Institute of Legislation and Comparative Law under the Government of the Russian Federation

Maria Magdalena KENIG-WITKOWSKA, Professor of legal sciences, University of Warsaw, Poland

Yann KERBRAT, Professor at the Paris I Panthéon-Sorbonne, Director of the Sorbonne Research Institute for International and European Law, France

Nicolas KICHIGIN, Leading research fellow of the Institute of Legislation and Comparative Law under the Government of the Russian Federation, Associate professor of the Vysokovsky Graduate School of Urbanism of National Research University High school of Economics, Russia

Louis J. KOTZE, Research Professor, North-West University, South Africa, Visiting Professor of Environmental Law, University of Lincoln in the United Kingdom, South Africa

Arnold KREILHUBER, Head of the International Environmental Law Unit in the Division of Environmental Law and Conventions of the United Nations Environment Programme (UNEP), Austria

Pascale KROMAREK, Lawyer, Member of the Environment Committee of the MEDEF, France

Swatanter KUMAR, Justice, Former Chairperson, National Green Tribunal, India

Aaron T. LAUR, Executive Officer, World Commission on Environmental Law of the IUCN, United States

Sophie LAVALLEE, Full Professor, Lawyer, Faculty of Law, Laval University, Quebec, Canada

Luc LAVRYSEN, Judge at the Constitutional Court of Belgium, President of the European forum of Judges for the Environment, Professor of Environmental Law at the Centre for Environmental & Energy Law, Ghent University, Belgium

Philippe LE PRESTRE, Full Professor of Political Science, Laval University, Québec, Canada

Qingbao LI, Associate Professor of law at the North China Electric Power University, China

Sébastien MABILE, Lawyer, Doctor in Law, Chairman of the IUCN Commission on Environmental Law and Policy, France

Sandrine MALJEAN-DUBOIS, Research director at the CNRS, Director of the mixed research unit International, Comparative and European Law, Professor in International Law at the University Aix-Marseille, France

Luis Fernando MACIAS GOMEZ, Lawyer in Environmental Law, Partner, Macías Gomez y Asociados, President of the Colombian Institute for Environmental Law, Colombia

Gilles J. MARTIN, Professor Emeritus, University Nice Sophia-Antipolis, CNRS, GREDEG, Associate Professor at Sciences Po Paris, France

Benoit MAYER, Assistant Professor, the Chinese Universty of Hong Kong (CUHK), Hong Kong

Makane Moïse MBENGUE, Professor of International Law at the Faculty of Law of the University of Geneva, Affiliated Professor at Sciences Po Paris (School of Law), Senegal

Pilar MORAGA SARIEGO, Associate Professor of Environmental Law at the Faculty of Law of the University of Chile, Santiago, Chili

Maria MUAVESI, Environmental Legal Officer, Pacific Centre for Environmental Governance, IUCN, Fidji

Shinya MURASE, Professor Emeritus, Sophia University Faculty of Law, Tokyo, Member and Special Rapporteur of the UN International Law Commission, Japan

Bouchra NADIR, Professor of Private Law at the University Mohammed V Rabat, Coordinator of the Master in Environmental Law and Sustainable Development, Morocco

Constance NALEGACH ROMERO, Senior Attorney Chief of cabinet, Ministry of Environment of Chile

Françoise NESI, Public Auditor to the criminal chamber of the French Court of Cassation, France

Laurent NEYRET, Professor, University Versailles Paris Saclay, Head of cabinet of the President of the Constitutional Council of the French Republic, France

Nilufer ORAL, Professor at the Istanbul Bilgi University Law Faculty, Member of the UN International Law Commission, Turkey

Luciano PAREJO ALFONSO, Administrative Law Professor Emeritus at Carlos III de Madrid University, Spain

Teresa PAREJO NAVAJAS, Associate Professor of Law at Carlos III de Madrid University, Spain, Senior Advisor UN SDSN, New York

Cymie PAYNE, Associate Professor, Rutgers University, Chair of the IUCN WCEL Oceans, Coasts, and Coral Reefs Specialist Group (OSG), United States

Jacqueline PEEL, Professor of Law and Associate Director of the Centre for Resources, Energy and Environmental Law, Melbourne Law School, Australia

Amedeo POSTIGLIONE, Director and Founder of ICEF, Honorary President of the Italian Court of Cassation, Italy

Tianbao QIN, Director, Research Institute of Environmental Law (RIEL), Wuhan University; Secretary-General, China Society of Environmental and Resources Law (CSERL), China

Fabienne QUILLERE MAJZOUB, Professor at the Rennes 1 University, Lebanon

Lavanya RAJAMANI, Professor at the Center for Policy Research in New Delhi, India

Rama S. RAO, Former Director of the World Intellectual Property Organization (WIPO) at the United Nations, India

Yvan RAZAFINDRATANDRA, Lawyer at the Paris Bar, Environmental Affairs Advisor, France

Vincent REBEYROL, Professor of Law at the EM Lyon Business School, Lawyer, France

Eckard REHBINDER, Professor emeritus of economic and environmental law, Research Centre for Environmental Law, Goethe University Frankfurt, Former Member and Chair of the German Advisory Council on the Environment, Former Regional Governor of the International Council of Environmental Law (ICEL), Germany

Nicholas A. ROBINSON, Professor at Elisabeth Haub School of Law, Pace University, Co-Director of the Global Center for Environmental Legal Studies (GCELS), Executive Governor International Council of Environmental Law (ICEL), United States

Lisa SACHS, Director of the Columbia Center on Sustainable Investment (CCSI), Columbia Law School – The Earth Institute, Columbia University, United States

James SALZMAN, Bren Distinguished Professor of Environmental Law, UCLA Law School, United States

Peter H. SAND, Institute of International Law, University of Munich, Formerly World Bank Legal Adviser for Environmental Affairs, Germany

Yacouba SAVADOGO, Expert Jurist in Environmental Law, IUCN, IUCN's Central and West Africa Regional Office, Member of the World Commission on Environmental Law, Coordinator of the Fracophone African Network of Environmental Jurists (RAFJE), Burkina Faso

Patricia SAVIN, Partner, DS Avocats, Doctor of Law, Associate Professor at the University of Créteil, France

Tullio SCOVAZZI, Professor of International Law at the Università degli Studi di Milano Bicocca, Italy

Dinah SHELTON, Professor, George Washington University, Former Member of the Inter-American Commission on Human Rights, United States

Patrick THIEFFRY, Lawyer at the Paris and New-York Bars, Thieffry & Associés, Associate Professor at the Sorbonne Law School, University Paris I Panthéon-Sorbonne, France

James THORNTON, Founding CEO of ClientEarth, Environmental lawyer and social entrepreneur, Republic of Ireland

Amado Jr. TOLENTINO, Professor of Environmental Law, Member of the Experts Group on Environment Law of the World Commission on Environment and Development (WCED) of the IUCN, Former Executive Governor (for developing countries), International Council of Environmental Law, Philippines

François-Guy TREBULLE, Professor, Director of the Sorbonne Law School, University Paris I Panthéon-Sorbonne, France

Eduardo VALENCIA OSPINA, Chair, International Law Commission of the United Nations, Former Special Rapporteur of the ILC on the Protection of Persons in the Event of Disasters, Colombia

Jorge E. VINUALES, Professor at the University of Cambridge (Harold Samuel Chair of Law and Environmental Policy), Director of the Cambridge Centre for Environment, Energy and Natural Resource Governance (C-EENRG), Chairman of the Compliance Committee of the UNECE/WHO-Europe Protocol on Water and Health, Argentina

Christina VOIGT, Professor at the University of Oslo, Chair of the IUCN Specialist Group on climate change, legal advisor to the Norwegian Ministry of Climate and the Environment, Norway

Canfa WANG, Professor at the China University of Political Science and Law, Director of the the Center for Legal Assistance to Pollution Victims (CLAPV), China

Catherine WARBURTON, Managing Director, Warburton Attorneys & IMBEWU Sustainability Legal Specialists (Pty) Ltd, South Africa

Michael D. WILSON, Associate Justice, Hawaii Supreme Court, Founding member of the Global Judicial Institute on the Environment, Adjunct faculty member of the Jindal Global University Law School in Sonipat in India, United States

Farhana YAMIN, International environmental lawyer, Founder and CEO of Track 0, United Kingdom

Margaret YOUNG, Associate Professor, Melbourne Law School, Australia

Jinfeng ZHOU, Secretary General of China Biodiversity Conservation and Green Development Foundation, China; Vice Chairman of World Green Design Organization, Belgium

Chapter 2: Phase II: Adoption of the Resolution (Sept. 2017 – May 2018)

The French delegation introduced the Global Pact on the sidelines of the 72nd session of the UN General Assembly (UNGA) in a high-level event titled "Summit on a Global Pact for the Environment."[1] Between September 2017 and May 2018, Member States held closed doors negotiations to draft a resolution unfolding the process of debating a potential global pact. In May 2018, the UNGA adopted a resolution titled "Towards a Global Pact for the Environment," by which Member States requested the UN Secretary-General to submit a report identifying and assessing possible gaps in international environmental law and environment-related instruments and to establish an ad hoc open-ended working group (OEWG) to consider the report and discuss options to address said gaps with a view to making recommendations.[2]

This chapter focuses on the process of adopting Resolution No. 72/277. Phase II, entitled Adoption of the Resolution, relates to the beginning of the discussions of a potential Global Pact at the United Nations, starting from the high-level event held by the French delegation in September 2017 to the adoption of the resolution in May 2018. Section I covers the high-level event held at the 72nd UNGA, in which French President Macron presented the Global Pact to UN delegates. Part II relates to the subsequent period at the UNGA, in which the diplomatic process for the adoption of a resolution unfolded behind closed doors. Additionally, several academic and diplomatic events were held to support the GPE, gathering support for the proposal. Section III focuses on the draft resolution submitted by the French government and its adoption in May 2018. Section IV includes a brief commentary on the resolution. Resolution No. 72/277 is reprinted at the end of this chapter.

The timeline below portrays Phase II.

1. Speech by M. Emmanuel Macron, President of the Republic: Summit on the Global Pact for the Environment, France Diplomatie, Sept. 19, 2017, http://www.diplomatie.gouv.fr/en/french-foreign-policy/united-nations/united-nations-general-assembly-sessions/unga-s-72nd-session/article/speech-by-m-emmanuel-macron-president-of-the-republic-summit-on-the-global-pact.
2. UNGA, Towards a Global Pact for the Environment, UN Doc. A/RES/72/277 (10 May 2018).

Figure 2: Phase II Timeline "Adoption of the Resolution" (Sept. 2017 – May 2018):

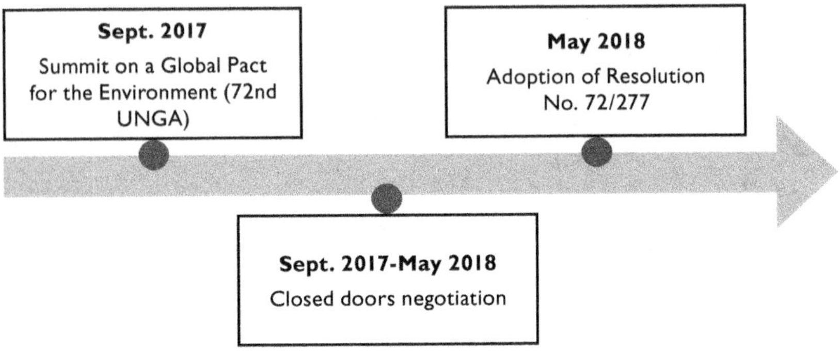

I. September 2017: 72nd United Nations General Assembly

The Summit on a Global Pact for the Environment was held at the UN headquarters in New York as a side event to the high-level segment of the 72nd session of the UNGA on September 19th, 2017.[3] The Secretary-General of the UN, 40 Heads of State and Government, Ministers, representatives from UN institutions and figures from civil society attended the Summit. French President Emmanuel Macron gave a speech announcing the Global Pact as the "next phase" in environmental protection.[4] Noting the protection of nature as a daily battle for the UN and its agencies, and the rise of statements, conventions, and protocols that promote joint efforts in environmental protection, President Macron said that it was our common responsibility to take the next step and go further in transforming our societies, taking resolute action for environmental protection.[5] He added:

> "A framework that will promote at the highest level peoples' and governments' ambitions for protecting the planet. A framework that will establish rights, but also duties for mankind as regards nature and therefore as regards itself. This collective framework is the Global Pact for the Environment.(…) I very strongly believe that the world is ready for this and that it's our responsibility; and rather than spend too much time wondering whether we should reopen

3. Macron, *supra* note 1.
4. UN / Global Pact Environment (UN Multimedia, Sept. 19, 2017), http://www.unmultimedia.org/avlibrary/asset/1972/1972090/.
5. Summit on a Global Pact for the Environment, Concept Note (Sept. 19, 2017), https://wedocs.unep.org/bitstream/handle/20.500.11822/21712/Global%20Pact%20for%20the%20environnement%20-%20Concept%20note%20%28France%29.pdf?sequence=1&isAllowed=y.

issues we've already closed, or decisions we've already taken, we've instead got to forge ahead and build the next step. This Global Pact for the Environment is the next step."[6]

The idea was received with great enthusiasm, with immediate encouragement of 17 countries.[7] UN Secretary-General António Guterres[8] and President of the European Council Donald Tusk spoke in support of the Global Pact.[9] Speakers included Bangladesh, Bolivia, China, Costa Rica, Croatia, Estonia, Fiji, Gabon, Guinea for the African Union, India, Mexico, Norway.[10] The initiative subsequently received ample coverage in the media,[11] as well as in academic and policy circles.[12]

Following the high-level summit, the Columbia Center on Sustainable Investment (CCSI) and the UN Sustainable Development Solutions Net-

6. Macron, *supra* note 1.
7. Columbia Center on Sustainable Investment, World Leaders Discuss a Global Pact for the Environment, STATE OF THE PLANET: EARTH INSTITUTE|COLUMBIA UNIVERSITY (Sept. 26, 2017), http://blogs.ei.columbia.edu/2017/09/26/world-leaders-discuss-a-global-pact-for-the-environment/.
8. UN News, French initiative to create global environment pact deserves support, says Secretary-General (Sept. 19, 2017), https://news.un.org/en/story/2017/09/565352-french-initiative-create-global-environment-pact-deserves-support-says.
9. European Council, Council of the European Union, Remarks by President Donald Tusk at the High-Level Event on the Global Pact for the Environment (Sept. 19, 2017), https://www.consilium.europa.eu/en/press/press-releases/2017/09/19/tusk-speech-un-high-event-environment/.
10. UNEP, Global Pact for the Environment—Update, https://wedocs.unep.org/bitstream/handle/20.500.11822/22190/Global%20Pact%20for%20the%20Environment%20-%20Concept%20note%20%2813%20November%29.pdf?sequence=3&isAllowed=y.
11. 'Wang Yi Attends Global Pact for the Environment Summit' (Ministry of Foreign Affairs of the People's Republic of China, 20 September 2017); H Xiao, 'China Lauds UN Environment Pact' (ChinaDaily, 20 September 2017); 'Macron Rilancia all'Onu un Patto Globale per il Clima' (La Stampa, 21 September 2017); 'Secretário-Geral da ONU Pede Apoio a Pacto Ambiental Proposto Pela França' (Naçoes Unidas no Brasil, 22 September 2017); Laurent Fabius and Yann Aguila, 'Un Pacto Medioambiental' (El País, 2 August 2018); 'Global Pact Will Boost International Environmental Governance' (The Guardian (Nigeria), 25 September 2018); 'Appel de 100 Juristes Pour l'Adoption d'un Pacte Mondial Pour l'Environnement' (Le Monde, 9 October 2018); Yann Aguila et al, 'The Time Is Now for a Global Pact for the Environment' (The Guardian, 9 October 2018); 'Uhuru: Kenya Committed to Fight Against Climate Change' (Daily Nation (Kenya), 11 November 2018).
12. *See, e.g.*, Marisol Anglés Hernández, et al., Global Perspectives on a Global Pact for the Environment § 2019 (Michael Burger, et al. eds., Sabin Center for Climate Change Law, Columbia University 2018). In addition, many meetings have been held around the world, including in Paris (Conference 'Towards a Global Pact for the Environment,' La Sorbonne, 24 June 2017), New York (Conference on the Global Pact for the Environment, Columbia University, 20 September 2017), Bogotá (Symposium on the Global Pact for the Environment Organized by the Attorney General of the Nation, 1 March 2018), Brasilia (Round Table on the Global Pact for the Environment, World Water Forum, 19 March 2018), Dakar (Conference 'L'Afrique S'Engage Pour la Planète,' 14 May 2018), Geneva (Conference on the Global Pact for the Environment at the UN International Law Commission, 10 July 2018), Santiago de Chile (Coloquio 'Pacto Mundial del Medio Ambiente, Derechos Humanos, y Constitución,' 28 August 2018), Québec (Conférence 'Une Opportunité Pour un Canada Plus Vert? Le Projet de Pacte Mondial Pour l'Environnement,' 21 September 2018), Ottawa ('Le Projet Onusien de Pacte Mondial Pour l'Environnement: Quelles Implications Pour le Canada?,' 24 September 2018), Beijing (Conference on the Legal Aspects of a Healthy Environment, 12 October 2018), Naples ('Une Patto Globale per l'Ambiente,' 19 October 2018).

work (SDSN) organized an academic conference to discuss the blueprint for a Global Pact at Columbia University.[13] The initiative received praise from academics like Prof. Boisson de Chazournes, who welcomed a document to unify the sprawling web of existing environmental law with core principles and Prof. Burkett, who hoped the Pact could catalyze a green audit of other areas of international governance such as trade, investment, and intellectual property.[14] Significantly, Prof. Susan Biniaz questioned some of the core premises of the Pact, including the idea of codifying principles into hard law, and presented concerns about its effects on different iterations of the principles drafted to address specific circumstances. Her concerns echoed a paper published a couple of weeks earlier, which summarized ten questions about the Global Pact, and was harshly critical of it.[15]

While she acknowledged the need for more action to protect the environment, she argued the Global Pact was not the "right vehicle" for enhancing environmental protection. She raised legal and policy questions, including how the Pact relates to other international agreements, whether it addresses the actual causes of inadequate environmental protection, and whether the provisions would solve any particular environmental problem. Amidst some confusion on the Pact's intended purpose (create a coherent body of law, provide legally binding effect to soft law principles, create an environment-oriented human-rights treaty or set out law that could be relied upon in courts) and scope, she questioned what the added value of adopting such an initiative would be. Her negative approach caused some pause, slowing down the momentum the Pact had built.

II. Sept. 2017 – May 2018: Informal Meetings

After the Global Pact was proposed by the French delegation to the General Assembly, an internal process unfolded at the UN. For the idea to move forward, the General Assembly had to vote on a procedural resolution to provide for the establishment of an open intergovernmental working group responsible for negotiating the Pact and setting out its parameters, such as its scope and legally binding nature.[16] Between September 2017 and May 2018,

13. Columbia Center on Sustainable Investment, Conference on the Global Pact for the Environment (Sept. 20, 2017), http://ccsi.columbia.edu/2017/09/20/conference-on-the-global-pact-for-the-environment/.
14. Nathan Lobel, World Leaders Discuss a Global Pact for the Environment § 2019 (CCSI 2017), *available at* http://ccsi.columbia.edu/2017/09/26/world-leaders-discuss-a-global-pact-for-the-environment/.
15. Susan Biniaz, 10 Questions to Ask About the Proposed "Global Pact for the Environment," *at* http://columbiaclimatelaw.com/files/2017/08/Biniaz-2017-08-Global-Pact-for-the-Environment.pdf.
16. Report of the Ad Hoc Committee on the Improvement of the Methods of Work of the General Assembly, U.N.G.A. 18th sess., 1256th Plen. Mtg., U.N. Doc. A/RES/1898 (XVIII) (Nov. 11, 1963).

several informal meetings occurred between delegates outlining the scope of a draft resolution in support of the Pact. The internal process unfolded behind closed doors. France and supportive nations planned to bring forward a resolution that would ignite a discussion on the Pact itself. Due to significant pushback from a few delegations, an agreement was reached to take a step back, and instead submit a watered-down resolution to the UNGA. The compromise reached between countries related to a procedural resolution that ignited a discussion on the current state of international environmental law. It set forward the process of considering the codification of environmental principles, asking first whether a Global Pact is needed.[17]

Additionally, several significant steps were taken to support the idea of a GPE, including expert gatherings,[18] a Sino-French Summit between French President Emmanuel Macron and Chinese President Xi Jinping in January 2018,[19] and a high-level discussion organized by the UN Environment in Geneva in March 2018.[20]

III. May 2018: Adoption of the UNGA Resolution A/72/L.51

Under point 14 of the Agenda of the UN General Assembly's plenary (Integrated and coordinated implementation of and follow-up to the outcomes of

See also Rules of Procedure of the General Assembly, U.N. Doc. A/520/Rev.18 (Feb. 21, 2017).

17. Macron, *supra* note 1.
18. *See, e.g.*, Hernández, et al. 2018. In addition, many meetings have been held around the world, including in Paris (Conference 'Towards a Global Pact for the Environment,' La Sorbonne, 24 June 2017), New York (Conference on the Global Pact for the Environment, Columbia University, 20 September 2017), Bogotá (Symposium on the Global Pact for the Environment Organized by the Attorney General of the Nation, 1 March 2018), Brasilia (Round Table on the Global Pact for the Environment, World Water Forum, 19 March 2018), Dakar (Conference 'L'Afrique S'Engage Pour la Planète,' 14 May 2018), Geneva (Conference on the Global Pact for the Environment at the UN International Law Commission, 10 July 2018), Santiago de Chile (Coloquio 'Pacto Mundial del Medio Ambiente, Derechos Humanos, y Constitución,' 28 August 2018), Québec (Conférence 'Une Opportunité Pour un Canada Plus Vert? Le Projet de Pacte Mondial Pour l'Environnement,' 21 September 2018), Ottawa ('Le Projet Onusien de Pacte Mondial Pour l'Environnement: Quelles Implications Pour le Canada?,' 24 September 2018), Beijing (Conference on the Legal Aspects of a Healthy Environment, 12 October 2018), Naples ('Une Patto Globale per l'Ambiente,' 19 October 2018).
19. 'Joint Declaration Between the People's Republic of China and the French Republic' (10 January 2018) para. 8 ('China and France Intend to Continue Their Constructive Dialogue on the Formulation of the Global Pact for the Environment'), translation available at http://www.xinhuanet.com/english/2018-01/11/c_136886038.htm.
20. UN Environment, High-Level Discussion on the Global Pact for the Environment Organized by the UN Environment in Geneva (Mar. 9, 2018, https://www.unenvironment.org/events/un-environment-event/high-level-discussion-global-pact-environment). The Geneva Environment Network looked at the contribution of the Global Pact to global environmental governance, informing participants on progress achieved, potential risks and opportunities identified so far in the process.

the major United Nations conferences and summits in the economic, social and related fields), the UN General Assembly held a meeting on May 10th, 2018 to debate a potential resolution to continue the dialogue on a Global Pact for the Environment.[21] France presented a Draft Resolution (A/72/L.51) which was sponsored by 71 States after intense diplomatic negotiations.[22] The Kenyan delegation proposed minor amendments (A/72/L.53), primarily aimed at ensuring that the process unfolds in Nairobi.[23]

Some delegations took the floor to oppose the project or aspects of it, mainly related to matters of process.[24] The United States claimed that Member States had not been able to consider how such a proposal would contribute to the existing environmental regime and would be willing to support the establishment of a working group to address gaps, but not the title of the draft resolution, which included specific reference to the Global Pact, or any language that would prejudge discussions before challenges had been identified.[25] The Philippines also noted the need to follow a transparent and consultative process, with extensive national inter-agency consultations. The Russian Federation noted that the drafting process was not participative and prevented the addition of comments and suggestions. Arguing that France did not consult with the Group of 77 and China to inquire whether they would vote as a group, and instead engaged countries bilaterally, the Philippines decided to vote against it.[26]

Some of the delegates' comments reflected the need to focus on the implementation of existing agreements rather than negotiating a new document. The Philippines noted that the 2030 Agenda already provided an integrative framework for bringing the global community together on the environment and that we should not renegotiate principles.[27] Also expressing their views on the resolution were representatives from Bulgaria (on behalf of the

21. United Nations Meetings Coverage and Press Releases, General Assembly Decides to Establish Working Group Aimed at Identifying Gaps in International Environmental Law § 2019 (United Nations UN Meeting Coverage, GA 12015, 10 May 2018 ed. 2018).
22. Lucien Chabason & Elisabeth Hege *What to Expect From a Global Pact for the Environment?* 2 (IDDRI, 2019), *available at* https://www.iddri.org/sites/default/files/PDF/Publications/Catalogue%20Iddri/D%C3%A9cryptage/201901-IB0119EN-pacte%20mondial%20env.pdf.
23. Emphasizing Nairobi's standing as the environmental capital of the United Nations, she said all substantive sessions—rather than just the initial one—must be held in the Kenyan capital. That would preserve the integrity of UNEP and the United Nations. The proposal to have Nairobi as the location of the substantive session was in accordance with all resolutions, including the decision adopted in Rio de Janeiro, Brazil, on 20-22 June 2012, contained in the document "The Future We Want."
24. United Nations Meetings Coverage and Press Releases, *supra* note 21.
25. *Id.*
26. Philippines, Explanation of Vote (10 May 2018), http://statements.unmeetings.org/media2/18559939/philippines-explanation-of-vote.pdf.
27. *Id.*

European Union, voicing disappointment with Kenya's amendment), Bolivia (commending the effort and reinforcing the principle of common but differentiated responsibilities), China (welcoming the initiative), Syria (pointing out that the concept of world environmental law was still legally controversial) and Mali (which had not taken part in the vote, but would have voted in favor of the text).[28]

The United States requested a recorded vote as "no transparent and open discussion had taken place for a new environment-related instrument."[29] The UNGA adopted Resolution A/72/L.51 by a large majority.[30] Out of the 193 UN Member States, 143 voted in favor of the resolution, five opposed it (Philippines, Russia, Syria, Turkey, the USA), seven abstained (Belarus, Iran,[31] Malaysia, Nicaragua, Nigeria, Saudi Arabia, Tajikistan) and 38 did not vote.[32] The resolution is reprinted at the end of this chapter. The next section provides a commentary.

IV. Commentary on the Resolution

Resolution No. 72/277, entitled "Towards a Global Pact for the Environment," represents a decisive first step in mobilizing the international community towards environmental protection, while also embodying a commitment from governments to explore existing gaps in international environmental law and potential ways to approach them.[33] However, the Resolution uses neutral language and provides an intentional distance from the draft proposed by the French government. Before analyzing a potential new agreement, it was necessary to assess whether there was a need for one.[34] Notwithstanding the title of the Resolution, "Towards a Global Pact for the Environment," the text does not actually mention a Global Pact or reference the original French draft text. The only allusion is by noting the convening of the high-level event held on the sidelines of the 72nd session of the UNGA in 2017, mentioned in its preamble. Politically, it was challenging to begin the process

28. United Nations Meetings Coverage and Press Releases, *supra* note 21.
29. *Id.*
30. UNGA, Towards a Global Pact for the Environment, UN Doc. A/RES/72/277 (10 May 2018).
31. Iran's vote was wrongfully recorded, The country wished to abstain rather than vote against it. United Nations Meetings Coverage and Press Releases, *supra* note 21.
32. UN, Voting Record, Item 14 A/72/L.51 as amended (Towards a Global Pact for the Environment), General Assembly 88th Plenary Meeting, UN (2018), *available at* http://papersmart.unmeetings.org/media2/18559921/vr-1.pdf.
33. Niko Urho, et al., International Environmental Governance: Accomplishments and Way Forward 16 (Nordic Council of Ministers. 2019). Elena Loredana Pîrvu, *The New Global Pact for the Environment*, 15 Acta Universitatis Danubius Juridica 5 (2019).
34. Christina Voigt, *How a 'Global Pact for the Environment' Could Add Value to International Environmental Law*, 28 Rev. Eur., Comp. & Int'l Envtl. L. 13;16 (2019).

of discussing a new international agreement that was unilaterally proposed by one government. Some countries immediately opposed the idea simply because France proposed it. Instead, to jumpstart the process, it was necessary to start from scratch.

The preamble of the Resolution introduced the context of the need to continue to address, comprehensively and coherently, the challenges posed by environmental degradation in the context of sustainable development (preamble). Accordingly, the Resolution sets out a linear and open-ended methodological approach to potential problems and solutions in international environmental law.[35] To gain more clarity on the need for additional action, States agreed to assess whether there are gaps or deficiencies in international environmental law, leaving it open to further deliberations whether to do something about those. The Resolution opened a two-step process: it requested a report from the Secretary-General to assess gaps in international environmental law and established a working group to discuss said report, considering possible gaps in international environmental law.

As a first step, the Resolution requested the Secretary-General (UNSG) to submit a technical and evidence-based report at the 73rd session of the General Assembly in 2018. The UNSG was tasked with identifying and assessing possible gaps in international environmental law and, to encompass non-legally binding documents, environment-related instruments. The investigation had the goal of strengthening the implementation of existing instruments at the core of the process. Beginning with the perceived problems followed a logical methodology.[36] However, the open-ended mandate has caused much debate among delegates. Supporters of a Global Pact expressed frustration with a perceived ambiguity in the Resolution, which set a mandate considered too generic and all-encompassing.[37] During the Nairobi sessions, States disagreed on the meaning of "technical and evidence-based," "gaps," and "environment-related instruments."[38] The question opened the door for a broad discussion on inefficiencies of international environmental law, including gaps in substantive instruments, the governance of international environmental law and its effective implementation.

35. Susan Biniaz, *The UNGA Resolution on a 'Global Pact for the Environment': A Chance to Put the Horse Before the Cart*, 28 Rev. Eur., Comp. & Int'l Envtl. L. 33 (2019).
36. *Id.* at 34.
37. Doran, et al., Summary of the First Substantive Session of the Ad Hoc Open-Ended Working Group Towards a Global Pact for the Environment: 14-18 January 2019. 2019. P. 13. Yann Aguila & Jorge E. Viñuales, *A Global Pact for the Environment: Conceptual Foundations*, 28 Rev. Eur., Comp. & Int'l Envtl. L. 3 (2019).
38. *See* Chapter 4, Section V "Analysis of Substantive Issues Discussed and How the Recommendations Came About."

The second step was to install an ad hoc open-ended working group (OEWG) under the UNGA's auspices to consider the matter. The group received three specific tasks: (i) consider the report, using it as a guide for discussions; (ii) debate possible options to address possible gaps in international environmental law and environment-related instruments, as appropriate; (iii) if deemed necessary, to deliberate the scope, parameters and feasibility of an international instrument, with a view to making recommendations to the General Assembly. These recommendations may include the convening of an intergovernmental conference to adopt an international instrument. It set a deadline to produce its conclusions to the Assembly during the first half of 2019.

The Resolution does not restrict the consideration of possible gaps identified in the Secretary-General's report.[39] Instead, the OEWG should use the report as a guide to consider whether there are possible "gaps" in existing environmental law and policy and, if so, to articulate ways of approaching them. The OEWG had full discretion in deciding how to move forward.[40] The Resolution does not presume there are gaps in international environmental law. If gaps exist, it leaves open to discussion the type of options that could be discussed to direct them. It also did not task the OEWG with negotiating a legally binding instrument. In fact, the working group's mandate does not anticipate the need for a new "international instrument." If it decides a new agreement is necessary, the Resolution does not specify its form, legal character or name.[41] Not prejudging a specific outcome was essential to provide a distance from the Global Pact. The OEWG's recommendations could include "the convening of an intergovernmental conference" to negotiate a binding or non-legally binding text, but this is just one of the options States could choose. A multi-pronged outcome was a possibility and discussions could lead to several different directions.[42] These included a new legally binding instrument covering a single issue or a wide range of topics, a new instrument of a political character aimed at one or more issues, actions (such as increased funding, a campaign or a high-level gathering) not involving a new instrument, a combination of the above, or no action.[43]

A few specific details established the contours of the mandate. The OEWG was open to participation by all Member States of the United

39. Biniaz, *supra* note 35, at 34.
40. Not All That Glitters Is Gold: An Analysis of the Global Pact for the Environment Project (2019).
41. Biniaz, *supra* note 35, at 34.
42. *Id.* at 34.
43. *Id.* at 34.

Nations and all members of specialized agencies.[44] Attendance to formal meetings as observers was open to relevant non-governmental organizations in consultative status with the Economic and Social Council, as well as to those that were accredited to relevant conferences and summits.[45] In addition to setting a deadline for formalizing concluding recommendations, it decided that the working group should hold at least two sessions, one procedural session in New York, focused on deciding the duration, number, and venue of following sessions, as well as one substantive session in Nairobi.[46] The Resolution requested the UNGA to appoint two co-chairs of the OEWG, specifying one would come from a developing country and one from a developed country, to oversee its consultations.[47] The OEWG should consult all Member States, regional groups, and relevant stakeholders, and be open, transparent and inclusive.[48] Finally, the resolution specified how to fund the working group based on voluntary contributions.[49] It also requested the Secretary-General to arrange for substantive support from UNEP based on voluntary contributions.[50]

Significantly, the Resolution recognizes that the process [i.e., the OEWG and its possible continuation by an intergovernmental conference] "should not undermine existing relevant legal instruments and frameworks and relevant global, regional and sectoral bodies."[51] The statement is meaningful, given the concern by several delegates about the potential effect of a new instrument on existing law. This relates to the delicate question of the relationship between a potential GPE and other existing agreements.[52] The requirement was reinforced in the UNSG's report and the final recommendations by the OEWG. In line with this statement, the Resolution reaffirmed the purposes and principles of the Charter of the United Nations, existing obligations and commitments under international environmental law, the principles of the Rio Declaration, the 2030 Agenda for Sustainable Development and the Sustainable Development Goals. It recalled the Declaration

44. Resolution, para. 3.
45. Resolution, para. 4. Reference is made to the non-governmental organizations that were accredited to the following relevant conferences and summits: the United Nations Conference on Environment and Development, the World Summit on Sustainable Development, the United Nations Conference on Sustainable Development and the United Nations summit for the adoption of the post-2015 development agenda.
46. Resolution, para. 5.
47. Resolution, para. 6.
48. Resolution, para. 6.
49. Resolution, para. 7.
50. Resolution, para. 8.
51. Resolution, para. 9.
52. Saint-Geniès. 2019. P. 6.

of the United Nations Conference on the Human Environment,[53] the Rio Declaration on Environment and Development,[54] Agenda 21,[55] the Programme for the Further Implementation of Agenda 21,[56] the Johannesburg Declaration on Sustainable Development[57] and the Plan of Implementation of the World Summit on Sustainable Development (Johannesburg Plan of Implementation)[58] and the outcome document of the United Nations Conference on Sustainable Development, entitled "The Future We Want,"[59] as well as the outcomes of all the major United Nations conferences and summits in the economic, social and environmental fields.

Scholars, delegates, and drafters of the Global Pact were harshly critical of the Resolution. One scholar questioned whether the Secretary-General raised the right questions.[60] Prof. Bodansky challenged the possibility of having an objective, evidence-based answer to the question of whether the lack of a general agreement is a gap, arguing it dangles on political and moral judgments.[61] A few delegates condemned the Resolution's invitation to look at gaps beyond international environmental law, arguing it opened "a can of worms."[62] Supporters of the Pact called the Resolution "ambiguous," deeming the mandate extensively broad. Prof. Biniaz, however, praised the Resolution for allowing States to step back and methodically consider the most critical missing pieces in environmental law and policy.[63] Prof. Boer interpreted the Resolution as an indication of the international community's readiness to accept that the fundamental importance of the environment warrants a new instrument.[64]

The Resolution is particularly noteworthy for inviting an unprecedented discussion on the state of international environmental law. Rather than jumpstarting a negotiation of a new instrument, it takes a step back. It

53. *See* Report of the United Nations Conference on the Human Environment, Stockholm, 5–16 June 1972 (A/CONF.48/14/Rev.1), part one, chap. I.
54. Report of the United Nations Conference on Environment and Development, Rio de Janeiro, 3–14 June 1992, vol. I, Resolutions Adopted by the Conference (United Nations publication, Sales No. E.93.I.8 and corrigendum), resolution 1, annex I.
55. *Id.* annex II.
56. Resolution S-19/2, annex.
57. Report of the World Summit on Sustainable Development, Johannesburg, South Africa, 26 August–4 September 2002 (United Nations publication, Sales No. 03.II.A.1 and corrigendum), chap. I, resolution 1, annex.
58. *Id.* resolution 2, annex.
59. Resolution 66/288, annex.
60. Biniaz, *supra* note 35, at 38.
61. Hernández, et al. 2018.
62. Doran, et al., Summary of the First Substantive Session of the Ad Hoc Open-Ended Working Group Towards a Global Pact for the Environment: 14–18 January 2019. 2019.
63. Biniaz, *supra* note 35, at 38.
64. Hernández, et al. 2018.

encourages debate on existing gaps and if/how the international community should address them. By providing a broad mandate, the General Assembly strikes an essential balance between the different political views of the Member States, which became apparent since the launch of the Global Pact at the Sorbonne. The wide-ranging question presumes there are no preliminary findings on an outcome. The Resolution is precise in the result the General Assembly intends to receive, and the deadline to achieve it. Additionally, it sets significant safeguards that protect the current framework of international environmental law, making sure not to undermine existing MEAs and institutions.

Document 3: Resolution No. A/72/L.51 "Towards a Global Pact for the Environment"

United Nations General Assembly
Resolution No. A/72/L.51 (7 May 2018)

Seventy-second session
Agenda item 14

Integrated and coordinated implementation of and follow-up to the outcomes of the major United Nations conferences and summits in the economic, social and related fields

Albania, Andorra, Angola, Bangladesh, Belgium, Benin, Bhutan, Bosnia and Herzegovina, Brazil, Bulgaria, Burkina Faso, Canada, Central African Republic, Chad, Chile, Colombia, Congo, Costa Rica, Croatia, Cyprus, Czechia, Denmark, Equatorial Guinea, Estonia, Finland, France, Gabon, Georgia, Germany, Ghana, Greece, Guatemala, Guinea, Guyana, India, Ireland, Italy, Jordan, Latvia, Lebanon, Libya, Lithuania, Luxembourg, Madagascar, Malta, Mauritania, Mexico, Monaco, Montenegro, Morocco, Netherlands, Niger, Norway, Paraguay, Peru, Portugal, Qatar, Romania, Senegal, Seychelles, Slovakia, Slovenia, Spain, Sri Lanka, Suriname, the former Yugoslav Republic of Macedonia, Tunisia, Turkmenistan, Tuvalu, United Arab Emirates and United Kingdom of Great Britain and Northern Ireland: draft resolution

Towards a Global Pact for the Environment

The General Assembly,

Reaffirming the purposes and principles of the Charter of the United Nations,

Recalling the Declaration of the United Nations Conference on the Human Environment,[1] the Rio Declaration on Environment and Development,[2] Agenda 21,[3] the Programme for the Further Implementation of Agenda 21,[4] the Johannesburg Declaration on Sustainable Development[5] and the Plan of Implementation of the World Summit on Sustainable Development (Johannesburg Plan of Implementation)[6] and the outcome document of the United Nations Conference on Sustainable Development, entitled "The future we want",[7] as well as the out-

---

1. *See* Report of the United Nations Conference on the Human Environment, Stockholm, 5–16 June 1972 (A/CONF.48/14/Rev.1), part one, chap. I.
2. Report of the United Nations Conference on Environment and Development, Rio de Janeiro, 3–14 June 1992, vol. I, Resolutions Adopted by the Conference (United Nations publication, Sales No. E.93.I.8 and corrigendum), resolution 1, annex I.
3. *Id.* annex II.
4. Resolution S-19/2, annex.
5. Report of the World Summit on Sustainable Development, Johannesburg, South Africa, 26 August–4 September 2002 (United Nations publication, Sales No. 03.II.A.1 and corrigendum), chap. I, resolution 1, annex.
6. *Id.* resolution 2, annex.
7. Resolution 66/288, annex.

comes of all the major United Nations conferences and summits in the economic, social and environmental fields,

Recognizing existing obligations and commitments under international environmental law,

Reaffirming all the principles of the Rio Declaration,

Reaffirming also its resolution 70/1 of 25 September 2015, entitled "Transforming our world: the 2030 Agenda for Sustainable Development", in which it adopted a comprehensive, far-reaching and people-centred set of universal and transformative Sustainable Development Goals and targets, its commitment to working tirelessly for the full implementation of the Agenda by 2030, its recognition that eradicating poverty in all its forms and dimensions, including extreme poverty, is the greatest global challenge and an indispensable requirement for sustainable development, its commitment to achieving sustainable development in its three dimensions — economic, social and environmental — in a balanced and integrated manner, and to building upon the achievements of the Millennium Development Goals and seeking to address their unfinished business,

Noting the convening of the high-level event held on the sidelines of the seventy-second session of the General Assembly on 19 September 2017, entitled "Summit on a Global Pact for the Environment",

Stressing the need to continue to address, in a comprehensive and coherent manner, the challenges posed by environmental degradation in the context of sustainable development,

1. *Requests* the Secretary-General to submit to the General Assembly at its seventy-third session in 2018 a technical and evidence-based report that identifies and assesses possible gaps in international environmental law and environment-related instruments with a view to strengthening their implementation;

2. *Decides* to establish an ad hoc open-ended working group, under the auspices of the General Assembly, to consider the report and discuss possible options to address possible gaps in international environmental law and environment-related instruments, as appropriate, and, if deemed necessary, the scope, parameters and feasibility of an international instrument, with a view to making recommendations, which may include the convening of an intergovernmental conference to adopt an international instrument, to the Assembly during the first half of 2019;

3. *Also decides* that the ad hoc open-ended working group shall be open to participation by all States Members of the United Nations and all members of the specialized agencies;

4. *Further decides* that attendance at the sessions of the ad hoc open-ended working group as observers will be opened to relevant non-governmental organizations in consultative status with the Economic and Social Council in accordance with the provisions of Council resolution 1996/31 of 25 July 1996, as well as to those

that were accredited to relevant conferences and summits,[8] on the understanding that participation means attending formal meetings, unless otherwise decided by the working group in specific situations, receiving copies of the official documents, making available their materials to delegates and addressing the meetings, through a limited number of their representatives, as appropriate;

5. *Decides* that the ad hoc open-ended working group shall hold the following sessions, with the provision of interpretation services, in accordance with established practice:

(a) An organizational session, to be held for a duration of three working days, by the end of the seventy-second session of the General Assembly, in New York, in order to examine matters related to the organization of the work of the ad hoc open-ended working group, including the duration, number and venue (preferably in Nairobi) of its sessions;

(b) An initial substantive session, to be held in Nairobi, at least one month after the submission of the report of the Secretary-General;

6. *Requests* the President of the General Assembly at its seventy-second session to appoint two co-chairs of the ad hoc open-ended working group, one from a developing country and one from a developed country, to oversee its consultations, in regular coordination and consultation with all Member States, regional groups and all relevant stakeholders, and underlines that the work of the working group must be open, transparent and inclusive;

7. *Decides* that the costs associated with the work of the ad hoc open-ended working group shall be met from voluntary contributions;

8. *Requests* the Secretary-General to arrange for substantive support to be provided by the United Nations Environment Programme, on the basis of voluntary contributions, without prejudice to the current voluntary funded programmatic activities of the Programme, including all assistance necessary for the performance of the work of the ad hoc open-ended working group, secretariat services and the provision of essential background information and relevant documents, complemented, as appropriate, by other relevant United Nations agencies, funds and programmes;

9. *Recognizes* that the process indicated above should not undermine existing relevant legal instruments and frameworks and relevant global, regional and sectoral bodies;

10. *Requests* the Secretary-General to establish a special voluntary trust fund in support of the process, and invites Member States, international financial institutions, donor agencies, intergovernmental organizations, non-governmental organizations

---

8. Reference is made to the non-governmental organizations that were accredited to the following relevant conferences and summits: the United Nations Conference on Environment and Development, the World Summit on Sustainable Development, the United Nations Conference on Sustainable Development and the United Nations summit for the adoption of the post-2015 development agenda.

and natural and juridical persons to make financial contributions to the voluntary trust fund;

11. *Also requests* the Secretary-General to establish a special voluntary trust fund for the purpose of assisting developing countries, in particular, the least developed countries, landlocked developing countries and small island developing States, in attending the sessions of the ad hoc open-ended working group, including daily subsistence allowance, in addition to defraying the costs of economy-class travel for one delegate per State for each session, and invites Member States, international financial institutions, donor agencies, intergovernmental organizations, nongovernmental organizations and natural and juridical persons to make financial contributions to the voluntary trust fund.

Chapter 3: Phase III: Fulfilling the Resolution (Sept. 2018 – Dec. 2018)

After Resolution No. 72/277[1] was adopted, steps were taken to comply with the requests of the UN General Assembly (UNGA). This chapter focuses on the first steps of compliance with the mandate of the UN Secretary-General (UNSG) and the open-ended working group (OEWG). Phase III, entitled Fulfilling the Resolution, starts from the appointment of the Co-Chairs of the OEWG in June 2018, and extends to the publication of a commentary on the UNSG's Report by the International Council of Environmental Law (ICEL) in December 2018. Section I relates to the UNGA choosing the permanent representatives of Portugal and Lebanon to lead the consultation on gaps in international environmental law in Nairobi. Section II briefly summarizes how the activities of the OEWG were financed. Part III focuses on the OEWG's September 2018 organizational session, held in New York to decide on a tentative calendar of meetings and programme of work for the Nairobi substantive sessions.

Section IV relates to the publication of the UNSG's Report at the end of November 2018. As the first publication on international environmental law at the Secretary-General's level, the report represented a landmark for the improvement of the field. Through a dialogue between principles, gaps and institutions, it set a blueprint for the progressive development of international environmental law. Section V provides a commentary on the report, highlighting its most significant conclusions. In December 2018, ICEL published a Note on the Report, as well as charts on the regional application of each principle included in the Global Pact. The Note is reproduced at the end of this chapter. Section VI includes a brief commentary on the aftermath of ICEL's Note.

The timeline below portrays Phase III.

1. UNGA, Towards a Global Pact for the Environment, UN Doc. A/RES/72/277 (10 May 2018).

Figure 3: Phase III Timeline "Fulfilling the Resolution" (June – Dec. 2018):

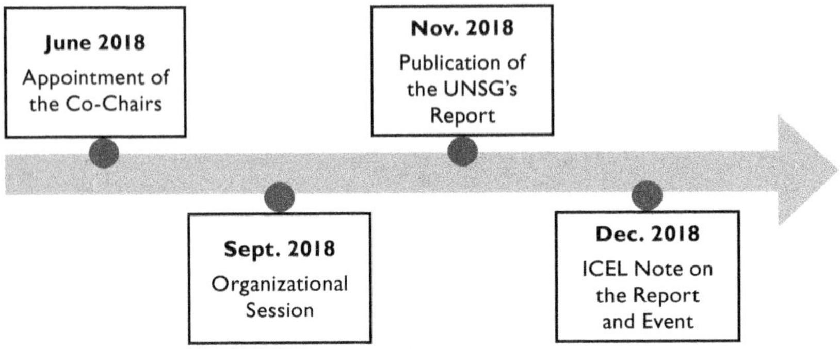

I. June 2018: Appointment of Co-Chairs of the Working Group

Through the Resolution No. 72/277, the General Assembly requested its President to appoint two Co-Chairs to oversee consultations of the OEWG. It required one to be chosen from a developing country and the other from a developed country.[2] On June 24th, 2018, UNGA's President Miroslav Lajcak appointed the permanent representatives of Portugal, Mr. Francisco António Duarte Lopes, and Lebanon, Ms. Amal Mudallali, to lead consultations on gaps in international environmental law.[3] The Co-Chairs were assisted by the legal representatives Sérgio Carvalho and Youssef Hitti.[4] The working group was responsible for negotiating a final text with the 193 member states.[5] During this process, the work carried out by the legal experts and the UNSG was used as a basis for discussions, which continued between States in collabora-

2. *Id.* para. 6.
3. Miroslav Lajcak, (All Permanent Representatives and Permanent Observers to the United Nations ed., The President of the General Assembly, 2018), *available at* https://www.un.org/pga/72/wp-content/uploads/sites/51/2018/06/Letter-to-MS-4-June.pdf (last accessed June 14, 2019) (appointing Ambassadors Duarte Lopes and Mudallali as co-chairs of the ad hoc working group on the Global Pact for the Environment negotiations).
4. Amal Mudallali (@AmbMudallali). "It was a great honor and pleasure to work on the negotiations for a Global Compact for the Environment with my friend & colleague amb. Francisco Duarte Lopes @Portugal_UN and his team especially Sérgio Carvalho who did a great job with Youssef Hitti our legal advisor & expert." July 10, 2019. Tweet.
5. Isabelle Hanne, A l'ONU, la France Pose les Jalons d'un Pacte Mondial Pour l'Environnement, Liberation (Sept. 20, 2017), http://www.liberation.fr/planete/2017/09/20/a-l-onu-la-france-pose-les-jalons-d-un-pacte-mondial-pour-l-environnement_1597671. Léia Santacroce, Le Pacte Mondial Pour l'Environnement Sur de Bons Rails, GEO (Sept. 20, 2017), http://www.geo.fr/photos/reportages-geo/le-pacte-mondial-pour-l-environnement-sur-de-bons-rails-179100.

tion with stakeholders from civil society.[6] The United Nations Environment Programme (UNEP) was asked to work closely with the General Assembly to guide the working group.[7]

The Permanent Representative of Portugal to the United Nations, Francisco António Duarte Lopes, presented his credentials to Secretary-General António Guterres on September 13th, 2017. Mr. Duarte Lopes is a career diplomat and previously served at Portugal's Ministry of Foreign Affairs in Lisbon. He had posts in Pakistan and Denmark, previously served as Director for Institutional Affairs at the Foreign Ministry, coordinator at Portugal's Permanent Representation to the European Union, diplomatic adviser to the Prime Minister, Chief of Staff to the Secretary of State for European Affairs and Director-General for European Affairs. He was promoted to the rank of Ambassador in December 2015.[8]

The Permanent Representative of Lebanon to the United Nations, Amal Mudallali, presented her credentials to Secretary General António Guterres in January 15th, 2018. She is the first woman to have been appointed by the Lebanese government as Ambassador to the United Nations.[9] Ms. Mudallali was the principal adviser on American Affairs for Prime Minister Saad Hariri of Lebanon since 2005. From 2013 to 2016, she was also a senior scholar at the Woodrow Wilson Center in Washington, D.C., focusing on American-Arab relations, the Middle East, Iran-Arab and Russian-Arab relations, the United Nations, and nuclear proliferation in the region. She was the founder and president of Bridges International Group, a political consulting firm based in Washington, D.C. Her work focuses on strengthening the relationship with the U.S. administration, Congress, the policy community, and the media. Between 2000 and 2005, she served as a foreign policy adviser to Prime Minister Rafiq Hariri. From 1998 to 2005, she also served as his spokesperson for foreign press and headed his international press office. Prior

6. Gary Tabor, President Macron Announces Global Pact for the Environment, Leonardo DiCaprio Foundation (July 24, 2017), https://www.leonardodicaprio.org/president-macron-announces-global-pact-for-the-environment/. Speech by M. Emmanuel Macron, President of the Republic: Summit on the Global Pact for the Environment, France Diplomatie (Sept. 19, 2017), http://www.diplomatie.gouv.fr/en/french-foreign-policy/united-nations/united-nations-general-assembly-sessions/unga-s-72nd-session/article/speech-by-m-emmanuel-macron-president-of-the-republic-summit-on-the-global-pact.

7. UNGA Resolution, *supra* note 1, para. 8. UN Environment, UN Environment New York Office, Gisele Bündchen Joins Heads of State to Launch the Global Pact for the Environment, http://www.unep.org/newyork/events/gisele-b%C3%BCndchen-joins-heads-state-launch-global-pact-environment (last accessed Feb. 19, 2019).

8. United Nations Meetings Coverage and Press Releases, New Permanent Representative of Portugal Presents Credentials (United Nations BIO/5022, Sept. 13, 2017), *available at* https://www.un.org/press/en/2017/bio5022.doc.htm.

9. The Kahlil Girab Chair for Values & Peace, Women Leaders, Dr. Amal Mudallali, *available at* https://pioneersandleaders.org/women-leaders/dr-amal-mudallali (last accessed July 21, 2019).

to joining the Prime Minister's team, she worked as a journalist in Washington, D.C. Awarded by President Jacques Chirac of France the Chevalier de l'Ordre de la Légion d'Honneur, Ms. Mudallali also holds a Doctor of Philosophy in political communication from the University of Maryland, a master's degree in political communication from Syracuse University and a bachelor's degree in mass communications from the Lebanese University.[10]

The Co-Chairs brilliantly guided the negotiations with specific questions that refocused discussions to the mandate bestowed upon them. After a broad debate on the UNSG's report, the Co-Chairs sent to delegates a specific list of questions intended to move the discussion forward and reach practical suggestions to the gaps envisioned. Additionally, the Co-Chairs provided an oral and written summary after each session, helping summarize the main arguments and set the stage for the following sessions. Through their diplomacy, the OEWG reached an outcome document by consensus.

II. Financing of the Activities of the Ad Hoc Open-Ended Working Group

The General Assembly requested the Secretary-General to establish two special voluntary trust funds in support of the process, one to support the process, including the Secretariat's functions, and the other to assist delegates from developing countries to participate in the substantive sessions in Nairobi.[11] At the organizational session in September 2018, Jamil Ahmad, Director ad interim of UNEP's New York Office, reported that the funds had been established by the Secretary-General.[12] The voluntary funds received USD 1.74 million (an additional USD 390,000 had been pledged for the period 2018-2019) from France, the EU, Germany, and Portugal.[13]

10. United Nations Meetings Coverage and Press Releases, New Permanent Representative of Lebanon Presents Credentials (United Nations BIO/5055, Jan. 15, 2018), *available at* https://www.un.org/press/en/2018/bio5055.doc.htm (last accessed July 21, 2019).
11. UNGA Resolution, *supra* note 1, para. 7; 8; 10; 11.
12. UNGA, Ad Hoc Open-Ended Working Group (Oewg) Established Pursuant to General Assembly Resolution 72/277, Organizational Session, New York, 5–7 September 2018, Report of the Ad Hoc Open-Ended Working Group Established Pursuant to General Assembly Resolution 72/277 of 10 May 2018 Entitled "Towards a Global Pact for the Environment," A/AC.289/2 (22 October 2018), para. 9.
13. Peter Doran, et al., *Summary of the Third Substantive Session of the Ad Hoc Open-Ended Working Group Towards a Global Pact for the Environment: 20-22 May 2019,* Vol. 35, No. 3, International Institute for Sustainable Development 3 (2019), *available at* http://enb.iisd.org/download/pdf/enb3503e.pdf.

III. September 2018: Working Group Organizational Session

The OEWG's organizational session convened from 5-7 September 2018 at the UN headquarters in New York, US, holding five meetings.[14] During the session, the countries approved its programme of work (A/AC.289/CRP.1), adopted the provisional agenda and other organizational matters, agreed on the schedule and agenda for the substantive sessions, and discussed the financing of the activities.[15] The meetings were attended by 98 countries, six intergovernmental organizations,[16] one specialized agency,[17] UN organs and bodies[18] and thirty-eight non-governmental organizations.[19] The main goal was to reach a consensus on the timing, number, and duration of the substantive sessions.[20]

The resolution required the OEWG to complete its work by June 2019, starting no sooner than one month after the submission of the report by the Secretary-General.[21] The EU called for allowing two to three months between the meetings to consider the Secretary-General's report, allowing sufficient time for drafting, and consulting among groups.[22] It was necessary to have a number of sessions that provided the working group with the time and space for a comprehensive discussion on the substance that enabled it to carry out its work and deliver on what was requested by the General Assem-

14. UNGA Resolution, *supra* note 1, para. 5.
15. Based upon the provisional agenda and annotations (A/AC.289/1), the agenda was adopted as follows: "1. Opening of the session. 2. Adoption of the provisional agenda and other organizational matters. 3. General discussion. 4. Agenda for the substantive sessions. 5. Information on documents to be considered by the substantive sessions. 6. Financing of the activities of the ad hoc open-ended working group. 7. Other matters. 8. Adoption of the report of the proceedings of the session. 9. Closure of the session." UNGA, Ad Hoc Open-Ended Working Group Established Pursuant to General Assembly Resolution 72/277, Organizational Session, New York, 5–7 September 2018, Provisional Agenda and Annotations, A/AC.289/1 (1 August 2018).
16. International Chamber of Commerce, International Committee of the Red Cross, International Federation of Red Cross and Red Crescent Societies, International Organization of la Francophonie, International Union for the Conservation of Nature and Natural Resources, and Organization for Economic Cooperation and Development. OEWG, A/AC.289/2, *supra* note 12.
17. International Fund for Agricultural Development.
18. United Nations Environment Programme, and United Nations Entity for Gender Equality and the Empowerment of Women.
19. OEWG, A/AC.289/2, *supra* note 12, para. 10-14.
20. OEWG, A/AC.289/1, *supra* note 15, item 3 ("The General Assembly also decided that the organizational session would examine matters related to the organization of the work of the ad hoc open-ended working group, including the duration and number of its substantive sessions, with a view to reporting back to the General Assembly during the first half of 2019.").
21. UNGA Resolution, *supra* note 1, para. 2.
22. Ana Maria Lebada, *Governments Commence Organizational Work on Global Pact for Environment,* 6 September 2018, IISD (2018), *available at* http://sdg.iisd.org/news/governments-commence-organizational-work-on-global-pact-for-environment/.

bly. Notably, there should be enough time "in-session" to allow for a fruitful exchange of views and efficiency in the way it carried out discussions, as well as to allow sufficient time for consultations.[23] Delegates expressed their preferences and agreed to the dates of three substantive sessions, as per the suggestion of the EU.[24]

The calendar took into consideration the need to avoid overlap with other environmental meetings,[25] as well as to take advantage of trips already in the delegates' agenda.[26] Explicitly, delegates expressed a desire to hold one session back-to-back with the fourth session of the United Nations Environment Assembly (UNEA-4). This suggestion was especially relevant to ensure full participation of developing countries and countries in special situations, especially the least developed countries (LDCs) and small island developing States (SIDS).[27] Underscoring that some countries lacked a permanent mission to UNEP, El Salvador called for an alternative that enabled New York-based missions to engage in the working group, such as by circulating documents at the UN Headquarters, and webcasting the Nairobi meetings.[28] They ultimately decided to hold three substantive meetings as follows: (i) the first substantive session from January 14-18, 2019, to give countries as much time as possible to consider the report of the Secretary-General; (ii) the second substantive session from March 18, 2019, for 3-5 days, taking place back-to-back with the UNEA-4; (iii) the third substantive session from May 20, 2019, for 3-5 days.[29]

Delegates extensively discussed how to set out the agenda of the substantive sessions on the second day of the organizational meeting.[30] G-77/China was against the idea of setting a formal agenda and anticipating the dis-

23. OEWG, A/AC.289/2, *supra* note 12, Annex, Decision 2018/1.
24. Colombia called for a "sufficient" number of sessions to discuss all the gaps in international environmental governance. Faye Leone, *Governments Set Dates for Global Pact Discussions, Begin Debating Agenda*, IISD (Sept. 7, 2018), *available at* http://sdg.iisd.org/news/governments-set-dates-for-global-pact-discussions-begin-debating-agenda/.
25. Philippines, supported by the G-77/China, EU, Costa Rica, Japan, Monaco and Senegal, raised concerns with the overlaps between the working group's sessions and other environmental meetings.
26. For example, El Salvador, supported by Thailand, suggested holding one of the substantive sessions back-to-back with the UN Environment Assembly (UNEA 4) in March 2019. Some countries expressed concern about a back-to-back meeting with UNEA-4 in March, especially for smaller delegations (Switzerland); and time needed to absorb discussions from one session and prepare for the next (EU and Australia).
27. These concerns were raised by Madagascar, supported by New Zealand (regarding the number of sessions), as well as Egypt for the Group of 77 and China (G-77/China) with China, Costa Rica, India, Madagascar and Philippines (regarding the need for support for representatives' participation in the working group).
28. Lebada, *supra* note 22.
29. OEWG, A/AC.289/2, *supra* note 12, Annex, Decision 2018/1.
30. Leone, *supra* note 24.

cussed items, and instead called for a "step-by-step approach." The delegates proposed beginning with examining the Secretary-General's report, then deciding how to proceed, defining each provisional agenda for the following session.[31] Each substantive session would thus adopt the subsequent session's provisional agenda and decide on its programme of work.[32] The working group adopted a provisional agenda for the first substantive session on the last day of the organizational session.[33] The organization session concluded its work on September 7, 2018. A report was made available shortly afterward.[34]

IV. November 2018: Publication of the UNSG's Report

On November 30, 2018 Mrs. Mrema, Director of UNEP's Law Division, announced the release of the UNSG's report entitled "Gaps in international environmental law and environment-related instruments: towards a global pact for the environment" (A/73/419).[35] The technical and evidence-based report reviewed and analyzed the corpus of international environmental law and environment-related instruments as well as the governance structure and implementation of international environmental law, identifying gaps and deficiencies. The report is divided into five substantive sections: (i) the scope and status of the principles of international environmental law; (ii) gaps relating to the sectoral regulatory regimes; (iii) environment-related instruments; (iv) gaps relating to the governance structure of international environmental law; and (v) gaps concerning the implementation and effectiveness of international environmental law. These will be specifically explored in the next section.

While welcomed by several delegations, the report was harshly criticized for going beyond its mandate. According to Prof. Christina Voigt, who helped draft the report, it adopts a wide interpretation of its mandate in three

31. *Id.*

32. Ana Maria Lebada, *Delegates Set Agenda for First Session on Global Pact for Environment*, IISD (2018), *available at* http://sdg.iisd.org/news/delegates-set-agenda-for-first-session-on-global-pact-for-environment/.

33. OEWG, A/AC.289/2, *supra* note 12, Annex, Decision 2018/2. ("Pursuant to General Assembly resolution 72/277, the ad hoc open-ended working group is to consider the report and discuss possible options to address possible gaps in international environmental law and environment-related instruments, as appropriate, and, if deemed necessary, the scope, parameters and feasibility of an international instrument, with a view to making recommendations, which may include the convening of an intergovernmental conference to adopt an international instrument, to the Assembly during the first half of 2019.").

34. OEWG, A/AC.289/2, *supra* note 12.

35. UN Secretary-General, Gaps in International Environmental Law and Environment-Related Instruments: Towards a Global Pact for the Environment, UN Doc. A/73/419 (30 November 2018).

ways.[36] First, it adopts a broad interpretation of what constitutes a "gap." This issue was central to the discussions in the first session in Nairobi, as will be detailed below. The report identifies a wide range of gaps and assesses deficiencies which impact the effectiveness of international environmental law. These deficiencies include: (i) "blank spots" in the coverage of MEAs; (ii) the status and content of environmental principles; (iii) gaps within and (iv) between MEAs; (v) gaps between MEAs and other international law; and (vi) gaps related to the implementation of MEAs. Second, it not only identifies and assesses regulatory (i.e. procedural and substantive) and governance gaps in international environmental law, but also assesses gaps in environment-related instruments, including international trade, investment, intellectual property, human rights, peace and security, migration, disaster management and armed conflict. Third, a narrow interpretation of paragraph 1 of the UNGA resolution might suggest that the question of how to address any potentially identified gaps would be subject to the OEWG deliberations and would therefore not be part of the mandate for the report. Nonetheless, the report makes several significant suggestions and recommendations, including specifically to clarify and reinforce principles of international law. This led some States to suggest that the UNSG report did not comply with its mandate.[37] These issues will be further detailed below.

Shortly after the report was circulated, ICEL, along with the World Commission of Environmental Law (WCEL), and the International Group of Experts for the Pact published a note on the report.[38] The Note commented on aspects of the report, while also explaining how and why the Nairobi consultations could reach consensus on the codification and progressive development of core principles of international environmental law. It included some additional gaps the report failed to examine, such as the implementation of the recommendations of Agenda 21. It called for a recognition of a unity of purpose in international environmental law, shared by States through a set of universally agreed principles.[39] Through an assessment of the adoption of environmental principles across regions, it showed that the principles which the Global Pact intends to codify are already accepted worldwide.[40] The Note is reprinted in full below.

36. Christina Voigt, *How a 'Global Pact for the Environment' Could Add Value to International Environmental Law*, 28 Rev. Eur., Comp. & Int'l Envtl. L. 13;16 (2019).
37. *Id.* at 16.
38. WCEL et al., Note on The United Nations Secretary-General's Report, Gaps in International Environmental Law and Environment-Related Instruments: Towards a Global Pact for the Environment (Dec. 10, 2018).
39. *Id.* at 6.
40. See Document 4: ICEL Note on the UNSG's Report (Dec. 10, 2018), below.

On December 10, 2018, ICEL organized a conference at the UN Headquarters, entitled "Strengthening Implementation of International Environmental Law - Commentaries on the UN Secretary General's Report on International Environmental Law for the Global Pact for the Environment."[41] The conference was organized on the 70th anniversary of the Universal Declaration of Human Rights (UDHR) and provided an opportunity for leading experts to comment on the UN Secretary-General's Report. The conference was moderated by Professor Nicholas A. Robinson, hosted by François Delattre, Permanent Representative of France, and included the following speakers: Abdoulaye Barro, Deputy Permanent Representative of Senegal, Roy S. Lee, Permanent Observer for the Asian-African Legal Consultative Organization, Claudia De Windt, Senior Legal Advisor for the American-States Organization, John C. Cruden, Former Assistant Attorney General for Environment and Natural Resources to US Department Justice, and Yann Aguila, Secretary General of the International Group of Experts for the Pact and Former Judge at the Conseil d'Etat (the administrative Supreme Court in France).

Mr. Delattre opened the event, emphasizing the fact that the Global Pact is solidly rooted in the UN Agenda and provides a way to implement the 2030 Agenda. The GPE offers a unique opportunity to look toward the future, continue to promote international law and recognize new rights such as the right to a healthy environment. Professor Robinson emphasized the need to address codification and progressive development of international environmental law. He pointed out the UNSG Report is a landmark in international environmental law, as the first report at this level published internationally. Mr. Lee said it was essential to understand the causes of deficiencies, especially being the result of divergent position and interest of states, trade-offs and watered-down formulations necessary to move forward. Ms. De Windt explained how principles are the guiding force for the jurists of international environmental law on a daily basis. Mr. Aguila highlighted the importance of the UN as an international legislator. He noted the report leads to a long "to-do list" for States, but the starting point must be the codification of the principles of law. The discussions resulted in the conclusion that the Global Pact for the Environment presents an opportunity to return to the spirit of the UDHR, within the environmental context.[42]

41. UN Web TV, Strengthening Implementation of International Environmental Law (Dec. 10, 2018), http://webtv.un.org/watch/strengthening-implementation-of-international-environmental-law/5977795659001/?lan=english.

42. Recap of the Event, Strengthening Implementation of International Environmental Law—Commentaries on the UN Secretary General's Report on International Environmental Law for the "Global Pact

In February 2019, the Council of Nordic Ministers (CNM) published a report which investigated international environmental governance in the context of the Global Pact and the UNSG's report.[43] The CNM assessed some of the improvements in international environmental law and governance, while looking forward to what was still lacking. The Report concluded that while the reform completed at Rio+20 significantly renewed UNEP's functions and enhanced synergies among MEAs, it had yet to address the normative foundation for keeping environmental challenges under control.[44] It highlighted lack of implementation of existing commitments and obligations as a pervasive feature of international environmental law, while fragmentation of the treaty system leads to a deadlock in its expansion.[45]

Despite harsh criticism by delegates and a few scholars, the report is a first step towards the recognition of significant gaps in international environmental law.[46] As the first analysis of international environmental at this level at the UN, the Report is welcomed, and should be a first in a series of similar investigations. Through an overview of the developments of the past decades, the UNSG provided a blueprint for how to improve the existing framework. The Report confirms a number of gaps in international environmental law in three separate categories: principles, gaps and institutions. It provided a useful basis to kickstart the debate at the Nairobi consultations, but should be used beyond it, to think creatively about where international environmental law should be heading. Through its piecemeal approach to multilateral treatymaking, international environmental law has often lacked such a broad analysis which looks at the past as much as the future. The Report provides a significant step towards the advancement of international environmental law, identifying our current leading challenges and proposing ways to address them.

V. The UNSG's Report (Dec. 10, 2018)

The technical and evidence-based report prepared by the Secretary General reviewed and analyzed the corpus of international environmental law and environment-related instruments as well as its governance structure and implementation. The report indicates that international environmental

for the Environment," https://globalpactenvironment.org/uploads/Conference-NY-EN-10122018.pdf (last visited Aug. 31, 2019).

43. Niko Urho, et al., International Environmental Governance: Accomplishments and Way Forward (Nordic Council of Ministers. 2019).

44. *Id.* at 14.

45. *Id.* at 14.

46. See substantive discussions below.

law developed in a reactive manner, in response to specific sectoral requirements. This incremental and piecemeal nature has resulted in a proliferation of largely sectoral regulatory regimes and a fragmented international legal framework for the protection of the environment.[47] Fragmentation, in turn, leads to a deficit in coordination at the law-making and implementation levels and a need for better policy coherence, mutual supportiveness and synergies in implementation.[48] This temporal aspect is an important factor in understanding what the report describes as "gaps", "fragmentation" and, consequently, the need for a comprehensive unifying mechanism.[49]

The Report revealed gaps and deficiencies at multiple levels, with five gaps identified.[50] First, there is no single overarching normative framework that sets out rules and principles of general application in international environmental law:

> "First, there is no single overarching normative framework that sets out what might be characterized as the rules and principles of general application in international environmental law even though such principles may help unify the current, sectoral, approach to international environmental law and help fill the gaps in the rules laid out in treaties. While some principles of international environmental law are now well recognized through their incorporation into issue-specific multilateral environmental agreements and have been affirmed by a number of international courts and tribunals, others enjoy neither clarity nor judicial consensus as to their applicability, nor recognition in binding legal instruments. This has an impact on the predictability and implementation of sectoral environment regimes."[51]

Second, international environmental law is piecemeal and reactive, characterized by fragmentation and a general lack of coherence and synergy among a large body of sectoral regulatory frameworks. The UNSG noted that "[t]his leads to an important deficit in coordination at the law-making and implementation levels and a need for better policy coherence, mutual supportiveness and synergies in implementation."[52]

---

47. UN Secretary-General, *supra* note 35, at 4.
48. *Id.* at 2.
49. Lucien Chabason & Elisabeth Hege *What to Expect From a Global Pact for the Environment?* (IDDRI, Issue Brief No. 5, 2019), ***available at*** https://www.iddri.org/sites/default/files/PDF/Publications/Catalogue%20Iddri/D%C3%A9cryptage/201901-IB0119EN-pacte%20mondial%20env.pdf.
50. UN Secretary-General, *supra* note 35, at 1.
51. *Id.* at 1.
52. *Id.* at 1-2.

Third, the articulation between multilateral environmental agreements and environment-related instruments remains problematic owing to the lack of clarity, content-wise and status-wise, of many environmental principles.[53]

Fourth, the structure of international environmental governance is characterized by institutional fragmentation and a heterogeneous set of actors, revealing important coherence and coordination challenges. International courts and tribunals often stress the lack of international consensus concerning environmental principles.[54]

Fifth, the implementation of international environmental law is challenging at both the national and international levels. At the national level, implementation is constrained by the lack of appropriate national legislation, financial resources, environmentally sound technologies and institutional capacities. At the international level, implementation is constrained by the lack of clarity of many environmental principles.

International environmental law lacks a single overarching framework that sets out rules and principles of general application. Customary international environmental law is sparse, since its identification remains a challenging task, with often a gap between what States say and what they actually do. These critical challenges led to the rise of an important body of non-binding instruments, including the Stockholm and Rio Declarations. These have provided important guidance, acting as precursors to the development of subsequent legally binding instruments.[55] To strengthen international environmental law and its implementation, the report suggested actions such as the clarification and reinforcement of principles of international environmental law; more effective reporting, review and verification measures and robust compliance and enforcement procedures and mechanisms, and the enhancement of the role of non-State actors at multiple levels.[56]

> "International environmental law and its effective implementation could be strengthened through such actions as the clarification and reinforcement of principles of international environmental law. This could be done through a comprehensive and unifying international instrument that gathers all the principles of environmental law. There should also be more effective reporting, review and verification measures and robust compliance and enforcement procedures and mechanisms, ensuring that those States that require support have adequate resources to enable them to effectively implement

53. *Id.* at 2.
54. *Id.* at 2.
55. *Id.* at 5.
56. *Id.* at 2.

their commitments, and the role of non-State actors should be enhanced at multiple levels."[57]

In its introduction, the report clarifies the context in which it was drafted, the development of international environmental law and some basic definitions. Noting the transboundary nature of environmental challenges, the UNSG recognizes the need for international cooperation in the advancement of international environmental law: "Most environmental challenges and problems and their impacts are transboundary, and some are global in nature, which led to the early recognition that international cooperation among States through appropriate legal frameworks was indispensable to the creation of effective responses and solutions." Anchored in the rules and principles of general public international law, a large body of international legal obligations to protect the environment emerged:

> "2. International treaties adopted at the regional and global levels, commonly referred to as multilateral environmental agreements, are the dominant sources of international environmental law. A vast body of multilateral environmental agreements, comprising more than 500 instruments, have been adopted so far. Each agreement addresses a specific environmental challenge and is legally and institutionally distinct from the others. The incremental and piecemeal nature of international environmental law-making has resulted in a proliferation of largely sectoral regulatory regimes and a fragmented international legal framework for the protection of the environment.3 Fragmentation has become a frequent phenomenon in international law, and is one of the consequences of multilateral decision-making."[58]

Still, there is "no single overarching normative framework in the area of international environmental law that sets out what might be characterized as rules and principles of general application."[59] Although customary international environmental law is sparse, some have already been codified in treaties and confirmed by international courts and tribunals.[60] Additionally, a significant body of non-binding instruments emerged.[61]

> "6. The normative and institutional fragmentation of international environmental law and the sectoral approach to environmental regulation have led over the years to proposals to enhance the coherence and coordination of global environmental governance, including successful proposals to enhance coordination among specific multilateral environmental agreements, and

57. *Id.* at 2.
58. *Id.* at 4, para. 2.
59. *Id.* at 4, para. 3.
60. *Id.* at 4-5, para. 4.
61. *Id.* at 5, para. 5.

less successful proposals to establish a World Environment Organization or to adopt an international covenant on environment and development. More recently, the idea of a global pact for the environment that synthesizes and codifies the principles of international environmental law in one document was proposed.10 On 10 May 2018, the General Assembly adopted resolution 72/277, entitled "Towards a Global Pact for the Environment", and requested that the Secretary-General submit, at its seventy-third session in 2018, a technical and evidence-based report that identifies and assesses possible gaps in international environmental law and environment-related instruments with a view to strengthening their implementation. The present report has been prepared pursuant to that request."

The report is then divided into five substantive sections: section II identifies and assesses the scope and status of the principles of international environmental law; section III addresses gaps relating to the sectoral regulatory regimes; section IV identifies and assesses some environment-related instruments; section V deals with gaps relating to the governance structure of international environmental law; and section VI addresses gaps concerning the implementation and effectiveness of international environmental law. The following segments summarize the main points made by the Secretary General in each of those sections.

A. *Gaps Concerning Principles of International Environmental Law*

Part II of the Secretary-General's Report addresses gaps concerning general principles of international environmental law. The section addresses: the (A) scope and (B) status of principles. The section begins by elucidating the scope and role of environmental principles. Principles may help unify the current sectoral approach to international environmental law, guide interpretation of environmental treaties, supplement or complement specific rules, and fill the gaps in the rules laid out in treaties.[62] The UNSG further clarifies:

> "9. Principles of international environmental law are an important building block and their usage is widespread. (...) [T]hose principles that are not contained in multilateral environmental agreements also play an important role in guiding the interpretation and further development of those agreements. (...) 10. More generally, environmental principles also serve to supplement or complement more specific rules. (...) The general character of the principles permits their application to the continuously evolving interrelationships between human activity and the environment. The principles also play a role with respect to potential gaps arising from the use of different legal sources.

62. *Id.* at 1.

(...) [E]nvironmental principles may help to unify international environmental law's current sectoral approach."[63]

Section B relates to the status of principles. It notes that "[w]hile some principles of international environmental law are now well recognized through their incorporation into issue-specific multilateral environmental agreements and have been affirmed by a number of international courts and tribunals, others enjoy neither clarity nor judicial consensus as to their applicability, nor recognition in binding legal instruments."[64] The degree of legal uncertainty surrounding many of these principles has a direct and indirect impact on the predictability and implementation of sectoral regimes.[65] The section covers the following principles: prevention, precaution, polluter pays, environmental democracy, cooperation, right to a clean and healthy environment, sustainable development, common but differentiated responsibilities and respective capabilities, non-regression and progression. The selection of principles is mainly based on the 1992 Rio Declaration, although the report also takes note of more recent developments.[66]

It reports that some principles are more well-established. Several international courts and tribunals have confirmed the existence of rules of customary international law relating to environmental protection, in particular the obligation to prevent environmental harm beyond national jurisdiction, the performance of due diligence, the duty to conduct an environmental impact assessment, and the obligation of reparation for environmental damage.[67] The status of other principles, however, remains debatable. For example, the legal basis of the precautionary principle continues to be a matter of controversy and debate.[68] Environmental democracy, which includes access to information, participation in decision-making and access to environmental justice, is unevenly implemented globally, with remarkably little geographic symmetry.[69] Differing expressions and understandings of principles exist in many issue-specific MEAs. While sustainable development is included in different MEAs and represents the basis of the 2030 Agenda, "questions remain as to the extent to which the sustainable development principles represent binding or non-binding rules or indeed whether they constitute a source of law."[70] The principle of common but differentiated responsibilities and respective

63. *Id.* at 1.
64. *Id.* at 1.
65. *Id.* at 42, para. 102.
66. Voigt, *supra* note 34, at 17.
67. UN Secretary-General, *supra* note 35, at 42, para. 101.
68. *Id.* at 8, para. 12.
69. *Id.* at 8-9, para. 14.
70. *Id.* at 12, para. 20.

capabilities responds to similar challenges, with a dynamic and flexible content that deems their general application hardly evident. Others, such as the right to a clean and healthy environment and non-regression, are not fully developed, and have only recently been recognized in a limited number of legal instruments.[71] Chabason & Hege argue the report lacks a comprehensive view of the effective implementation of the principles established in soft law, which could help assess the added value in translating principles into legal provisions in the form of a new legal instrument."[72]

When enshrined in legally binding MEAs, the scope and content of the relevant principles are confined to that particular MEA. Its dynamic function of gap-filling, an important element in the continuously evolving development of international environmental law, can only be fulfilled when principles are general in character.[73] The Report concludes that there is a need to further clarify environmental principles, without prejudice to the legal developments already achieved in the issue-specific contexts of various MEAs.[74] More clarification of their content and scope would make them more effective, predictable and strengthen their implementation. The Report goes as far as suggesting a "comprehensive and unifying international instrument,"[75] giving rise to the criticism of exceeding its mandate as expressed below. The UNSG argues that a comprehensive and unifying international instrument that gathers all the principles of environmental law could provide for better harmonization, predictability and certainty.[76]

B. *Gaps Relating to Existing Regulatory Regimes*

Section B of the Report conveys gaps relating to existing regulatory regimes of international environmental law. It analyzed the following sectors: protection of the atmosphere, conservation of biological diversity and protection of soils, protection of freshwater resources, protection of oceans and seas, and regulation of hazardous substances, wastes and activities. It covered existing agreements in each sector, noting, when relevant, existing gaps within those. The notion of gaps in existing agreements was significantly criticized by delegates in Nairobi. They argued these should be debated by the governance bodies of the different conventions, and that several perceived gaps were the intended product of negotiations. Profs. Chabason and Hege suggested that

71. *Id.* at 42, para. 102.
72. Chabason & Hege, *supra* note 49, at 2.
73. UN Secretary-General, *supra* note 35, at 6, para. 10.
74. *Id.* at 43, para. 102. Voigt, *supra* note 34, at 17-18.
75. UN Secretary-General, *supra* note 35, at 42, para. 102.
76. *Id.* at 42, para. 102.

sectoral legal gaps should be excluded from the outset from future negotiations. Since the institutional topics were dealt with during the Rio +20 Summit in 2012, the only topics of negotiation that should be retained are the horizontal principles, environmental policy integration, for instance in trade agreements, and implementation and effectiveness issues.[77] This discussion is further detailed in Chapter 4.

The UNSG notes that the adoption of MEAs faces a significant challenge "to encourage the participation of all relevant actors while at the same time ensuring that the commitments are ambitious enough to provide for an effective response to the problem, and to ensure that parties comply with their obligations."[78] Political compromises and the notions of fairness feature prominently in negotiation of sectoral agreements and ensure broad participation. The Report predicts that "because the national circumstances and capabilities of States differ significantly, the future development of international environmental law is likely to require more, rather than less, differentiation and flexibility."[79]

Substantive gaps identified in this section include: gaps related to liability and compensation in the regime of the Paris Agreement;[80] need for harmonization of multiple climate change treaties,[81] no control of short-lived chemical pollutants and nitrous oxide (N_2O), some specific uses of controlled substances, such as uses in feedstock and for quarantine and pre-shipment; and the disposal of controlled substances that are in banks, such as insulation foams or equipment;[82] gaps in monitoring and verification in the regulation of the stratospheric ozone layer;[83] gaps in monitoring and verification of data related to the regulation of mercury;[84] linkages and coordination between the Mimata Convention and other multilateral environmental agreements that relate to the regulation of mercury;[85] gaps in geographical coverage, regulated activities, regulated substances and applicable principles and rules related to the regulation of air pollution;[86] with respect to the problem of acid rain and other dispersed pollutants, there are no rules on liability, some of the protocols have not entered into force and the geographical scope is limited;[87]

77. Chabason & Hege, *supra* note 49, at 3.
78. UN Secretary-General, *supra* note 35, at 13, para. 23.
79. *Id.* at 14, para. 25.
80. *Id.* at 15, para. 29.
81. *Id.* at 15, para. 29.
82. *Id.* at 15-16, para. 30.
83. *Id.* at 16, para. 31-32.
84. *Id.* at 16-17, para. 33.
85. *Id.* at 17, para. 34.
86. *Id.* at 18, para. 35.
87. *Id.* at 18, para. 36.

lack of an overall strategy and coherent structure for conservation of biodiversity, with many issues lacking a specific, legally binding regulation, including on the conservation and sustainable use of forests, the pollution of marine areas by land-based plastic waste, the protection of soil, the use of pesticides, noise pollution, human rights and biodiversity, the Arctic area, nanomaterials and some geo-engineering processes;[88] limitation of the jurisdictional scope of the Aichi Targets to areas within national jurisdiction;[89] lack of cooperation with international agreements in other fields such as trade, intellectual property rights and plant genetic resources for food and agriculture, regulation of invasive alien species and of issues of synthetic biology and digital sequence information;[90] limited international legal responses related to land and soil degradation;[91] gaps related to the lack of general framework of freshwater governance and legal integration;[92] uncertainty in the applicability of principles in the field of water resources protection;[93] lack of coordination and cooperation among the regional seas frameworks and relevant global multilateral environmental agreements;[94] gaps related to the material or geographical scope of instruments related to ocean management;[95] underdeveloped rules governing the transport of hazardous substances by different modes of transport, and limited geographical application;[96] significant gaps remain with respect to regional coverage as well as the regulation of the disposal of marine plastic litter and microplastics, mine tailings and associated wastes from mining operations, and wastes form deep seabed mining, land-based disposal, recovery, recycling and reuse;[97] and significant gaps in the regulatory regimes of hazardous substances, wastes and activities.[98]

C. *Environment-Related Instruments*

With respect to environment-related instruments, the UNSG analyzed gaps in trade, investment, intellectual property, and human rights, as those related to international environmental law.[99] The mandate was significantly ques-

88. *Id.* at 19, para. 41.
89. *Id.* at 19, para. 42.
90. *Id.* at 20, para. 42.
91. *Id.* at 21, para. 48.
92. *Id.* at 23, para. 54.
93. *Id.* at 23, para. 55.
94. *Id.* at 25, para. 58.
95. *Id.* at 25-26, para. 61.
96. *Id.* at 27-28, para. 64.
97. *Id.* at 28-29, para. 67.
98. *Id.* at 29, para. 69.
99. *Id.* at 30-32.

tioned by Member States during the Nairobi session, as will be detailed in Chapter 4. Delegates argued these should be discussed within their own frameworks and were beyond the mandate of the OEWG.

The UNSG noted that normative gaps in disputes concerning environment-related trade measures have been evident, despite mutual supportiveness in environmental treaties featuring trade components. Specifically, the WTO Appellate Body has been reluctant to apply environmental principles to justify measures that are inconsistent with trade obligations.[100] The UNSG concluded that "significant challenge of reaching consensus on the implementation of mutual supportiveness of trade and environment suggests a widening gap between these two normative regimes."[101]

State practices on environmental clauses in investment treaties vary widely, with a few developed States systematically including them and a trend towards its inclusion and newly concluded investment treaties, particularly in Africa.[102] Observing a global decline in the frequency of approaches that include references to environmental concern in investment agreements, the UNSG notes that "normative gaps arise because the specific environmental concerns explicitly addressed in these agreements are limited, and have generally not evolved to include more recent concerns such as climate change and biodiversity."[103]

With respect to intellectual property instruments, the UNSG observed a normative gap between patent law and the plant-breeders' rights regimes which promote these rights, a gap between WIPO institutional norms that promote innovation and the provisions of the Convention on Biological Diversity (CBD) regarding access and benefit-sharing, the rights of traditional knowledge holders and biodiversity conservation, and between the regimes of the TRIPS Agreement and the CBD.[104]

On human rights, the Report notes the obligation of States under international human rights law to prevent foreseeable human rights harms, including those caused by environmental degradation.[105] Several principles from human rights instruments are applied in the context of environmental law, and explicitly reference the environment or environmental concerns. The Report specifically notes the framework of principles on human rights and the environment by the Special Rapporteur on the issue of human rights

100. *Id.* at 30, para. 71.
101. *Id.* at 30, para. 71.
102. *Id.* at 30, para. 72.
103. *Id.* at 30-31, para. 72.
104. *Id.* at 31, para. 73.
105. *Id.* at 32, para. 74.

obligations relating to the enjoyment of a safe, clean, healthy and sustainable environment articulates the application of existing human rights norms in the environmental context.[106] Human rights instruments further reflect a wide array of principles applied by regional human rights and environmental democracy treaties. While UN resolutions include a right to a healthy environment, it is not explicitly present in the International Covenant on Economic, Social and Cultural Rights. Resolutions from the Human Rights Council have addressed the issues of human rights and the environment generally, and regional courts have filled gaps between sources of human rights law and environmental law.[107]

D. *Gaps Relating to the Governance Structure of International Environmental Law*

According to the Report "[t]he structure of international environmental governance is characterized by institutional fragmentation and a heterogeneous set of actors. Although States remain the primary actors, international environmental governance is a multi-actor governance system that includes international institutions, treaty bodies, non-governmental organizations, the scientific community and the private sector."[108] In addition to UNEP and UNEA, several UN programmes, funds, and specialized agencies have acquired considerable environmental responsibilities since UNEP was established. This problem is exacerbated by a proliferation of environmental agreements with separate mandates that "ignore the unity, interconnectedness and interdependence of the Earth's ecosystem", and "create potential for overlap and conflict, institutional and policy incoherence and increased financial and administrative burdens on states parties."[109] These create potential for overlap and conflict, institutional and policy incoherence and increased financial and administrative burdens on State parties.[110] Institutional fragmentation and a lack of coordination are key challenges with regard to the current international environmental governance[111] and enhanced coordination might be necessary within the field of international environmental law and between MEAs and other instruments that directly or indirectly affect the environment.[112]

106. *See* UN Doc. A/HRC/37/59 (24 January 2018).
107. UN Secretary-General, *supra* note 35, at 31-32, para. 74-76.
108. *Id.* at 33, para. 77.
109. *Id.* at 34, para. 80.
110. *Id.* at 34, para. 80.
111. *Id.* at 34, para. 81.
112. *Id.* at 34-35, para. 82.

The Report suggested a few options to improve efficiency and address institutional fragmentation, such as: "(a) creating clusters and synergies between conventions; (b) mapping existing global and regional action plans and agreements to create an overview of coverage and identify interlinkages; (c) avoiding duplication of reporting and/or monitoring processes by using the same reporting channels and not creating additional burdens ("integrated reporting"); (d) sharing lessons learned and best practices; (e) developing implementation guidelines for multilateral environmental agreements; and (f) sharing information among the different scientific bodies that support the work of related multilateral environmental agreements. Potential conflicts between treaty regimes can be managed by using legal means, including conflict clauses, mutual supportiveness or the application of the general rule of treaty interpretation contained in article 31, paragraph 3(c), of the Vienna Convention on the Law of Treaties."[113]

Finally, despite a trend in broadening the range of actors recognized as having a legitimate role in environmental governance, "compared to the international human rights mechanisms there exists a significant gap in international environmental law regarding effective participation by non-State actors in international law-making and implementation."[114]

E. *Gaps Relating to the Implementation and Effectiveness of International Environmental Law*

The Report identified the lack of effective national implementation of MEAs as a major gap in addressing environmental challenges. Implementation deficits arise for many reasons, including "knowledge gaps; a lack of adequate means of implementation, such as finance, capacity-building or technology; the need for facilitation for compliance; a lack of coordination between relevant government departments as well as with other sectors; insufficient monitoring and law enforcement; a lack of political will; and the inadequate engagement of different stakeholders, such as civil society and women's organizations." The challenges at the international level are similar to those at the national level, where different ministries may be responsible for the implementation of different MEAs. Coherence, synergy and coordination at the international level could ease implementation at the national level.[115] To address gaps in effectiveness and enable compliance, the Report suggested improving access to means of implementation, such as financial

113. *Id.* at 35, para. 83.
114. *Id.* at 35, para. 84.
115. *Id.* at 36, para. 86.

resources, environmentally sound technologies and technical and institutional capacities.[116]

Gaps in the implementation of international environmental law also appear in inter-State dispute settlements.[117] Since there is no international environmental court, disputes are addressed by a variety of international courts and tribunals, revealing a variety of gaps. Additionally, compliance mechanisms and procedures within MEAs vary greatly between them and generally do not enforce their findings.[118] Gaps are also observed in the enforcement of rights and obligations regarding the global commons and shared natural resources and in disputes concerning natural resources which do not originate from environmental treaties.[119] There has been limited development in the area of liability and redress for transboundary environmental harm.[120] Finally, the rules of State responsibility may need to be further developed if they are to play any significant role as a tool for redressing transboundary environmental harm.[121] For example, very few treaties provide for international liability for transboundary environmental damage.[122] The regimes of civil liability lack an agreed international standard for a de minimis threshold of environmental damage,[123] environmental damage in areas beyond the limits of national jurisdiction is not covered in many cases, and liability is limited in terms of the amount of compensation payable.[124]

F. *Conclusions*

The UNSG concluded that "[t]here are significant gaps and deficiencies with respect to the applicable principles of environmental law; the normative and institutional content of the sectoral regulatory regimes, as well as their articulation with environment-related regimes; the governance structure of international environmental law; and the effective implementation of compliance with and enforcement of international environmental law."[125]

The UNSG noted "important deficiencies with respect to principles of international environmental law" with "instances where there is no clarity as to the nature and content of a principle, or no judicial consensus as to its

116. *Id.* at 36, para. 87.
117. *Id.* at 8, para. 90-91.
118. *Id.* at 38, para. 92.
119. *Id.* at 39, para. 93.
120. *Id.* at 39, para. 94.
121. *Id.* at 40, para. 96.
122. *Id.* at 41, para. 97.
123. *Id.* at 41, para. 99.
124. *Id.* at 42, para. 99.
125. *Id.* at 42, para. 100.

applicability, or no recognition in binding legal instruments, or all of the above."[126] The degree of legal uncertainty surrounding many of these principles has a direct and indirect impact on the predictability and implementation of sectoral environmental regimes. "There is a need to further clarify the principles of environmental law, without prejudice to the legal developments already achieved in the issue-specific contexts of various MEAs. A comprehensive and unifying international instrument that gathers all the principles of environmental law could provide for better harmonization, predictability and certainty."[127]

The UNSG noted fragmentation in MEAs and in the governance structure of international environmental law and suggested "better coordination at both the law-making and implementation levels [is needed] in order to ensure policy coherence, mutual supportiveness and synergies in implementation."[128] Gaps and deficiencies were also found in specific sectoral regulatory regimes, with issues remaining without a "specific, legally binding regulation."[129] These include "regulations on the conservation and sustainable use of forests, the pollution of marine areas by land-based plastic waste, the protection of soil, human rights and climate change, biodiversity, nanomaterials and some geo-engineering activities."[130] Some gaps are also found within existing MEAs, with an identified need for harmonization of treaties, a global approach to issues dealt with at the regional level, principles to harmonize the application of a patchwork of agreements, improved compliance mechanisms, and better articulation between MEAs and environment-related instruments.[131] Compliance mechanisms and means of implementation need to be strengthened to promote the effective implementation of MEAs.[132] At the international level, implementation is constrained by the lack of clarity of environmental principles.[133] Implementation at the international level could be strengthened through more effective reporting, review and verification processes, robust compliance and enforcement procedures and mechanisms, and increased role of non-State actors in law-making, implementation monitoring and compliance procedures.[134]

126. *Id.* at 42, para. 102.
127. *Id.* at 43, para. 102.
128. *Id.* at 43, para. 103.
129. *Id.* at 43, para. 104.
130. *Id.* at 43, para. 104.
131. *Id.* at 43-45, para. 104-09.
132. *Id.* at 45, para. 110-11.
133. *Id.* at 45, para. 112.
134. *Id.* at 45, para. 112.

The UNSG finalized: "Building upon the creative approaches that States have thus far adopted to protect the environment, it is essential that States and the United Nations work together to address gaps in international environmental law. We must collectively seize the opportunity to use international environmental law in new and dynamic ways to provide a strong and effective governance regime with a view to better safeguarding the environment for future generations."[135]

135. *Id.* at 45, para. 113.

Document 4: ICEL Note on the UNSG's Report (Dec. 10, 2018)

World Commission on Environmental Law of the
International Union for the Conservation of Nature
International Council of Environmental Law
International Group of Experts for the Pact

NOTE
on the
United Nations Secretary-General's Report, "Gaps in international environmental law and environment-related instruments: towards a global pact for the environment"
(A/73/419, 3 December 2018)

10 December 2018

Executive Summary

The Secretary-General's historic first Report of 3 December 2018 on international environmental law is a welcome analysis of legal endeavors worldwide to protect the Earth's environment. Without this field of law, the impacts of climate change, biodiversity loss, and pollution would have been worse. States have adopted many agreements to frame their cooperation to safeguard the environment. Each agreement contains general principles of environmental law. ICEL has compiled rosters of these principles from all the global and regional agreements and recorded them in the ICEL Charts, which are presented here for the first time. These principles have the potential to accelerate implementation of the UN Sustainable Development Goals (SDGs). This Note explains how and why the consultations in 2019 in Nairobi could reach consensus on the codification and progressive development of core principles of international environmental law. The Note offers commentary also on other aspects of the Secretary-General's Report.

This Note sets forth an independent assessment by a working group of expert members of the World Commission on Environmental Law (WCEL) of the International Union for the Conservation of Nature (IUCN),* and of the International Council of Environmental Law (ICEL),** in concert with the International Group of Experts for a Global Pact for the Environment (IGEP).*** The opinions expressed in this Note are the individual scholarly or professional judgments of these experts, and are not statements on behalf of either WCEL-IUCN, ICEL, or IGEP. This Note offers information and expert perspectives as a contribution for the forthcoming consultations about international environmental law that will convene in Nairobi, Kenya, in 2019.

We dedicate the Note to the memory of Elisabeth Haub and Wolfgang E. Burhenne, founders of IUCN's environmental law programme, and in honor of Prof. Charles Okidi,[1] and of the other laureates of the Elisabeth Haub awards in environmental law and diplomacy,[2]all of whom made enormous contributions to establishing the field of environmental law across all regions of the Earth.

* The International Union for the Conservation of Nature (IUCN), founded in 1948, established its World Commission on Environmental Law in 1963. Its Law Commission's Members were instrumental in the development of several agreements, such as CITES and the Convention on Biological Diversity, as well as soft law instruments, such as the World Charter for Nature. IUCN participates in the work of the UN General Assembly through its Permanent Observer Mission to the UN in New York, and its headquarters in Gland, Switzerland. Contact via the WCEL Administrative Officer at wcel@iucn.org.

** ICEL was founded in New Delhi in 1969, and is constituted under Article 60 of the Swiss Civil Code (Canton of Geneva). It has been accredited to the UN Economic and Social Council (ECOSOC) since 1973, and maintains representatives in Bonn, Geneva, and New York. It sponsors the Journal *Environmental Policy & Law*. It is a Member of IUCN. Contact via ICEL Executive Governor at nrobinson@law.pace.edu.

*** The Commission on the Environment of the *Club des Juristes* launched preparation of the draft Global Pact for the Environment in 2016-17. It convened a group of more than 100 environmental law experts, many also are members of the IUCN CEL and ICEL, who deliberated during the first half of 2017 and met in Paris in June of 2017 to refine and approve the text of the Global Pact for the Environment. *See also* "Renforcer l'Efficacité du Droit International de l'Environnement—Devoirs des Etats, Droits des Individus," http://www.leclubdesjuristes.com/rapport-renforcer-lefficacite-du-droit-international-de-lenvironnement-devoirs-des-etats-droits-des-individus/ (2015) (a summary of the report and the full report are available in English). The International Group of Experts for the Pact (IGEP) is an association of these experts. Contact via Secretariat at globalpact@globalpactenvironment.org.

1. Patricia Kakeri-Mbote and Collins Odote, eds., Blazing the Trail—Professor Charles Okidi's Enduring Legacy in the Development of Environmental Law (University of Nairobi, 2019).
2. http://www.juridicum.su.se/ehp/laureates.html for law and https://law.pace.edu/elisabeth-haub-award for diplomacy. The two awards were merged in 2018, and will continue as one award recognizing the shared contributions leaders in both fields make for strengthening international environmental law.

Note on the UN Secretary General's Report on International Environmental Law

Welcoming the Secretary-General's Report

This Note welcomes the first report ever issued by the Secretary-General of the United Nations concerning the field of international environmental law, A/73/419 (30 November 2018). The UN General Assembly mandated preparation of the Report in resolution 72/277 (10 May 2018), entitled "Towards a Global Pact for the Environment." The Report is a major contribution to the further development of international environmental law. It would be of value for the UN General Assembly to request further such reports, on a periodic basis, on the progressive development of international environmental law, a realm of cooperation among States that did not exist when the United Nations was established.

The genesis of the General Assembly's request for the preparation of this Report was the submission by France of a proposed draft of a "Global Pact for the Environment,"[3] which had been prepared in 2017 by an international group of experts on international environmental law. Their draft reflected analysis of the development of normative principles of international environmental law since the 1972 Stockholm Declaration on the Human Environment.[4] The General Assembly put the draft Pact to one side and requested that the Secretary-General undertake an independent review of the instruments that comprise contemporary international environmental law, and identify gaps and relationships with other related fields of law. In addition to the 1972 Stockholm Declaration, the General Assembly resolution references the 1982 World Charter for Nature,[5] the 1992 Rio Declaration on Environment and Development,[6] Agenda 21 and the Programme for the Further Implementation of Agenda 21,[7] the Johannesburg Declaration on Sustainable Development,[8] the outcome document ("The Future We Want") of the 2012 UN Conference on Sustainable Development,[9] the 2015 Sustainable Development Goals,[10] as well as the outcomes of other UN conferences and summits in economic, social and environmental fields.

3. Global Pact for the Environment; White Paper: Toward a Global Pact for the Environment (September 2017), both available at http://pactenvironment.org.
4. Stockholm Declaration on the Human Environment, *at* http://www.un-documents.net/unchedec.htm.
5. World Charter for Nature, Res 37/7 (1982), *at* http://www.un.org/documents/ga/res/37/a37r007.htm37/7 (1982).
6. Rio Declaration, A/CONF.151/26 (Vol. I), *at* http://www.un.org/documents/ga/conf151/aconf15126-1annex1.htm.
7. Agenda 21 (1992), *at* https://sustainabledevelopment.un.org/outcomedocuments/agenda21.
8. Johannesburg Declaration on Sustainable Development, 2002, *available at* http://ec.europa.eu/environment/archives/wssd/documents/wssd_pol_declaration.pdf.
9. "The World We Want," Outcome Document of the Rio 2012 Summit on Sustainable Development, *at* https://sustainabledevelopment.un.org/futurewewant.html.
10. UN General Assembly, Transforming Our World: The 2030 Agenda for Sustainable Development, A/RES/70/1 (21 October 2015), *available at* https://www.refworld.org/docid/57b6e3e44.html (accessed 7 December 2018).

At the outset, we find that the Secretary-General's analysis is sound and we share the Report's over-all analysis and conclusions. As the Report falls into the mainstream of scholarly and professional analysis about environmental law, as confirmed by the many expert references that we cite in this Note, we are able to promptly respond to this Report and proffer these additional further perspectives.

The state of international environmental law has been extensively set forth and succinctly summarized in the 26 chapters of UNEP's "Training Manual on International Environmental Law" (2006), which was prepared by experts from each region around the world.[11] This Manual provides a standard description of international environmental law, in an easily understood and non-technical presentation. The Secretary-General's Report necessarily assumes that its readers have some familiarity with the field of environmental law. For those who may not have this background, this UN Environment Programme (UNEP, UN Environment) Manual provides context and can serve as a reference in relation to the recommendations in the Secretary-General's Report.

An Urgent and Common Concern for the Earth

Why does the Secretary-General's Report matter, to States, to us in our chosen discipline of environmental law, and ultimately to world security and order?

Former UNEP Executive Director Klaus Töpfer introduced UNEP's Manual in 2006 stating that: "Today's world is facing an unprecedented environmental crisis. Deterioration of the Earth's environment increasingly threatens the natural resource base and processes upon which all life on Earth depends. Without strong and multifaceted action by all of us, the biosphere may become unable to sustain human life and future generations will suffer deprivation and hardship unless current patterns of production, consumption and water management dramatically change. The urgency of balancing development with the Earth's life support systems is being finally recognized and understood. Now it is time to act upon this understanding." The UNEP "Global Environmental Outlook 5" (GEO-5) report in 2012 confirmed that Earth's environment is degrading faster and further than was the case in 2006.[12]

The recent Special Report of the Intergovernmental Panel on Climate Change (IPCC), "Global Warming of 1.5°*C*" (October 2018),[13] soberly reported that the time to act to avert harm has passed. IPCC (Intergovernmental Panel on Climate Change) studies revealed that unless remedial action is taken in the next decade, all States face irrevocable damage. Adverse impacts of climate change, extreme weather events, fires, droughts, and floods, today are eroding development gains

11. Training Manual on International Environmental Law (UNEP, 2006), ISBN 92-807-2554-8; online at https://digitalcommons.pace.edu/lawfaculty/791/. Currently being updated by UN Environment and the IUCN Academy of Environmental Law.
12. UNEP, Global Environment Outlook 5: Environment for the Future We Want (2012), *available at* http://wedocs.unep.org/handle/20.500.11822/8021.
13. IPCC Special Report, "Global Warming of 1.5°C," *at* https://www.ipcc.ch/sr15/ (last accessed December 4, 2018).

that took years to acquire. The IPCC attributed the recent record-breaking floods, droughts, and coastal impacts from rises in sea levels, to the .87°C rise in global atmospheric temperature since the pre-industrial era (1850-1900). The IPCC advised that the aim of the 2015 Paris Agreement, to hold the rise in temperature to "well below a 2°C increase above pre-industrial levels" and to pursue efforts to limit the temperature increase to 1.5°C above pre-industrial levels, is insufficient to avert severe disruption globally. The IPCC's recent report advised limiting temperature increases to below 1.5°C, but acknowledged that to do so would require "unprecedented changes" in all aspects of socio-economic life.[14]

Natural disasters are not new, but they are becoming more severe and more people are in harm's way. 1998 is recalled as the year that "the world burned."[15] Two decades on, regional climates have become drier and hotter, and wildfires were even worse this past year. Significant new levels of flooding, and powerful hurricanes and typhoons, also recur. In light of prospects for an increased scale of disasters, States have cooperated to develop the "*Sendai Framework on Disaster Risk Reduction*."[16] The Sendai Framework would benefit from having a stronger environmental law foundation and treaty mechanisms to help States prepare for and build resilience to recover from disasters. Recognizing an international Principle of Resilience could animate States to adopt more effective national policies to avert, to prepare for, and to recover from natural disasters.[17]

As the global population of humans is projected to grow from 7.5 billion today to 9 billion in 2050, all States will benefit from enhanced cooperation to sustain a healthy environment, provide for food production, and cope with the ecological impacts of rapid declines in biological diversity. There are many ways to do so.[18] As President Xi Jinping of China has observed, "It is high time that we intensified eco-environmental protection. And we are capable of accomplishing this task now."[19] China is moving

---

14. Intergovernmental Panel on Climate Change Special Report 15, "Global Warming of 1.5° C 6 October 2018, *at* www.ippc.org. To attain acceptable temperature levels, by 2030 global carbon dioxide emissions need to fall to 45% of 2010 levels, and by 2050 it will be necessary to scrub the greenhouse gases from the atmosphere by vastly wider use of photosynthesis by plants (from marine phytoplankton to forests). As Joyeeta Gupta and Karin Arts indicate, "The reality is that transformational changes in development patterns are required for achieving a 2ºC world and yet more radical changes if one is to reach the ore stringent target of 1.5ºC." Joyeeta Gupta, & Karin Arts, Int. Env. Agreements (2018) 18:11. http://doi.org/10.1007/s10784-017-9376-7.
15. *See* Nicholas A. Robinson, *Forest Fires as a Common International Concern: Precedents for the Progressive Development of International Environmental Law*, 18 Pace Envtl. L. Rev. 459 (2001), *at* http://digitalcommons.pace.edu/lawfaculty/375/.
16. Sendai Framework for Disaster Risk Reduction, *at* https://www.unisdr.org/we/inform/publications/43291.
17. See also the International Law Commission's draft articles on the protection of persons in the event of disasters; Official Records of the General Assembly, Seventy-First Session, Supplement No. 10 (A/71/10); UN GA res. A/res/71/141 (13 December 2016) (recommending to the General Assembly the elaboration of a convention on the basis of the draft articles on the protection of persons in the event of disasters).
18. See, e.g., the studies of the Stockholm Resilience Center, at www.stockholmresilience.org.
19. Xi Jinping, The Governance of China II (Foreign Languages Press, 2017), p. 425.

toward a principled stewardship program of "ecological civilization,"[20] which aligns government practices and budgets with ecological stewardship. Other guides, such as the Earth Charter,[21] also establish normative foundations for global environmental stewardship. In responding to the Secretary-General's Report, States have an opportunity to enhance the effectiveness of international environmental law. The ad hoc open-ended working group scheduled to meet in Nairobi under UN General Assembly resolution 72/277 will provide an opportunity for States to develop an effective global approach.

Peace, security, and sustainable development depend on maintaining a healthy and stable environment. The destabilizing effect of events like recurrent wildfires can be seen both domestically as human lives and nature are impacted and also when transboundary pollution spreads the harm more widely, people are displaced, and regional ecological integrity is threatened.[22] In 2018, wild fires were more severe again, afflicting alike, without distinction, both developed and developing States. This "new normal" requires new responses from governments. The IPCC attributes this escalating scale and severity of natural disasters to climate change. The pattern of increasing threats to the environment makes it plain that more consensus is needed to accelerate efforts to implement the SDGs through the United Nations 2030 Agenda. Principles of environmental law have a key role to play in this effort.

Furthering the Progressive Development of Environmental Law

Following the 1972 Stockholm Conference, States have increasingly promoted the field of international environmental law to prevent environmental degradation and guide socio-economic development toward sustainability. The 1987 UN World Commission on Environment and Development ("Brundtland Commission"), in its report "Our Common Future," called for the elaboration of environmental law.[23] Agenda 21 delineated steps that States should undertake to strengthen national and international environmental law in chapters 8 ("Integrating environment and development in decision-making"), 37 ("National mechanisms and international cooperation for capacity building in developing countries"), 38 ("International institutional arrangements"), and 39 ("International institutional arrangements"). States agreed to these recommended measures by consensus. The motivation for consensus at the 1992 Rio Conference on Environment and Development is characterized by Russian Federation President Boris Yeltsin: "Our common aspiration should be not

---

20. Zhu Guangyao, *Ecological Civilization—A National Strategy for Innovative, Concerted, Green, Open and Inclusive Development*, OUR PLANET (UN Environment March 2016); *see also* Paul Baressi, *The Role of Law and the Rule of Law in China's Quest to Build an Ecological Civilization*, 1:1 CHINESE J. ENVTL. L. 9-36 (2017).
21. *See* www.earthcharter.org.
22. *See* SHUNMUGAM JAYAKUMAR, TOMMY KOH, ROBERT BECKMAN, AND HAO DUY PHAN, TRANSBOUNDARY POLLUTION, EVOLVING ISSUES OF INTERNATIONAL ENVIRONMENTAL LAW (Edward Elgar, 2015).
23. Our Common Future (1987), *at* http://www.un-documents.net/our-common-future.pdf. The Report had a detailed appendix on the need for further environmental law development. Those recommendations remain to be fully implemented.

just the survival but the life – a life worthy of mankind – of our great homeland, the uniquely beautiful planet Earth."[24]

The thoughtful recommendations of Agenda 21 for international environmental law and governance deserve to be revisited. They have not been fully implemented. These pending recommendations represent a kind of "gap" which is not examined in the Secretary-General's report. Many recommendations in Agenda 21 have been implemented, resulting in improved cooperation between States on international institutional arrangements for environmental goals, evidence of its potential.

Between 1972 and 2018, States have cooperated progressively to develop the field of environmental law. The multilateral environmental agreements (MEAs), along with the many regional agreements, are founded upon a set of agreed principles and obligations.[25] The fact that States share a set of universally agreed principles is not widely recognized, because international environmental law is often thematic and largely directed to managing, protecting, or conserving specific parts of the biosphere, such as the stratospheric ozone layer or the Antarctic Ocean; or on human impacts, such as the release of toxic chemicals that are persistent organic pollutants, or the trade in endangered species. Despite this appropriate regional and sectoral focus, all aspects of international environmental law are guided by a shared vision, which is to organize human activity to safeguard the biosphere. This unity of purpose is obscured because international environmental law is often seen through its parts, not its whole.

States understandably focus on the separate parts of international environmental law because of the importance they give to the national implementation of each agreement. However, in practice, States generally assign implementation of their international environmental obligations to different ministries or authorities, and rarely have a single cabinet-level office to oversee all of them. The Secretary-General's Report is valuable in providing States an overview of international environmental law, which is otherwise difficult to obtain. Moreover, environmental ministries within States and at the local level are typically under-resourced and hard-pressed to implement their duties. There is little opportunity to share best practices with authorities in other regions, or internationally. For these reasons, it is difficult for governments to learn how others cope with the same problems. Too few are aware that other States have adopted and embraced the same general principles of environmental law across all sectors. International secretariats and UN Environment lack the resources to play such an informational role and address this situation.

24. Agenda Item 9, Letter dated 9 June 1992, from the Deputy Head of the Delegation of the Russian Federation to the Secretary-General of the United Nations Conference on Environment and Development, transmitting the Address of the President of the Russian Federation, A/CONF.151/18 10 June 1992, reproduced at pp. 885-88, vol. 4, AGENDA 21 AND THE UNCED PROCEEDINGS (Nicholas A. Robinson, editor, Oceana Publications, 1993, in 6 volumes, the *traveaux préparatoires* of UNCED).

25. For more information on the institutions created within the MEA's, see BHARAT DESAI, MULTILATERAL ENVIRONMENTAL AGREEMENTS. LEGAL STATUS OF THE SECRETARIATS (Cambridge Univ. Press, 2010).

As the UN Secretary-General's Report accurately indicates, international environmental law consists of specialized agreements. This is a strength. Although increased coordination between related sectoral conventions is desirable, it is not appropriate to characterize the wide range of specialized agreements as representing some kind of dysfunctional fragmentation. Shared principles and comparable administrative programs produce effective remedial measures in similar ecological conditions, in all regions. For example, implementation of the Vienna Convention to Protect the Stratospheric Ozone Layer, and its Montreal Protocol and other derivative agreements[26] is a justly celebrated example of integrated global action to collectively protect a common resource. Regional cooperation is also productive, but few regions have occasion to learn what other regions do. For example, even in the case of legal regimes for one medium, the marine environment, it is perhaps not surprising that the Regional Seas Programme for the Baltic (Helsinki Agreement)[27] is not much in contact with the Regional Seas Programme for the Mediterranean (Barcelona Agreement)[28] or with the Agreements for the Wider Caribbean Sea[29] or the Gulf (Kuwait Agreement) or the Red Sea or with the cooperative programmes in the South Pacific (SPREP) or North Atlantic (OSPAR).[30] As the Report of the UN Secretary-General observes, there would be benefits from a "comprehensive and unifying international instrument clarifying all the principles of environmental law."[31]

Providing References to Principles for the 2019 Consultations in Nairobi

The General Assembly requested that its *ad hoc* open-ended working group report on its forthcoming consultations by June 2019. As Ambassador Macharia Kamau has observed, "Most of what we have come to accept as the body of international norms and legislation that govern our global system of cooperation, humanitarian support, and peace and security is negotiated, endorsed, legislated, and enforced through this system of agencies, council and offices. Mastering the functions and operations of this global multilateral system takes years, if not decades, of engagement and practice."[32] Because States have already share a wide consensus about principles of international environmental law, previous investments of diplomatic time and capacity mean that the General Assembly's time-table is realistic.

26. *See* Handbook for the Montreal Protocol on Substances the Deplete the Ozone Layer (2006), *at* https://unep.ch/ozone/Publications/handbook/MP__Handbook_2006.pdf.
27. Helsinki Convention for the Protection of the Baltic Sea Area (HELCOM), *at* http://www.helcom.fi/about-us/convention.
28. The Barcelona Convention for the Protection of the Mediterranean Sea (which also helped promote the wider Mediterranean Union), *at* https://web.unep.org/unepmap/1-barcelona-convention-and-amendments.
29. The 1983 Cartagena Convention for the Wider Caribbean, *at* http://www.cep.unep.org/cartagena-convention.
30. See these regional seas agreements at https://unep.ch/conventions/rscaplist.htm.
31. UN Secretary-General, Gaps in International Environmental Law and Environment-Related Instruments: Towards a Global Pact for the Environment, UN Doc. A/73/419, 43, para. 10, at 7 (30 November 2018).
32. Macharia Kamau, Preface to M. Kamau, P. Chasek and D. O'Connor, Transforming Multilateral Diplomacy—The Inside Story of the Sustainable Development Goals (Routledge, 2018).

States' delegates have a brief period of time in which to study the Secretary-General's report and prepare for the forthcoming 2019 consultations on International Environmental Law. They have only 45 days, followed by the six months of consultations. Their mission deserves cooperation and support, for the reasons cited in Res. 72/277. Accordingly, a working group of experts convened by ICEL, in cooperation with the IUCN World Commission on Environmental Law and the International Group of Experts for the Global Pact for the Environment, has prepared this Note and supporting studies.

ICEL has undertaken studies to provide States with the tools that enable them to secure this overview of existing commitments, in cooperation with the Vance Center of the New York City Bar and the international law firm of White & Case. ICEL has assembled this information in a set of Charts (the "**ICEL Charts**," 5 September 2018).[33] The Charts identify general principles adopted within multilateral environmental agreements and regional agreements for: the African Union (AU), the Association of South East Asian States (ASEAN), the Caribbean Community (CARICOM), the Commonwealth of Independent States (CIS), the League of Arab States (Arab League), the Organization of American States (OAS), the South Asian Cooperative Agreement (SACEP) and the Pacific Islands Forum and similar studies are underway for all other regional groups. The States of the European Union are party to the same set of agreements,[34] and Brazil, China, Japan, Russia and the United States have accepted most of the same principles. ICEL has assembled a Chart indicating the legal foundation provided by these agreed principles of international environmental law for each of the UN Sustainable Development Goals.

The ICEL Charts reveal the consensus on principles and objectives in international environmental law. They complement the discussion in the Secretary-General's Report. This Note touches upon several of the recommendations in the UN Secretary-General's report:

(a) the progressive development of international law with respect to general principles of international environmental law and their codification;

(b) gaps in existing international environmental agreements;

(c) the relationships of environmental agreements with instruments in other fields of international law;

(d) gaps in the governance frameworks;

---

33. See the Appendix to this Note for the links providing access to the ICEL Charts. The ICEL Charts may be accessed on the websites of the Law Library at the Elisabeth Haub School of Law, New York (https://libraryguides.law.pace.edu/icel), and IUCN's World Commission on Environmental Law (https://www.iucn.org/news/world-commission-environmental-law/201812/global-pact-gap-report-released-un-environment).

ICEL also is disseminating its ICEL Charts to States as references for their participation in the Nairobi consultations.

34. *See* Environmental Law, Magazine *Environment* for Europeans (19 January 2018), *at* https://ec.europa.eu/emvironmnet/efe/themes/evironmental_law_en; and Jan H. Jans and Hans H.B. Vedder, European Environmental Law (2009. 3rd edition).

(e) the implementation and effectiveness of international environmental law, and

(f) the role of international environmental law in ensuring attainment of the UN Sustainable Development Goals and the 2030 Development Agenda.

A. General Principles of International Environmental Law

Part II of the Secretary-General's Report addresses general principles of international environmental law. The Report's useful observations can be endorsed and also expanded upon.

International recognition of the principles of environmental law has roots in the 1972 UN Stockholm Conference on the Human Environment, which adopted the Stockholm Declaration. The Declaration's preamble states that "Man is both creature and moulder of his environment, which gives him physical sustenance and affords him the opportunity for intellectual, moral, social and spiritual growth. In the long and tortuous evolution of the human race on this planet a stage has been reached when, through the rapid acceleration of science and technology, man has acquired the power to transform his environment in countless ways and on an unprecedented scale. Both aspects of man's environment, the natural and the man-made, are essential to his well-being and to the enjoyment of basic human rights the right to life itself."[35]

In light of these and other considerations, the Stockholm Conference proclaimed an environmental right and duty in its first principle. This was based on the assumption that the Earth's environment was stable and capable of being sustained: "Man has the fundamental right to freedom, equality and adequate conditions of life, in an environment of a quality that permits a life of dignity and well-being, and he bears a solemn responsibility to protect and improve the environment for present and future generations." Principle 2 provided that: "The natural resources of the earth, including the air, water, land, flora and fauna and especially representative samples of natural ecosystems, must be safeguarded for the benefit of present and future generations through careful planning or management, as appropriate."[36] These principles set the stage for subsequent deliberations about how to more clearly recognize and observe the right to the environment.

Since 1972, principles of international environmental law have been elaborated and refined. Their virtue, as ICEL Member Winfried Lang noted, is that they serve to build agreement and cooperation. Surveying the views of other ICEL members for an article in the Max Planck UN Year Book,[37] he stated: "[Alexandre] Kiss-[Dinah]

35. Preamble paragraph 1, Stockholm Declaration on the Human Environment, *at* www.un-documents.net/unchedec.htm; *see* Ben Boer, *Environmental Principles and the Right to Environment, in* Ludwig Krämer and Emanuela Orlando (eds.), PRINCIPLES OF ENVIRONMENTAL LAW, Elgar Encyclopedia of Environmental Law, Vol. VI, 52, 57 (2018).

36. Stockholm Declaration, Principle 1.

37. Winfried Lang, *UN-Principles and International Environmental Law,* MAX PLANCK YEAR BOOK OF UNITED NATIONS LAW, UNYB 3 (1999), *at* http://www.mpil.de/en/pub/publications/periodic-publications/max-planck-yearbook/volume-3.cfm.

Shelton linked the adoption of principles to the progressive development of international law, but as professional lawyers they agree that such principles cannot stand alone but need transformation into binding obligations in order to play their role in international life. [Paul] Szasz, with his life-long experience in law-making in the UN context, stressed the important role of legislative declarations as they may be precursors to and guide a later treaty-making process and are designed to influence the conduct of states directly."[38] Lang further observed that "French scholars distinguished by the mid-eighties between '*principes directeurs*' and '*principes inspirateurs*.' Among the former they included environmental impact assessments, information and consultation, early warning in case of accidents, non-discrimination and equal treatment. In the second group were mentioned sovereignty in exploiting one's natural resources, solidarity and cooperation, equitable utilization of common resources, safeguarding of the common heritage of mankind."[39] Lang goes on to identify principles as they appear in different environmental agreements, not unlike the ICEL Charts.

Since Lang wrote, the consensus about existing principles of international environmental law has become wider and more refined.[40] Many principles are now "accepted" (e.g. public participation in environmental decision-making) while others remain as "emerging" (e.g. inter-generational equity, and duties to future generations). Moreover, as Emanuela Orlando and Ludwig Krämer observed "alongside widely recognized environmental principles at the international law level, and across different jurisdictions world-wide other environmental principles have emerged in particular legal systems, reflecting the needs, aspirations and objectives of that particular culture and legal traditions. This is the case for example in the 'protection first' principle in China, or the public trust doctrine, which inherited from the US, is being increasingly used in environmental cases by courts in India and in Sri Lanka.'"[41]

The present consultations on principles of international environmental law, therefore, may need to evaluate those which are widely accepted and those which are emerging. Of the former, it is appropriate to codify them in a single agreed text. In cases where more than one expression of the principle is found a single agreed text would "provide for better harmonization, predictability and certainty" in international environmental law.[42] Some emerging principles may be important enough to acknowledge in such text as the progressive development of the law is necessary as real-world conditions change.

38. *Id.* p. 158.
39. *Id.* at p. 161. *See also* Maurice Kampto, *Les Nouveaux Principes du Droit de l'Environnement*, Revue Juridique de l'Environnement 18:1 (1993), at 11-21.
40. Philippe Sands, Principles of International Environmental Law (Cambridge 2d ed., 2003).
41. Ludwig Krämer and Emanuela Orlando, *Introduction*, *in* Ludwig Krämer and Emanuela Orlando (eds.), Principles of Environmental Law, Elgar Encyclopedia of Environmental Law, Vol. VI, 2 (2018).
42. UN Secretary-General's Report on "Gaps in International Environmental Law and Environment-Related Instruments: Towards a Global Pact for the Environment" (A/73/419, 30 November 2018), para. 102, p. 43.

As Shailendra Kumar Gupta includes the following principles as being widely accepted:[43]

"(1) Principle 21 of the Stockholm Declaration and Principle 2 of the Rio Declaration, namely that states have sovereignty over their natural resources and the responsibility not to cause environmental damage;

(2) The principle of preventive action;

(3) The principle of good neighborliness and international co-operation;

(4) The principle of sustainable development;

(5) The precautionary principle;

(6) The polluter-pays principle; and

(7) The principle of common but differentiated responsibility."

There is a large body of additional principles that some scholars would add to these.[44] The UNEP Manual described these principles in Chapter 3. The additional principles are (1) Sustainable Development; (2) Inter-Generational and Intra-Generational Equity; (3) Responsibility and Transboundary Harm; (4) Transparency, public participation and access to information and remedies; (5) Cooperation and Common But Differentiated Responsibilities; (6) Precaution; (70 Prevention; (8) Polluter pays; (9) Common Heritage and Common Concern of Mankind; (11) Good Governance. There are significant commentaries about how to observe and use principles to promote sustainable development, as for example in China through environmental management practices.[45]

The Secretary-General's Report describes nine principles (paragraphs 11-22). In addition to the principles set forth above, the Report adds the right to a healthy environment, and the Principles of Non-Regression and Progression, but does not

---

43. Shailendra Kumar Gupta, "Principles of International Environmental law and Judicial Response in India," at p. 3 (Benares Hindu University, Varanasi, India).

44. UNEP Manual, chapter 3. *See* Marie-Claire Cordonier Segger, *Commitment to Sustainable Development Through International Law and Policy*, *in* Marie-Claire Cordonier Segger and H.E, Judge C.G. Weeramantry, eds.,_SUSTAINABLE DEVELOPMENT PRINCIPLES IN THE DECISION OF INTERNATIONAL COURTS AND TRIBUNALS 1992-2012 (Routledge, 2017), pp. 29-98. *See also* Nico Schrijver, *Advancement in the Principles of International Law on Sustainable Development*, *in* Marie-Claire Cordonier Segger and H.E, Judge C.G. Weeramantry, eds., SUSTAINABLE DEVELOPMENT PRINCIPLES IN THE DECISION OF INTERNATIONAL COURTS AND TRIBUNALS 1992-2012, pp. 99-108.

45. *See* Xiangbai He, *Setting the Legal Enabling Environment for Adaptation Mainstreaming Into Environmental Management in China: Applying Key Environmental Law Principles*, 17 ASIA PAC. J. ENVTL. L. 23 (2014). *See also* Yuhong Zhao, *Environmental Principles in China*, PRINCIPLES OF ENVIRONMENTAL LAW, ELGAR ENCYCLOPEDIA OF ENVIRONMENTAL LAW, Vol. VI (Elgar, 2018), pp. 424-36; Olga Dubovik and Alla Röhrict, *Principles of Russian Environmental Law*, *in* PRINCIPLES OF ENVIRONMENTAL LAW, ELGAR ENCYCLOPEDIA OF ENVIRONMENTAL LAW, Vol. VI, pp. 437-48; Samudu Atapattu, *Environmental Law Principles in Asia*, *in* PRINCIPLES OF ENVIRONMENTAL LAW, ELGAR ENCYCLOPEDIA OF ENVIRONMENTAL LAW, Vol. VI, pp. 433-75; Hennie Strydom, *Environmental Principles in Africa*, *in* PRINCIPLES OF ENVIRONMENTAL LAW, ELGAR ENCYCLOPEDIA OF ENVIRONMENTAL LAW, Vol. VI, pp. 494-506.

address Inter-Generational or Intra-Generational Equity. The 1972 Stockholm Declaration embraces the right to the environment as a fundamental principle, as well as the principles associated with the duties of States to care for the environment and to enact effective laws to safeguard the environment. Principle 17 of the Rio Declaration obliges States to undertake environmental impact assessment in national decision-making impacting on the environment, and this norm has become accepted as customary international law;[46] the draft Global Pact and the Secretary-General's Report list this duty as one aspect of the Principle of Prevention. The Expert Group that prepared the draft Global Pact for the Environment includes the principle of caring for the Earth in Article 2 and set forth the Principle of Resilience in Article 16, and although both are implicit in other principles (e.g. prevention and precaution), there is value in expressing them in their own right.

This brief description of the international principles of environmental law lends support to the observation in the Secretary-General's Report regarding the importance of States coming to agreement on a common set of core principles to guide international environmental law. Agreeing to principles in a new Global Pact would provide certainty to the relations among States. The Nairobi consultations could agree on and restate the core principles of international environmental law. This is part codification, and part progressive development of law, which is within the General Assembly's mandate under article 13(1) of the UN Charter.

Expert commentaries about these general principles tend to agree on a core set of principles and diverge as to new or emerging principles. States themselves have determined the roster of accepted principles by including them in international agreements. This is considered the best evidence of core principles that are candidates for codification. The ICEL Charts found in the Appendix to this Note list these agreed principles.[47]

The most cited provision of the 1972 Stockholm Declaration is Principle 21, governing State obligations and rights. Principle 21 provides that: "States have, in accordance with the Charter of the United Nations and the principles of international law, the sovereign right to exploit their own resources pursuant to their own environmental policies, and the responsibility to ensure that activities within their jurisdiction or control do not cause damage to the environment of other States or of areas beyond the limits of national jurisdiction." This poses a problem: how can States know when their conduct may harm a neighbor of the commons? It would seem that the principles of prevention and precaution preclude such transboundary harm, and observing Rio Principle 17 on environmental impact assessment would enable States to observe their duty not to harm neighbors of the commons. In order to guide State practice and to build capacity for States to observe Principle

46. Pulp Mills on the River Uruguay (Argentina v. Uruguay), Judgment, I.C.J. Reports 2010, www.icj-cij.org/en/case/135; Responsibilities and Obligations of States Sponsoring Persons and Entities With Respect to Activities in the Area, Advisory Opinion, Case No. 17, International Tribunal for the Law of the Sea Reports 2011.

47. *See also* Cymie R. Payne, *A Global Pact for the Environment*, 22:12 Am. Soc. Intl L. Insights (2018), *available at* https://www.asil.org/insights/volume/22/issue/12/global-pact-environment.

21, States will need to understand their reciprocal and shared duties. For this reason alone, States should formally acknowledge that they share a common set of principles that would further this objective.

B. *Gaps in Existing International Environmental Agreements*

The analysis in Part II of the Secretary-General's Report is sound. A multifaceted response is called for and we encourage the several conferences of the parties under international agreements, as well as the UN General Assembly, to address the gaps identified where they have authority to do so. A response to this part of the Report requires substantially more time than provided for the Nairobi consultations in 2019. It is worth noting that, despite some gaps and limitations, there is positive international cooperation under all of the international environmental agreements. This reflects the findings that Nobel Laureate Dr. Elinor Ostrom established,[48] that when parties understand their shared dependence on common pool resources, they evolve ways to cooperate effectively together. The Secretary-General's Report is prudent in citing Ostrom's research,[49] which rebuts the theory that there is always a "tragedy of the commons." Ostrom's studies indicate that agreeing on clear rules leads to cooperation to sustain shared resources. The General Assembly has experienced this phenomenon in both the consensus on the SDGs and also in the on-going negotiation regarding conservation and sustainable use of biodiversity in areas beyond national jurisdiction (BBNJ). State practice under the Montreal Protocol for protection of the Stratospheric Ozone layer also reflects Ostrom's findings. The consultations in Nairobi may wish to recommend that priority be given to enhancing the effectiveness of international law in the areas identified in section II of the Secretary-General's Report.

C. *Environment-Related Instruments: Relationships of Environmental Agreements With Instruments in Other Fields of International Law*

The UN Secretary-General's report assesses the lack of coherence and synergy among environment-related instruments—specifically on trade, investment, intellectual property and human rights—to conclude that "the articulation between multilateral environmental agreements and environment-related instruments remains problematic owing to the lack of clarity, content-wise and status-wise, of many environmental principles."[50]

48. Elinor Ostrom, Understanding Institutional Diversity (2005), at p. 286.

49. UN Secretary-General's Report on "Gaps in International Environmental Law and Environment-Related Instruments: Towards a Global Pact for the Environment" (A/73/419, 30 November 2018), para. 22, Note 77, citing E. Ostrom, Governing the Commons: The Evolution of Institutions for Collective Action (1990).

50. UN Secretary-General's Report on "Gaps in International Environmental Law and Environment-Related Instruments: Towards a Global Pact for the Environment" (A/73/419, 30 November 2018), Summary. *See* Gilles J. Martin, *Principles and Rules*, *in* Principles of Environmental Law, Elgar Encyclopedia of Environmental Law, Vol. VI 13-22. *See also* Teresa Fajardo, *Environmental Law Principles and General Principles of International Law*, *in* Principles of Environmental Law, Elgar Encyclopedia of Environmental Law, Vol. VI 38-51.

With respect to trade and environment, the UN Secretary-General's report notes "a widening gap between these two normative regimes."[51] On the trade side, the Doha Round of negotiations had agreed to confer about how to reconcile international law regimes for environmental protection and for trade, but this never happened. Article XX of the General Agreement on Tariffs and Trade remains a critical norm. However, national implementation of the GATT Article XX's phytosanitary controls is often inconsistent and would benefit from harmonization. Current implementation is proving too weak to prevent infection across borders. On the environmental law side, the Convention on International Trade in Endangered Species (CITES)[52] is a robust regime that provides norms and procedures to ensure that trade does not cause the extinction of species. The Montreal Protocol has a successful fund that assists developing nations to phase out the manufacture and trade in ozone depleting substances and to finance national focal points to implement trade restrictions on banned substances.[53] While the principle of sustainable development has become an integral part of the world trading system,[54] and provides "color, texture and shading" to the interpretation trade agreements, there is no binding agreement articulating the prerequisites for sustainable trade practices. A coherent set of environmental law principles could contribute to stabilizing world trade law and averting future environment-related trade disputes. In sum, "environmental principles can play a role in reconciling international law with trade law, and balancing trade with environmental interests."[55]

This is also the case for investment and intellectual property legal instruments. The UN Secretary-General's report notes normative gaps "because the specific environmental concerns explicitly addressed in these agreements are limited."[56] In particular, gaps between the regimes of the Trade-Related Aspects of Intellectual Property Rights (TRIPS Agreement) under the World Trade Organization and the Convention on Biological Diversity are evident.[57] The consultations to harmonize rules and practices under these two regimes came to a halt after the Doha Round

51. UN Secretary-General's Report on "Gaps in International Environmental Law and Environment-Related Instruments: Towards a Global Pact for the Environment" (A/73/419, 30 November 2018), para. 71.
52. https://www.cites.org.
53. Donald Kaniaru, "The Montreal Protocol: Celebrating 20 Years of Environmental Progress: Ozone Layer and Climate Protection," UNEP/Earthprint 2007.
54. *See* Markus Gehring and Alexandre Genest, *Disputes on Sustainable Development in the WTO Regimes, in* Marie-Claire Cordonier Segger and H.E, Judge C.G. Weeramantry, eds., SUSTAINABLE DEVELOPMENT PRINCIPLES IN THE DECISION OF INTERNATIONAL COURTS AND TRIBUNALS 1992-2012, pp. 382-83. *See also* Kati Kulovesi and Sabaa Khan, *Environmental Principles in Trade Relations, in* PRINCIPLES OF ENVIRONMENTAL LAW, ELGAR ENCYCLOPEDIA OF ENVIRONMENTAL LAW, Vol. VI, pp. 644-57.
55. *See* Kati Kulovesi and Sabaa Khan, *Environmental Principles in Trade Relations, in* PRINCIPLES OF ENVIRONMENTAL LAW, ELGAR ENCYCLOPEDIA OF ENVIRONMENTAL LAW, Vol. VI, p. 656.
56. UN Secretary-General's Report on "Gaps in International Environmental Law and Environment-Related Instruments: Towards a Global Pact for the Environment" (A/73/419, 30 November 2018), para. 73. *See also* David M. Ong, *Environmental Principles in International Investment Law, in* PRINCIPLES OF ENVIRONMENTAL LAW, ELGAR ENCYCLOPEDIA OF ENVIRONMENTAL LAW, Vol. VI, pp. 658-72.
57. Makane Moïse Mbengue and Urs O. Thomas, *The Precautionary Principle: Torn Between Biodiversity, Environment-Related Food Safety and the WTO*, INT'L J. GLOBAL ENVTL. ISSUES, 5.1-2 (2005), pp. 36-53.

of Trade negotiations stalled. A comprehensive and unifying set of environmental law principles would guide the search for ways to reconcile competing economic, social and environmental objectives.[58]

With respect to human rights, while the connections between a healthy environment and the effective enjoyment of human rights are well recognized by human rights bodies and tribunals,[59] as noted in the UN Secretary-General's report, gaps exist between sources of human rights law and environmental law.[60] In this regard, clarification and reinforcement of principles of international environmental law, as well as the recognition of a stand-alone right to a healthy environment, could provide a more balanced reconciliation of economic, social, and environmental rights.[61] Moreover, this reconciliation approach of different rights at the intersection of environment and development—"the very essence of sustainability"[62]—would be a useful contribution to the implementation of the sustainable development goals and the UN 2030 Agenda.

Recognition of the right to a healthy environment as a human right has been acknowledged since the 1972 Stockholm Conference. The right to development dates back to the 1980s, and since 1992, as ICEL member Ben Boer has argued, "the principle of sustainable development suggests that the right to development is to be balanced with and constrained by the right to a clean, safe, healthy and sustainable environment."[63] To ensure that this is understood juridically, States should "agree on a legal instrument that reflects the current regional agreements which include recognition of the right to a quality environment, with focus both on the substantive elements as well as on robust means of implementation. The barriers to proclaiming a clearly articulated and unambiguous right to a quality environment at a global level are falling away. The question is now not if, but when, a global instrument containing such a right will be opened for signature and eventually enter into force."[64]

D. *Gaps Relating to the Governance Structure of International Environmental Law*

---

58. *See* Henning Grosse Ruse-Khan, *The Principle of Integration in WTO/TRIPS Jurisprudence, in* Marie-Claire Cordonier Segger and H.E, Judge C.G. Weeramantry, eds., SUSTAINABLE DEVELOPMENT PRINCIPLES IN THE DECISION OF INTERNATIONAL COURTS AND TRIBUNALS 1992-2012, p. 398.
59. MANUAL ON HUMAN RIGHTS AND THE ENVIRONMENT (2d Edition, 2012, Council of Europe), *at* www.echr.coe.int/Library/Docs/DH_DEV_Manual.
60. UN Secretary-General's Report on "Gaps in International Environmental Law and Environment-Related instruments: Towards a Global Pact for the Environment" (A/73/419, 30 November 2018), para. 76.
61. Stephanie Safdi and Sébastien Jodoin, *The Principle of Sustainable Development in the Practice of UN Human Rights Bodies, in* Marie-Claire Cordonier Segger and H.E, Judge C.G. Weeramantry, eds., SUSTAINABLE DEVELOPMENT PRINCIPLES IN THE DECISION OF INTERNATIONAL COURTS AND TRIBUNALS 1992-2012, p. 467.
62. *Ibid.*, p. 468.
63. *See* Ben Boer, *Environmental Principles and the Right to a Quality Environment, in* PRINCIPLES OF ENVIRONMENTAL LAW, ELGAR ENCYCLOPEDIA OF ENVIRONMENTAL LAW, Vol. VI, p. 73.
64. *Ibid.*

International Environmental Law has evolved rather quickly over the last four decades. Developing nations have played a leading role in the design and implementation of new environmental law as they have seen factual evidence of environmental harm.[65] These agreements are generally issue-specific or targeted to conditions in particular geographic areas. As noted above, this gives the field the appearance of being fragmented. An internationally agreed set of overarching principles would help give unity to instruments of varied scope and legal nature.

Clarity and consistency in defining these core principles, in a legal instrument, would simplify the complex task of operationalizing environmental agreements. The multiplicity of agreements has made it difficult for States to provide sufficient national civil servants and diplomats to participate in all the international regimes. It has also led to concerns about legal inconsistencies and institutional fragmentation[66] and a lack of legal certainty. Scholars around the world have noted this situation widely.[67] There is an "urgent need to strengthen the UN's environmental institutions and governance framework".[68]

There are more than 500 international environmental agreements[69] that directly or indirectly relate to the environment. This variety of normative instruments cover a diverse spectrum of issues, such as loss of biological diversity, atmospheric pollution, the deterioration of the oceans or the soil, or the problem of deforestation, among many others.[70] To this profusion of norms, a plethora of policymaking organs has to be added to complete the dominant heterogeneity. Indeed, the MEAs have created their own specific set of institutions (such as the Conference of the Parties, Secretariats, etc.) to ensure the proper functioning of the agreements.[71] The severity of the state of the environment[72] caused by

65. *See, e.g.*, Parvez Hassan, *Role of the South in the Development of International Environmental Law*, Chinese J. Envtl. L. 1 (2017) 133-57; and Adil Najam, *Developing Countries and Global Environmental Governance: From Contestation to Participation to Engagement*, *in* International Environmental Agreements: Politics, Law and Economics (September 2005), Vol. 5, Issue 3, pp. 303-21.
66. Joost Pauwelyn, *Bridging Fragmentation and Unity: International Law as a Universe of Inter-Connected Islands*, Mich. J. Int'l L. 25 (2003): 903.
67. Including the Global South: Adil Najam, Ioli Christopoulou, and William R. Moomaw, *The Emergent "System" of Global Environmental Governance*, Global Envtl. Pol. 4.4 (2004): 23-35.
68. Bharat H Desai, "The Quest for a UN 'Specialized Agency' for the Environment" (2012) 1010 (60) The Round Table 171, and *On the Revival of the United Nations Trusteeship Council With a New Mandate for the Environment and the Global Commons*, Y.B. Int'l Envtl, L., Vol. 27, No. 1 (2016) 16.
69. Kanie, Norichika, *Governance With Multilateral Environmental Agreements: A Healthy or Ill-Equipped Fragmentation?*, Green Planet Blues: Critical Perspectives on Global Environmental Politics (2014): 137.
70. Geoffrey Palmer, *New Ways to Make International Environmental Law*, 86 Am. J. Int'l L. 259, 263 (1992).
71. Indeed, international environmental institutions acquire their own character once they are established and start functioning. *See* Bharat Desai, Institutionalizing International Environmental Law (Transnational Publishers, 2004).
72. IPCC *Global Warming of 1.5 °C. Summary for Policymakers* (2018).

anthropogenic stress on the Earth, evidences the critical need for reform within this institutional framework.[73]

Among the numerous global and regional institutions, UNEP was intended to be the "leading environmental authority in the United Nations system".[74] Since its creation in 1972,[75] UNEP has tried to consolidate robust environmental standards and practices while guaranteeing compliance with them. However, it has faced many problems,[76] mostly due to its own organizational structure and to the lack of proper funding,[77] which has led to various restructuring attempts.[78]

A variety of proposals have been made to provide States with more coherent oversight of international governance for the Earth's environmental systems. Among the proposals to improve the effectiveness of the international environmental governance is the establishment of a World Environment Organization[79] as a UN specialized agency rather than a UN programme.[80] A WEO is envisioned as a more centralized institution that would improve decision-making processes, implementation and co-ordination in international environmental governance.[81] Other proposals would merge UNDP and UNEP, constituting a UN Sustainability Programme. It would report to the UN Economic and Social Council, which would function as an Ecological, Social and Economic Council. Alternatively, ICEL member Bharat H. Desai has urged that oversight be vested in a UN "Environmental" Trusteeship Council.[82] Currently, the UN Environment Assembly and the UNGA Second Committee are responsible for oversight of global environmental governance and policy. The UN General Assembly launched the High-Level Political Forum in July of each year, to measure implementation of the UN Sustainable Development Goals. One

73. *See* Maria Ivanova, *Global Governance in the 21st Century: Rethinking the Environmental Pillar*, Stakeholder F. (2011).
74. UNEP, United Nations Environmental Program, https://www.un.org/youthenvoy/2013/08/unep-united-nations-environment-programme/.
75. Institutional and financial arrangements for international environmental cooperation, UN Doc. A/res/27/2997 (1972), *available at* http://www.un-documents.net/a27r2997.htm.
76. The current UNEP is not strong and ambitious enough to tackle the environmental problems. *See* Bharat H. Desai, International Environmental Governance: Towards UNEPO (Brill/Nijhoff, 2015).
77. Bharat H. Desai, *UNEP: A Global Environmental Authority?*, Env. Pol'y & L., 36/3-4 (2006) 140.
78. Maria Ivanova, *Institutional Design and UNEP Reform: Historical Insights on Form, Function and Financing*, Int'l Aff. 88.3 (2012): 565-84.
79. A wide range of issues must be considered before any new inter-governmental body is to be constituted. *See* C.F. Amerasinghe, Principles of Institutional Law of International Organization (Cambridge 1996, 2d ed.). *See also* Nicholas A. Robinson, *Befogged Vision: International Environmental Governance a Decade After Rio*, 27 Wm. & Mary Envtl. L. & Pol'y Rev. 299 (2002), http://digitalcommons.pace.edu/lawfaculty/372/.
80. Louis Kotzé, *A Global Environmental Constitution for the Anthropocene?*, Transn'l Envtl. L. (2019): 1-23.
81. S. Oberthür & T. Gehring, *Reforming International Environmental Governance: An Institutionalist Critique of the Proposal for a World Environment Organisation (2004)* 4 Int'l Envtl. Agreements: Pol., L. & Econ., pp. 359–81.
82. Bharat H. Desai, *On the Revival of the United Nations Trusteeship Council With a New Mandate for the Environment and the Global Commons*, 27 Y.B. Int'l Envtl. L. 3 (2016).

efficient way to achieve global coherence could be provided by the adoption of a common set of agreed principles.

Whatever governance approaches may be considered, there is increasing recognition of the role of non-state actors in international environmental law, acknowledging that international relations have evolved beyond States and the "Westphalian model"[83] of state sovereignty. Non-state actors are increasingly participating in international environmental negotiations,[84] albeit often in an informal fashion, without clear rules regarding the scope of their involvement. In a world of social media, it is possible also to engage local communities in debates about their environmental futures. Systems of international environmental law need to explore further how to observe Rio Declaration Principle 10, on "public participation in environment decision-making."[85]

There is a wide consensus in support of more effective coordination among international environmental instruments and institutions. The IPCC Special Report "Global Warming of 1.5°C" projects that States have only ten years to improve coordination, before harms become insufferable. The accelerating warming of Earth's atmosphere does not allow any further procrastination. Strengthening international environmental legal systems is essential to achieving the 2030 Agenda on sustainable development. States would benefit from having more robust institutions that could more effectively respond to their environmental problems. Codification of a set of principles would stimulate international cooperation toward the new governance structures that gradually will fill the existing gaps within the international environmental law system, "....as the legal foundation for environmental justice, global ecological integrity, and a sustainable future for all."[86]

E. *Implementation and Effectiveness of International Environmental Law*

1) National Implementation

Effective implementation of international environmental law is a key element to guarantee the effective protection of the environment. States play an essential role[87] as they have full sovereignty over their territory, only limited by the suprem-

83. The Peace of Westphalia (1648) established the state sovereignty system, which becme the contemporary international system of states. *See* Derek Croxton, *The Peace of Westphalia of 1648 and the Origins of Sovereignty*, 21 Int'l Hist. Rev. 569 (1999).

84. Kal Raustiala, *The Participatory Revolution in International Environmental Law*, Harv. Envtl. L. Rev. 21 (1997): 537.

85. See, for example, "World Wide Views on Climate and Energy," 10,000 citizens, 97 Debates in 76 countries (2015, Danish Board for Technology Foundation), organized through Missions Publiques, www.missionspubliques.com.

86. IUCN, World Commission on Environmental Law, *World Declaration on the Environmental Rule of Law* (2016), *available at* https://www.iucn.org/sites/dev/files/content/documents/world_declaration_on_the_environmental_rule_of_law_final_2017-3-17.pdf.

87. As Ana Barreira, et al. indicate, "the States are the principal subjects in Environmental Law. They create, adopt and apply the principles and rules, establish the international organizations and allow the participation of other actors during the international legal process." Ana Barreira, Paula Ocampo, and María Eugenia Recio. *Medio Ambiente y Derecho Internacional: Una Guía Práctica*, Obra Social, Caja Madrid, 2007, p.13.

acy and exclusivity of other State's sovereignty (principle of non-intervention, article 2.4 UN Charter).[88] Also, despite the fact that some international agreements are self-executing, most States must enact implementing regulations.[89] But even this does not ensure achieving results. Empirical studies indicate that most States fail in compliance due to factors that vary according to the specific circumstances of the State. Agenda 21 (chapter 8, Integrating environment and development in decision-making) addressed the lack of implementation and poor compliance with regulations and MEAs[90] by strengthening domestic laws and institutions and building up national capacity.[91] Solutions require promoting coordination, cooperation, legal support, education and training in environmental law matters, respecting the national priorities and specific conditions of each nation.

2) *Means of Implementation: Financial Resources, Technology Transfer and Capacity-Building*

Effective MEA implementation requires efforts in education, technical assistance, voluntary compliance programmes, and importantly, financial assistance.[92] Indeed, effective implementation of MEAs requires strategic investment. Existing funding of MEAs needs to be re-evaluated and additional funding provided. The multiplication and lack of coordination among financing resources has eroded the effectiveness of efforts at sustainable development. The Addis Ababa Action Agenda[93] of the 3rd International Conference on Financing for Development was endorsed by the General Assembly on 27 July 2015. The Addis Ababa Action Plan can be advanced by reference to the principles of international environmental law. A codified Global Pact for the Environment would accelerate international cooperation to attain both the Addis Ababa Action Agenda and the Sustainable Development Goals. As long as each separate international environmental agreement has its own scarce funding stream, there will be "duplications and contradictions" within the system.[94] Agreement on a set of general principles of international environmental law can guide States toward a more coherent financing system, which could save costs and encourage more (in quantity and effectiveness) environmental action.[95] An example

---

88. Maziar Jamnejad and Michael Wood, *The Principle of Non-Intervention*, Leiden J. Int'l L. 22.2 (2009): 345-81.
89. Brigitte L. Okley, *Legislation and Implementation of International Environmental Law by African Countries: A Case Study of Ghana*, LLM Theses (2004): 8.
90. Agenda 21 (chapter 8). *See also* The Montevideo Program, https://www.unenvironment.org/explore-topics/environmental-governance/what-we-do/strengthening-institutions-0 (last visited Dec 4, 2018).
91. UNEP, Possible Elements for a Programme in the Area of Environmental Law for a Specific Period Beginning in 2020, UNEP/ENV.LAW/MTV.4/FP.3, Geneva, 12-14 September 2018.
92. UNEP, *Training Manual of International Environmental Law. 4. Compliance and Enforcement of Multilateral Environmental Agreements*, https://autlawiel.files.wordpress.com/2014/10/unep-tm-ch-4-compliance-and-enforcement-of-multilateral-environmental-agreements.pdf (last accessed, Dec. 4, 2018).
93. https://www.oecd.org/dac/gender-development/Action%20Plan%20on%20Financing%20Gender%20Equality.pdf.
94. Adil Najam, Mihaela Papa, Nadaa Taiyab, "Global Environmental Governance. A Reform Agenda," IISD, Ministry of Foreign Affairs of Denmark, 2006, p. 53.
95. *Id.*

of a very effective funding mechanism, as noted previously, is the Multilateral Fund for the Implementation of the Montreal Protocol, with a total budget of US $540 million for the 2018-2020 triennium, plus additional voluntary contributions.[96]

Nearly all international environmental law regimes are but minimally funded today. Yet military institutions, including NATO, have long recognized the link between the environment and security.[97] Environmental security will increasingly need to be resourced at a scale comparable to what States provide to their defense agencies. States recognized the need for such funding in Agenda 21 (Chapter 33), particularly for the developing countries. Climate change impacts will bring disruptions to all States. However, given the need to invest to build resilience and prepare, there is an unequal situation in the case of developing nations, especially small island States, which the common but differentiated responsibilities principle has acknowledged over the course of the history of international environmental law.[98] Therefore, the financial question is fundamental for the developing countries, and will be a topic of consultation in Nairobi.[99]

3) Dispute Resolution and Enforcement Mechanisms

The UN Secretary-General's report acknowledges gaps relating to the implementation and effectiveness of international environmental law in several aspects of inter-State dispute settlement, MEA implementation, and in the enforcement of rights and obligations regarding the global commons and shared natural resources, such as the high seas, Antarctica, and outer space. Furthermore, practices under international trade and investment regimes also reveal gaps in the implementation and effectiveness of environmental norms, and such gaps in regime interaction also arise insofar as many environmental treaties do not address their relationships with economic treaties, which may give rise to distinct sources of applicable law or jurisdiction in a given dispute.

While enforcement of international environmental obligations is largely dependent on the effectiveness of national rule of law and administrative resources and systems in order to oversee their proper application, "it would be incorrect to dismiss or ignore the actual and potential influence that international legal principles and mechanisms may bring to bear on states to respect their basic duty to adhere to international environmental obligations."[100] Further, it should be noted that such

96. Multilateral Fund for the Implementation of the Montreal Protocol, http://www.multilateralfund.org/default.aspx (last visited, 4 Dec. 4, 2018).
97. James Mcquaid and Arpad Vincze, *Countering Threats to Environmental Security: The Role of NATO*, *in* S. Stec and B. Baraj (eds.) Energy and Environmental Challenges to Security (NATO Science for Peace and Security Series) (Springer, Dordrecht, 2009).
98. Lavanya Rajamani, *The Changing Fortunes of Differential Treatment in the Evolution of International Environmental Law*, Int'l Aff., 88.3 (2012), 605-23, p. 623.
99. Adil Najam, Mihaela Papa, Nadaa Taiyab, "Global Environmental Governance, A Reform Agenda," IISD, Ministry of Foreign Affairs of Denmark, 2006, pp. 3-54.
100. *See* Martin Hedemann-Robinson, *Environment and Sanctions*, *in* Principles of Environmental Law, Elgar Encyclopedia of Environmental Law, Vol. VI, pp. 673-97.

principles also strengthen non-compliance mechanisms.[101] At the national level, there are now more than 1,500 specialized courts and tribunals that function to ensure the observance of national environmental laws. The IUCN World Commission on Environmental Law, the Organization of American States, and UN Environment have facilitated the establishment of an International Judicial Institute on the Environment, through which the courts can exchange best practices and share how they interpret the principles of environmental law across legal systems.[102] Innovative remedies, such as the use, as in the courts of South Asia, of judicially appointed commissions, are applications of international environmental law principles in specific contexts.[103]

4) Liability and Redress for Transboundary Environmental Damage

Compliance provisions in International Environmental Law have limits that help explain the failure of States to observe their Rio Declaration Principle 21 duty to prevent transboundary harm from activities under their jurisdiction and control. The Secretary-General's Report notes the halting progress of international courts and tribunals in addressing environmental harm, explaining their limitations with respect to legal principles for dealing with the particular features of such cases, and their imperfect ability to handle the scientific evidence. In contrast, it is useful to consider the arbitral tribunal in *Burlington Resources Inc. v. Republic of Ecuador,*[104] with its extensive legal analysis, and the valuation of both market and non-market environmental damage by the United Nations Compensation Commission.[105] Remedies for environmental liability and redress are only partially implemented through general international law and a handful of treaties dealing in very limited way with damage to areas beyond national jurisdiction: space, the high seas, and Antarctica; very few specify liability for risk-intensive but lawful activities.

In a world of transnational activities, this leaves the environment vulnerable, especially when a State has limited domestic enforcement capacity. Dire Tladi has addressed "the moral argument that the risks for damage should be borne by those who profit ... and that a binding international regime could make this possible in a way that domestic regulation could never achieve", in the context of devel-

101. *Ibid. See also* Suzanne Kingston, *Environment Principles and Environmental Disputes and Their Settlement, in* Principles of Environmental Law, Elgar Encyclopedia of Environmental Law, Vol. VI, pp. 698-709; Marie-Claire Cordonier Segger and H.E, Judge C.G. Weeramantry, eds., Sustainable Development Principles in the Decision of International Courts and Tribunals 1992-2012.

102. Global Judicial Institute on the Environment, *at* https://www.iucn.org/commissions/world-commission-environmental-law/wcel-resources/global-judicial-institute-environment.

103. See, for example, the experience of the High Court of Lahore, Pakistan. Parvez Hassan, Resolving Environmental Disputes in Pakistan: The Role of Judicial Commissions (Pakistan Law House, 2018).

104. ICSID Case No. ARB/08/5, Decision on Counterclaims (7 Feb. 2017).

105. United Nations Compensation Commission, Report and Recommendations made by the Panel of Commissioners concerning the Fifth Instalment of "F4" Claims, U.N. Doc. S/AC.26/2005/10 (30 June 2005).

oping State positions during the Nagoya - Kuala Lumpur Supplementary Protocol negotiations.[106]

The Secretary General Report's explanation of the role of state responsibility in redressing transboundary environmental damage might be rounded out by noting further that the due diligence standard of care does not apply to every international wrongful act. For example, where one State entered the territory of another and damaged vegetation and other environmental features, the ICJ did not apply a due diligence standard to the intentional act of the responsible government (*Certain Activities*);[107] nor did the award in the *Trail Smelter* case, where atmospheric pollution from one State caused transboundary harm to another.[108] It is only recently that the duty to prevent transboundary harm has in some circumstances been limited to the due diligence obligation to ensure that national law provides an adequate apparatus to prevent harm.

F. *International Environmental Law, the Sustainable Development Goals and the 2030 Development Agenda*

Adoption of the UN Sustainable Development Goals (SDGs) is among the greatest outcomes of inter-governmental cooperation in recent years. However, the General Assembly could stimulate faster implementation of the SDGs by recognizing a set of shared environmental law principles.[109] The UN Secretary-General's Report underscores that sustainable development principles have been incorporated into the larger global agenda by the 2030 Agenda for Sustainable Development.[110] The incomplete character of international environmental law is likely to retard the attainment of all of the SDGs. If States collectively can acknowledge the environmental law principles that most of them already explicitly embrace, they are apt to cooperate more effectively in the 2030 Agenda. Moreover, adhering to these general principles of law can guide conduct in subject areas where treaties or national legislation are still lacking. The principles also would afford guidance for tribunals and specialized agencies in their decision-making.

As Macharia Kamau has explained, the global consensus on the SDGs and the 2030 Agenda is a landmark achievement.[111] Implementation is the next step. Environ-

106. Dire Tladi, *Civil liability in the Context of the Cartagena Protocol: to Be or Not to Be (Binding)?*, INT'L ENVIRON AGREEMENTS (2010) 10:15–27, 20.
107. Joined cases concerning Certain Activities Carried Out by Nicaragua in the Border Area (Costa Rica v. Nicaragua) and Construction of a Road in Costa Rica Along the San Juan River (Nicaragua v. Costa Rica), Judgment, 2015.
108. Trail Smelter Case (United States, Canada).
109. See International Council of Environmental Law, Vance Center and White and Case, Analysis of the Adoption and Implementation of the Environmental Principles in the Proposed Global Pact for the Environment (Global Pact) in the Sustainable Development Goals (SDGs), set forth in the Appendix to this Note.
110. UN Secretary-General's Report on "Gaps in International Environmental Law and Environment-Related Instruments: Towards a Global Pact for the Environment" (A/73/419, 30 November 2018), para. 20.
111. M. KAMAU, P. CHASEK, D. O'CONNOR, TRANSFORMING MULTILATERAL DIPLOMACY—THE INSIDE STORY OF THE SUSTAINABLE DEVELOPMENT GOALS (Routledge, 2018).

mental law provides the essential means for doing so. The SDGs make clear the gravity of today's environmental and social problems. In the coming decade, as the UN Environment's GEO-5 report records, States will be confronted with the reality that Earth's natural systems are at a categorical turning point. Agreement on the principles, such as the right to a healthy environment, and clarification of the other principles, can equip States to build resilience and capacity amidst present and future environmental adversity.

For example, the UN Secretary-General's report stresses the importance of effective implementation of the legal framework established by the UN Convention on the Law of the Sea (UNCLOS) and its implementing agreements in order to achieve Sustainable Development Goal 14, oceans, seas and marine resources.[112] However, general principles and MEAs are not yet linked to all SDGs. For example, the principles found in the Convention on Biodiversity or the Ramsar Convention on Wetlands, are not tied to the terrestrial goals expressed in SDG 15; and there is not an SDG for freshwater, which is central to both treaties. Whereas, governance, access to justice and information principles are central to all the SDGs, as set forth in SDG 16.[113] Clarification and reinforcement of principles will promote the links between international and national environmental law and sustainable development, facilitate SDG integration and gap-filling, and contribute to a transformative realization of sustainability goals.

Agreement on shared environment law principles would also help to clarify why capacity-building is urgently needed in many States. Thus, such agreement can contribute to a significant enhancement in development assistance and in international and national environmental governance[114] towards a coherent and effective protection system, aimed at the real achievement of a sustainable future.[115]

Since the adoption of the 2030 Agenda and the Sustainable Development Goals, the overarching aim of environmental law and policy implementation – of both national law and MEAs – is attaining the SDGs via the 2030 Agenda. To deliver on this overarching aim, the UNGA endorsed the Addis Ababa Action Agenda,[116]

112. UN Secretary-General's Report on "Gaps in International Environmental Law and Environment-Related Instruments: Towards a Global Pact for the Environment" (A/73/419, 30 November 2018), para. 60 and 71.

113. *See* Marcos Orellana, *Governance and the Sustainable Development Goals: The Increasing Relevance of Access Rights in Principle 10 of the Rio Declaration*, Rev. Eur., Comp. & Int'l L., vol. 25, No. 1 (2016).

114. Professor Pilar Moraga, Universidad de Chile (Chile), indicates that: "In turn, the enshrinement of the principles of environmental law included in the Pact would make it possible to shed light on domestic rights, and consequently illuminate the work of national case law." *See* http://blogs.law.columbia.edu/climatechange/2018/09/20/global-perspectives-on-a-global-pact-for-the-environment/#Alex%20L.%20Wang (accessed November 2018).

115. Professor Marisol Anglés, UNAM (Mexico) stresses the sustainability element of the Pact by indicating that "the content and scopes proposed in the Pact may be perfected to build a long-term vision of development for all nations, encompassing present and future generations." *See* http://blogs.law.columbia.edu/climatechange/2018/09/20/global-perspectives-on-a-global-pact-for-the-environment/#Alex%20L.%20Wang (accessed November 2018).

116. The Addis Ababa Action Agenda of the Third International Conference on Financing for Development (Addis Ababa Action Agenda), adopted by the General Assembly on 27 July 2015 (resolution

which is an integral part of the 2030 Agenda for Sustainable Development. Full implementation of the Addis Ababa Action Agenda is critical for the realization of the SDGs and targets, and for addressing the gaps noted in the Secretary-General's report.

Also integral to the 2030 Agenda are the Istanbul Declaration and Programme of Action,[117] the SIDS Accelerated Modalities of Action (SAMOA) Pathway[118] and the Vienna Programme of Action for Landlocked Developing Countries for the Decade 2014–2024,[119] and the African Union's Agenda 2063 and the programme of the New Partnership for Africa's Development.[120] As agreed by the UNGA, the scale and ambition of the new Agenda requires a revitalized Global Partnership to ensure its implementation: "This Partnership will work in a spirit of global solidarity, in particular solidarity with the poorest and with people in vulnerable situations. It will facilitate an intensive global engagement in support of implementation of all the Goals and targets, bringing together Governments, the private sector, civil society, the United Nations system and other actors and mobilizing all available resources."[121]

Arguably, the greatest hindrance to implementing environmental laws, both national and MEAS, as well as the 2030 Agenda, is the lack of shared commitment by States to making the fulfillment of environmental law and the 2030 Agenda an over-arching priority. This has impeded sustainable development in the past and will also work to undermine the successful achievement of the SDGs. Providing a set of common governing principles has the capacity to broaden this focus into a widely shared perspective. The endorsement of a Global Pact will set the stage for making agreement on giving priority to the 2030 Agenda. Each of the Pact's principles can be aligned behind different SDGs and their agreed indicators.

Some urge a "no action" alternative, to let the existing systems go on "as is," but this is inconsistent with the 2030 Agenda and the SDGs. "No action" undermines the SDGs. Clarifying already applicable principles of law does not generate new commitments. It is a "least difficult" step in support of UNGA Res. 70/1. Further, observing the restated principles of environmental law is essentially the task of national governments. States themselves will individually decide how to observe them, as is the case with other general principles of law. Having an agreed set of principles will "level the playing field" and encourage cooperation among States, which are assured that all others have a similar outlook. It will enable sharing "best practices" and foster capacity-building.

As UN Environment, the Organization of American States, and the IUCN World Commission on Environmental Law have explained, the "environmental rule of

---

69/313, annex).

117. Report of the Fourth United Nations Conference on the Least Developed Countries, Istanbul, Turkey, 9–13 May 2011 (A/CONF.219/7), chaps. I and II.
118. Resolution 69/15, annex.
119. Resolution 69/137, annex II.
120. A/57/304, annex.
121. Res. 70/1, para. 29.

law" is a proven pathway for attaining the Sustainable Development Goals. In 2016, the World Commission on Environmental Law of the International Union for the Conservation of Nature (IUCN) and UN Environment[122] called the basic norms of procedural environmental rights part of the "Environmental Rule of Law."[123] UN Environment describes it, as follows: "Environmental rule of law is central to sustainable development. It integrates environmental needs with the essential elements of the rule of law, and provides the basis for improving environmental governance. It highlights environmental sustainability by connecting it with fundamental rights and obligations. It reflects universal moral values and ethical norms of behavior, and it provides a foundation for environmental rights and obligations. Without environmental rule of law and the enforcement of legal rights and obligations, environmental governance may be arbitrary, that is, discretionary, subjective, and unpredictable."[124]

Conclusions

As the UN Secretary-General stated in November 2018 at the Paris Peace Forum, anticipating the issuance of his Report: "codifying the fundamental principles of environmental law would provide predictability and clarity." We agree.

The Secretary-General's Report is a milestone in the progressive development of international environmental law. As practitioners, teachers, and scholars of this still young legal field, we urge everyone to study the Secretary-General's Report. We further commend to all, the authorities whom we have cited in this Note.

Implementing the SDGs is the best way forward to averting future environmental disasters. Codifying and progressively elaborating the international principles of environmental law will substantially improve the odds that the SDGs can be attained. Keeping this as the priority for the Nairobi consultations can build consensus. Once confidence is built, then the process can advance to capacity building. Recommending a set of common principles is the essential initial step.

It is possible to address the gaps in international environmental law, gaps in relationship to environment-related instruments, and gaps in financing. This will take more time. The five months provided for the consultations in Nairobi do provide adequate time to draft and agree upon a new Global Pact for the Environment. States already agree on many principles, as the **ICEL Charts** in the Appendix to this Note demonstrate. Recognition of our shared principles can then guide capacity building.

Resolution 72/277 has launched a remarkable quest to strengthen international environmental law. The promise of Agenda 21's recommendation on law and governance are at last recognized. The consultations in Nairobi can productively

122. https://www.un.org/ruleoflaw/thematic-areas/land-property-environment/environmental-law/.
123. https://www.iucn.org/sites/dev/files/content/documents/english_world_declaration_on_the_environmental_rule_of_law_final.pdf.
124. https://www.unenvironment.org/explore-topics/environmental-governance/what-we-do/strengthening-institutions/promoting-1.

examine the "scope, parameters and feasibility of an international instrument" that both codifies and clarifies the various international principles and basic duties for safeguarding Earth's natural environment. We have modest confidence that the forthcoming consultations in Nairobi will afford States an opportunity to review how much agreement already exists within international environmental law. This recognition will facilitate cooperation toward a deeper consensus to agree on the principles that strengthen international environmental law and contribute to attaining the UN Sustainable Development Goals.

Signatories

(as of 10 December 2018)

The names of the environmental law experts originating this Note are listed in alphabetical order (institutions and countries provided for identification purposes only)

Experts' signatures received as of 9 January 2019 will be included in the release of this Note at the consultations of the General Assembly's ad hoc open working group in Nairobi. The Note will be available for signature at the web page of the World Commission on Environmental Law of the International Union for the Conservation of Nature (IUCN), at https://iucn.org/sites/dev/files/noteforunsgenvllawrptdec2018_final.pdr and the signature link is at https://goo.gl/forms/expWxdLTehd0TKYUZ2

See also generally www.iucn.org/commissions/wcel.

Yann Aguila, International Group of Experts for the Pact (France)
Denise Antolini, Professor, Richardson School of Law University of Hawaii (USA)
Milena Bellini Sheppard, ICEL Representative to the United Nations Offices in Geneva (Switzerland)
Antonio Herman Benjamin, Chair, IUCN World Commission on Environmental Law (Brazil)
Ben Boer, Distinguished Professor, Wuhan University (China), and Professor *emeritus*, University of Sydney (Australia)
Trevor Daya-Winterbottom, University of Waikato (New Zealand)
Agustín de Assís Roig, Associate Professor, Carlos III de Madrid University (Spain)
Rose-Lisa Eisma-Osorio, Professor, College of Law, University of Cebu (Philippines)
Antonio Fortes, Associate Professor, Carlos III de Madrid University (Spain)
Fabrisio Fracchia, Professor, Department of Law, Bocconi University (Italy)
Parvez Hassan, Chair *emeritus*, IUCN World Commission on Environmental Law (Pakistan)
Patricia Kameri-Mbote, Professor, University of Nairobi (Kenya)
Koh Kheng Lian, ICEL Representative to ASEAN (Singapore)
Donald Kaniaru, ICEL Representative in Nairobi (Kenya)
Reinhard Josef Krapp, ICEL Representative in Bonn (Germany)

Herman-Kasper Gillisen, Professor, Utrecht University (Netherlands)
Isabel Hernández San Juan, Assistant Professor of Law, Carlos III de Madrid University (Spain)
Nilufer Oral, Istanbul Bilgi University and International Law Commission (Turkey)
Richard L.Ottinger, Dean *emeritus*, Elisabeth Haub School of Law at Pace University (USA)
Luciano Parejo Alfonsi, Professor of Law *emeritus*, Carlos III de Madrid University (Spain)
Teresa Parejo Navajas, Associate Professor of Law, Carlos III de Madrid University (Spain), and UN SDSN Senior Advisor (New York, USA)
Cymie R. Payne, Professor, Rutgers University (USA)
Robert V. Percival, Professor, University of Maryland Francis King Carey School of Law (USA)
Eckard Rehbinder, Professor *emeritus*, Goethe-University Frankfurt am Main (Germany)
H. F.M. W (Marleen) van Rijswick, Professor, Utrecht University (Netherlands)
Nicholas A. Robinson, Professor *emeritus*, Elisabeth Haub School of Law at Pace University (New York, USA)
Victor M.Tafur, ICEL Representative to the United Nations (New York, USA)

Appendix
The Icel Charts

Below please find links to charts that set forth the correspondence between the Draft Global Pact for the Environment and the Sustainable Development Goals, general principles of international soft law, multilateral environmental agreements, and various regional environmental agreements. They have been prepared by the International Council of Environmental Law (ICEL)—an expert international organization established in 1969 and in consultative status with UN ECOSOC since 1973—together with the Vance Center for International Justice (sponsored by the New York City Bar Association) and White & Case, an International Law Firm.

ICEL has prepared the attached charts as a resource and reference for the UN Ad hoc Open-ended Working Group that will deliberate in 2019 about the state of international environmental law today, and how gaps or limitations retard measures to attain the SDGs.

The charts simply gather, conveniently in one place, most if not all of the principles that States have already accepted in their international agreements. They are publicly available, without charge, through the Law Library of the Elisabeth Haub School of Law at Pace University (New York), at https://libraryguides.law.pace.edu/icel.

States may refer to these agreements as they evaluate the Report of the UN Secretary-General's technical and evidence-based report on how gaps in international environmental law with a view to strengthening implementation of this field, available at https://www.iucn.org/sites/dev/files/content/documents/global_pact_report.advance.30_november_2018.pdf.

Links To The Icel Charts

Analysis of the Adoption and Implementation of the Environmental Principles in the Proposed Global Pact for the Environment (Global Pact) in the Sustainable Development Goals (SDGs)

https://libraryguides.law.pace.edu/ld.php?content_id=45886809

https://www.iucn.org/sites/dev/files/global_pact_review__sustainable_development_goals.pdf

Analysis of the Adoption and Implementation of the Environmental Principles in the Proposed Global Pact for the Environment (Global Pact) in soft law instruments

https://libraryguides.law.pace.edu/ld.php?content_id=45886737

https://www.iucn.org/sites/dev/files/global_pact_review_-_soft_law_instruments.pdf

Analysis of the Adoption and Implementation of the Environmental Principles in the Proposed Global Pact for the Environment (Global Pact) in multilateral environmental agreements (MEAs)

https://libraryguides.law.pace.edu/ld.php?content_id=45886731

https://www.iucn.org/sites/dev/files/global_pact_review_-_multilateral_environmental_agreements.pdf

Analysis of the Adoption and Implementation of the Environmental Principles in the Proposed Global Pact for the Environment (Global Pact) in Regional Instruments: African Union States

https://libraryguides.law.pace.edu/ld.php?content_id=45886314

https://www.iucn.org/sites/dev/files/global_pact_regional_review_-_african_union_states.pdf

Analysis of the Adoption and Implementation of the Environmental Principles in the Proposed Global Pact for the Environment (Global Pact) in Regional Instruments: Association of Southeast Asian Nations (ASEAN)

https://libraryguides.law.pace.edu/ld.php?content_id=45886672

https://www.iucn.org/sites/dev/files/global_pact_regional_review_-_asean.pdf

Analysis of the Adoption and Implementation of the Environmental Principles in the Proposed Global Pact for the Environment (Global Pact) in Regional Instruments: Caribbean Community (CARICOM) Environmental and Natural Resources Policy Framework (July 2017-June 2022)

https://www.iucn.org/sites/dev/files/global_pact_regional_review_-_caricom.pdf

Analysis of the Adoption and Implementation of the Environmental Principles in the Proposed Global Pact for the Environment (Global Pact) in Regional Instruments:
China
https://libraryguides.law.pace.edu/ld.php?content_id=45886682
https://www.iucn.org/sites/dev/files/global_pact_regional_review_-_china.pdf

Analysis of the Adoption and Implementation of the Environmental Principles in the Proposed Global Pact for the Environment (Global Pact) in Regional Instruments: Commonwealth of Independent States (CIS)
https://libraryguides.law.pace.edu/ld.php?content_id=45886689
https://www.iucn.org/sites/dev/files/global_pact_regional_review_-_commonwealth_of_independent_states.pdf

Analysis of the Adoption and Implementation of the Environmental Principles in the Proposed Global Pact for the Environment (Global Pact) in Regional Instruments: League of Arab States (Arab League)
https://libraryguides.law.pace.edu/ld.php?content_id=45886695
https://www.iucn.org/sites/dev/files/global_pact_regional_review_-_league_of_arab_states.pdf

Analysis of the Adoption and Implementation of the Environmental Principles in the Proposed Global Pact for the Environment (Global Pact) in Regional Instruments: Pacific Islands Forum
https://libraryguides.law.pace.edu/ld.php?content_id=45886718
https://www.iucn.org/sites/dev/files/global_pact_regional_review_-_pacific_islands_forum.pdf

Analysis of the Adoption and Implementation of the Environmental Principles in the Proposed Global Pact for the Environment (Global Pact) in Regional Instruments: South Asian Association for Regional Cooperation (SAARC)
https://libraryguides.law.pace.edu/ld.php?content_id=45886852
https://www.iucn.org/sites/dev/files/content/documents/2018/globalpactsaarcfeb2018.pdf

Analysis of the Adoption and Implementation of the Environmental Principles in the Proposed Global Pact for the Environment (Global Pact) in Regional Instruments: South Asian Association Cooperative Environment Program (SACEP)
https://libraryguides.law.pace.edu/ld.php?content_id=45887131

Chapter 4: Phase IV: Nairobi Sessions and Adoption of Recommendations (Jan. 2019 – June 2019)

After the adoption of the General Assembly Resolution no. 72/277 and the OEWG's organizational session held at the UN Headquarters, three substantive sessions followed at the headquarters of the UNEP in Nairobi, Kenya. This chapter focuses on the content of these discussions. Phase IV, entitled "Nairobi Sessions and Adoption of the Recommendations," relates to the work done by the working group between January and May 2019. Sections I to IV follow the Nairobi sessions chronologically, identifying the factual information related to the meetings. Section I covers the first substantive session in January 2019, which was characterized as a "stocktaking" opportunity, as delegates considered the UNSG's report while examining the current state of international environmental law. Section II covers the second substantive session in March 2019. The second session included a more focused discussion about potential recommendations from the working group on options to respond to possible gaps in international environmental law and environment-related instruments. To guide the discussion, the Co-Chairs posed specific questions designed to facilitate initial reflections on the main themes of the working group: principles, governance, implementation, and specific regulatory regimes of environment-related instruments. Section III relates to the draft recommendations circulated by the Co-Chairs in between sessions. Section IV covers the third and final substantive session in May 2019 and the subsequent adoption of recommendations by the working group.

Section V then specifically analyzes the main challenges in international environmental law and policy raised by the delegates during the Nairobi sessions. Given that many topics raised in Nairobi were discussed on more than one session, these are analyzed jointly by topic, referring, when relevant, to how the UNSG's report also portrayed them. The section addresses the following points: (A) what is a gap; (B) fragmentation of international environmental law; (C) matters of process; (D) governance of international environmental law; (E) implementation; (G) environment-related issues; and (H) environmental principles. These show how delegates view these issues and their most significant concerns, showing how they were ultimately addressed in the final recommendations. Section VI offers a geopolitical analysis of the position of States on whether they were favorable to the adoption of a new instrument related to the codification of principles. This section provides an overview of where we currently stand politically, showing how such a proposal is supported. The Nairobi Outcome Document and ICEL's Analysis of the Nairobi Outcome Document are reprinted at the end of this chapter (Document 4 and 5, respectively).

The timeline below portrays Phase IV.

Figure 4: Phase IV Timeline "Nairobi Sessions and Adoption of OEWG's Recommendations" (Jan. – June 2019)

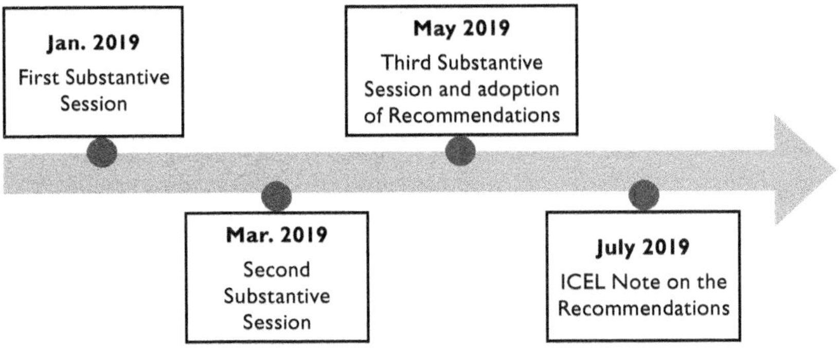

I. January 2019: First Substantive Session

The first substantive session of the OEWG convened from 14-18 January 2019.[1] Based on the agenda and programme of work, the week-long gathering consisted of ten meetings.[2] These were mostly dedicated to discussing

1. *See* Amal Mudallali and Francisco Duarte Lopes, Letter to UN Members from the co-chairs of the Ad Hoc Open-Ended Working Group Established by the General Assembly Resolution 72/277 inviting Member States to participate in the first substantive session (Dec. 6, 2018), *available at* https://wedocs.unep.org/bitstream/handle/20.500.11822/27168/Invitation.pdf?sequence=1&isAllowed=y.
2. Based on the provisional agenda agreed at the organizational session, the agenda was adopted as follows: "1. Opening of the session. 2. Adoption of the agenda and programme of work. 3. Financing of the activities of the ad hoc open-ended working group. 4. General statements. 5. Consideration of the report of the Secretary-General. 6. Provisional agenda and dates for the second substantive session. 7. Other matters. 8. Closure of the first substantive session." UNGA, Ad hoc Open-Ended Working Group Established Pursuant to General Assembly Resolution 72/277, First Substantive Session, Nairobi, 14–18 January 2019, Provisional Agenda and Annotations Thereto for the First

each section of the UN Secretary-General's Report, "Gaps in international environmental law and environment-related instruments: towards a global pact for the environment."[3] The all-encompassing Report provided delegates with an opportunity to engage in a "stocktaking" exercise, examining the current state of international environmental law[4] based on the UNSG's findings.[5] Approximately 288 participants attended the meeting, including government delegates from 109 countries, representatives of UN bodies, secretariat units and convention secretariats,[6] representatives of international organizations,[7] and members from 67 non-governmental organizations.

Delegates received the UNSG's Report with mixed reviews. Many delegations welcomed its findings, considering it provided a comprehensive overview of the existing gaps and was a sound basis for further discussion.[8] Others were wary of its limited effect and invited a more extensive dialogue on challenges, using the Report only as an initial guide.[9] Some Member States expressed concern about its contents, requesting more up-to-date information and the use of empirical evidence to confirm its outcomes.[10]

Substantive Session of the Ad Hoc Open-Ended Working Group Established Pursuant to General Assembly Resolution 72/277, A/AC.289/3 (6 December 2018).

3. UNGA, A/AC.289/6/Rev. 1 (June 13, 2019), Report of the Ad Hoc Open-Ended Working Group Established Pursuant to General Assembly Resolution 72/277 (para. 6).
4. The provisional agenda was adopted as follows: (1) Opening of the session; (2) Adoption of the agenda and programme of work; (3) Financing of the activities of the ad hoc open-ended working group; (4) General statements; (5) Consideration of the report of the Secretary-General; (6) Provisional agenda and dates for the second substantive session; (7) Other matters; (8) Closure of the first substantive session. OEWG, A/AC.289/3, Provisional Agenda and Annotations Thereto for the First Substantive Session of the Ad Hoc Open-Ended Working Group Established Pursuant to General Assembly Resolution 72/277 (Dec. 6, 2018).
5. UN Environment, Member States Debate the Need for a Global Pact for the Environment (January 28, 2019), *available at* https://www.unenvironment.org/news-and-stories/story/member-states-debate-need-global-pact-environment.
6. Department for General Assembly and Conference Management; Office of the United Nations High Commissioner for Human Rights (OHCHR); Secretariat of the Basel Convention on the Control of Transboundary Movements of Hazardous Wastes and Their Disposal, the Rotterdam Convention on the Prior Informed Consent Procedure for Certain Hazardous Chemicals and Pesticides in International Trade and the Stockholm Convention on Persistent Organic Pollutants; Secretariat of the Convention on Wetlands of International Importance especially as Waterfowl Habitat; Secretariat of the Minamata Convention on Mercury; Secretariat of the Montreal Protocol on Substances That Deplete the Ozone Layer; United Nations Development Programme; United Nations Office at Nairobi.
7. International Chamber of Commerce, International Committee of the Red Cross, International Federation of the Red Cross and Red Crescent Societies, League of Arab States.
8. UN Environment, *supra* note 5.
9. Amal Mudallali and Francisco Duarte Lopes, Letter to UN Members from the co-chairs of the Ad Hoc Open-Ended Working Group Established by the General Assembly Resolution 72/277 circulating the oral summary of the first substantive session (Jan. 29, 2019), *available at* http://wedocs.unep.org/bitstream/handle/20.500.11822/27261/Co-chairs.letter.25%20January%202019.pdf?sequence=110&isAllowed=y; Annex available at http://wedocs.unep.org/bitstream/handle/20.500.11822/27261/Oral%20summary.FINAL.pdf?sequence=124&isAllowed=y.
10. UN Environment, *supra* note 5.

A few delegations considered that the Report could have provided a more in-depth and objective analysis of specific areas and a more considerable justification for some of its findings. One of the most significant criticism concerned its inclusion of recommendations to address the gaps identified. Since the UNGA specifically called upon the OEWG to suggest recommendations, these delegations argued the UNSG went beyond its mandate.[11]

The meaning of gaps was an essential point of debate.[12] There was a significant concern about the methods followed by the OEWG and its potential effect on existing instruments, bodies, and processes. Delegations called for a commitment to MEAs, without duplicating or undermining them.[13] The Co-Chairs highlighted the need for a constructive, open, transparent, and inclusive discussion. It was essential to reach a consensus-based outcome that was both pragmatic and realistic, without prejudging the result.[14] Section V extensively debates these issues.

The Co-Chairs invited delegates to submit additional inputs during the inter-sessional period. Taking all views expressed into consideration, the Co-Chairs would provide elements to structure and guide the discussions for the following session.[15] The Co-Chairs agreed to synthesize the feedback supplied by delegates into a non-paper to serve as a basis for deliberations at the second substantive session. Finally, they provided an oral summary, with a written version circulated on Jan. 25, 2019.[16]

II. March 2019: Second Substantive Session

The second substantive session of the OEWG convened from 18-20 March 2019, totaling six meetings. Nearly 300 participants, including delegates from 102 countries, representatives of UN bodies, secretariat units and convention secretariats,[17] intergovernmental organizations[18] and 38 non-governmental organizations attended. Participants were invited to engage

11. Mudallali and Duarte Lopes, *supra* note 9.
12. UN Environment, *supra* note 5.
13. *Id.*
14. Mudallali and Duarte Lopes, *supra* note 9.
15. *Id.*
16. *Id.*
17. Food and Agriculture Organization of the United Nations; Office of the United Nations High Commissioner for Human Rights; Secretariat of the Basel Convention on the Control of Transboundary Movements of Hazardous Wastes and Their Disposal, the Rotterdam Convention on the Prior Informed Consent Procedure for Certain Hazardous Chemicals and Pesticides in International Trade and the Stockholm Convention on Persistent Organic Pollutants; Secretariat of the Minamata Convention on Mercury; Secretariat of the Montreal Protocol on Substances That Deplete the Ozone Layer; UNEP; United Nations Office at Nairobi.
18. International Chamber of Commerce, League of Arab States.

in a "results-oriented" discussion on options to respond to possible gaps in international environmental law and environment-related instruments.[19] The meetings focused mainly on item 4 of the agenda,[20] entitled "Discussion of possible options to address possible gaps in international environmental law and environment-related instruments, as appropriate."[21]

The Co-Chairs guided the discussions through four specific questions. These were designed to form a bridge from the preliminary "stocktaking" exercise in January to a process of formulating precise responses and possibly designing alternatives to recommend to the UNGA.[22] Based on the exchanges thus far, the questions focused on (i) principles of international environmental law; (ii) the governance structure of international environmental law; (iii) the implementation of international environmental law; and (iv) specific regulatory regimes or environment-related instruments.[23] These included suggestions on the form and content of options, ranging from legally to non-legally binding instruments, a high-level declaration or other UNGA outcome that might capture and collate the international community's current ambition to renovate the international environmental law system and environment-related instruments.[24] The Co-Chairs invited thoughts from delegates on the following issues:

> "What options can be considered to address the possible gaps or challenges related to principles of international environmental law mentioned by delegations without duplicating nor undermining existing law and ongoing efforts/processes? What would be the objective of such options? What methodology should be used to develop them?

---

19. Doran, et al., Summary of the Second Substantive Session of the Ad Hoc Open-Ended Working Group Towards a Global Pact for the Environment. *Global Pact for the Environment.* Vol. 35 No. 2, *available at* http://enb.iisd.org/unep/globalpact/oewg2/.
20. Based on the provisional agenda agreed at the first substantive session, the agenda was adopted as follows: "1. Opening of the session. 2. Adoption of the agenda and programme of work. 3. Financing of the activities of the ad hoc open-ended working group. 4. Discussion of possible options to address possible gaps in international environmental law and environment-related instruments, as appropriate. 5. Provisional agenda and dates for the third substantive session. 6. Other matters. 7. Closure of the session." UNGA, Ad hoc Open-Ended Working Group Established Pursuant to General Assembly Resolution 72/277, Second Substantive Session, Nairobi, 18–20 March 2019, Provisional Agenda and Annotations Thereto for the First Substantive Session of the Ad Hoc Open-Ended Working Group Established Pursuant to General Assembly Resolution 72/277, A/AC.289/4 (5 February 2019).
21. Amal Mudallali and Francisco Duarte Lopes, Letter to UN Members from the Co-Chairs of the Ad Hoc Open-Ended Working Group Established by the General Assembly Resolution 72/277 circulating the oral summary of the second substantive session and the provisional agenda for the third substantive session (Mar. 26, 2019), *available at* https://wedocs.unep.org/bitstream/handle/20.500.11822/27870/PGA_Letter-March2019.pdf?sequence=1&isAllowed=y.
22. Doran, et al., *supra* note 19.
23. *Id.*
24. *Id.*

What options can be considered to address gaps related to the governance structure of international environmental law, including challenges in coordination and mutual supportiveness as well as risks of incoherence highlighted by delegations?

What options can be considered to addressing gaps or challenges relating to the implementation of existing rules and principles of international environmental law?

What options can be considered to address possible gaps related to specific regulatory regimes or environment-related instruments with a view to strengthening the implementation of international environmental law?"[25]

At the end of the session, the Co-Chairs invited delegations to submit concrete proposals for consideration of draft recommendations at the third session. On Mar. 26, 2019, the Co-Chairs circulated a summary of the second substantive session to provide a synthesis of the views expressed, to be read in conjunction with the interventions made by delegations throughout the session.[26] These included views on principles in international environmental law and the negotiation of a new instrument, with different views on its nature and format. Delegates also expressed views that the nature of the instrument can be determined later, namely in the context of a negotiation process launched to develop such an instrument.

III. April 2019: Draft Recommendations Ad-Hoc Working Group

On April 25, 2019, the Co-Chairs of the OEWG circulated draft elements of recommendations to be submitted to the General Assembly at the end of its mandate. These were based on views expressed by governments during the first two substantive sessions.[27] Hoping to attract broad support, the Co-Chairs recommended considering the elements "as a package" and welcomed active participation. Considering the main concerns of delegates, the recommendations included three categories: (i) elements related to the objectives

25. Amal Mudallali and Francisco Duarte Lopes, Letter to UN Members from the Co-Chairs of the Ad Hoc Open-Ended Working Group Established by the General Assembly Resolution 72/277 circulating the oral summary of the first substantive session and and guiding questions for the second substantive sessions (Feb. 28, 2019), *available at* https://wedocs.unep.org/bitstream/handle/20.500.11822/27614/Pact_trasmittal.pdf?sequence=1&isAllowed=y.

26. *Id.*

27. Ana Maria Lebada, Draft Elements Proposed for Resolution on Global Pact for Environment, IISD (2019), *available at* https://sdg.iisd.org/news/draft-elements-proposed-for-resolution-on-global-pact-for-environment/.

informing the recommendations; (ii) elements related to the substantive recommendations; (iii) elements related to the process.[28]

Elements of these "draft recommendations" addressed, inter alia: (i) a broad understanding of gaps in international environmental law, and whether these are lacunae, deficiencies, or challenges; (ii) principles, their interpretation, and the consistency of their application; (iii) options for a new instrument and its legally or non-legally binding nature, including a high-level declaration and/or a UNGA compendium document on international environmental law principles; (iv) governance and enhancing cooperation, synergies, and coordination of existing MEAs, scientific regimes, and system-wide mainstreaming of the environment; (v) strengthening and revisiting the role of UNEP, UNEA, and other bodies charged with enhancing the impact and coordination of elements within the existing regime of international environmental law; and (vi) options to address the implementation gap caused by a lack of capacity-building, finance, technology, and political will.[29] Negotiations were set to begin on the basis of this draft at the third substantive session in May 2019.

IV. May 2019: Third Substantive Session and Final Recommendations

The third and final substantive session of the OEWG convened from 20-22 May 2019, preceded by pre-sessional consultations. Around 300 participants attended, including delegates from 107 countries, representatives of UN bodies, secretariat units and convention secretariats,[30] intergovernmental organizations,[31] and 24 non-governmental organizations. Following the provisional agenda,[32] the working group completed its mandate, and adopted

28. Amal Mudallali and Francisco Duarte Lopes, Letter to UN Members from the Co-Chairs of the Ad Hoc Open-Ended Working Group Established by the General Assembly Resolution 72/277 (Apr. 25, 2019), *available at* https://www.un.org/pga/73/wp-content/uploads/sites/53/2019/04/25-April-ad-hoc-open-ended-working-group-002.pdf.
29. Doran, et al., *supra* note 19.
30. Secretariat of the Basel Convention on the Control of Transboundary Movements of Hazardous Wastes and Their Disposal, the Rotterdam Convention on the Prior Informed Consent Procedure for Certain Hazardous Chemicals and Pesticides in International Trade and the Stockholm Convention on Persistent Organic Pollutants; Secretariat of the Convention on Wetlands of International Importance Especially as Waterfowl Habitat; Secretariat of the Montreal Protocol on Substances That Deplete the Ozone Layer; UNEP.
31. International Chamber of Commerce, International Organization of la Francophonie, Arab Organization for Agricultural Development, League of Arab States.
32. Based on the provisional agenda agreed at the first substantive session, the agenda was adopted as follows: "1. Opening of the session. 2. Adoption of the agenda and programme of work. 3. Statement on the financing of the activities of the ad hoc open-ended working group. 4. Consideration of the draft recommendations of the ad hoc open-ended working group. 5. Consideration of the draft report of

recommendations to the UNGA.[33] Delegates arrived at agreement after a series of formal and informal negotiations. The UNGA Resolution had provided for the Working Group to consider, if necessary, the scope, parameters and feasibility of an international instrument, with a view to making recommendations to the UNGA during the first half of 2019.[34] The final recommendations encompassed the views presented by delegations and set out: (i) objectives, including the reinforcement of environmental protection for present and future generations and strengthening international environmental law and environment-related instruments; (ii) substantive recommendations; and (iii) consideration of further work.[35]

At the beginning of the session, Duarte Lopes presented the Co-Chairs' non-paper noting it was developed based on divergent views and sought delegates' support in reaching consensus with text-based negotiations to then achieve a concrete outcome.[36]

Many delegations indicated that they were open to considering working on the consolidation of principles of international environmental law, noting the possibility of developing a new instrument with that purpose. Different views were shared with respect to the nature of such instrument, including

the ad hoc open-ended working group. 6. Other matters. 7. Closure of the session." UNGA, Ad Hoc Open-Ended Working Group Established Pursuant to General Assembly Resolution 72/277, Third Substantive Session, Nairobi, 20–22 May 2019, Provisional Agenda for the Third Substantive Session of the Ad Hoc Open-Ended Working Group Established Pursuant to General Assembly Resolution 72/277, A/AC.289/5 (25 March 2019).

33. UN Ga President (@UNGA). "Sincere thanks @LebanonUN and @Portugal_UN for your work as co-chairs of the working group created by resolution 72/277 towards a global pact for the environment. I commend you and all delegations on the agreement of recommendations by consensus #Environment4All #UN4ALL" May 29, 2019. Tweet. Amal Mudallali (@AmbMudallali). "The role of the PGA @ UN_PGA was instrumental in bringing this process to a successful end. Her efforts and support was invaluable especially her reaching out to thr conference in Nairobi and urging a positive outcome. Thank you @UN_PGA PGA. N" May 29, 2019. Tweet. Portugal na ONU (@Portugal_UN). "The #Nairobi #OEWG3 on the #GlobalPactEnvironment concluded its work and agreed, by consensus, to recommend, inter alia, a political declaration at a @UN high level meeting in 2022 @UN_PGA @ LebanonUN" May 23, 2019. Tweet. Amal Mudallali (@AmbMudallali). "The #OEWG3 concluded it's work on #GlobalPactEnvironment in Nairobi by consensus on recommendations to #UNGA PGA on way forward in process. Thanks to my co-facilitator PR Francisco Duarte Lopes, to Sérgio Carvalho, Portugal, , UNEP & our legal expert Youssef Hitti for good work." May 25, 2019. Tweet. Amal Mudallali (@AmbMudallali). "The WG toward a Global Pact of Environment successfully concluded its final session @ UNEP, Nairobi, with consensus on recommendations 4 #UNGA & @ UN_PGA. My Co- Facilitator PR Lopes and I are grateful to all who helped make it success esp. ambs of Columbia & Norway in Kenya." May 24, 2019. Tweet. Amal Mudallali (@AmbMudallali). "We gaveled! The WG toward a Global Pact for the Environment succeeded in reaching consensus on a outcome document of recommendations to the GA. It was a difficult process but result is testimony that we all want to work together 4 environment no matter what our differences are." May 24, 2019. Tweet.

34. Lebada, Draft Elements Proposed for Resolution on Global Pact for Environment. 2019.

35. Lynn Wagner, Global Pact Talks Forward Recommendations to UNEA-5, 28 May 2019, IISD (2019), *available at* https://sdg.iisd.org/news/global-pact-talks-forward-recommendations-to-unea-5/.

36. Doran, et al., *supra* note 19. Mudallali and Duarte Lopes, *supra* note 9.

whether it should be legal in nature. However, some delegations observed that the Report failed to offer a substantial justification for such a proposal.[37] Several delegations pointed out the need for further discussions on the concrete added-value of such an instrument, whether binding or non-binding, and how its development could contribute to strengthening environment protection.[38] Iran cautioned against the creation of a comprehensive new instrument without recognizing root causes of gaps in international environmental law and called for creativity in reviving existing environmental instruments. Cuba and the Republic of Korea were suspicious of an overarching framework as a response to a wide range of environmental problems. The US specifically criticized the report arguing it was biased towards the option of a global pact. Likewise, the Russian Federation emphasized that the OEWG should not set up a new framework.[39] Additionally, delegations indicated that there is no agreement at this stage on the conclusion of the Report that "a comprehensive and unifying international instrument clarifying all the principles of environmental law would contribute to making them more effective and strengthen their implementation". Given this push-back, any mention of an agreement on the codification of principles was ultimately not included in the final recommendations. This evaluation is further developed in the geopolitical analysis below.

A. *Recommendations to the UNGA*

The consensus-based final recommendations include a section identifying its objectives, substantive recommendations, and consideration of further work. Section 1 pertains to five objectives guiding the recommendations and reinforces some of the concerns presented by delegates during the Nairobi sessions. The first objective reinforces the protection of the environment for present and future generations. The second refers to upholding existing obligations and commitments under international environmental law, thus making sure not to undermine prior agreements. The third objective is a commitment to contribute to strengthening the implementation of international environmental law and environment-related instruments. The fourth refers to supporting the full implementation of the 2030 Agenda for Sustainable Development. Finally, the fifth objective concerns the governance structure of international environmental law, with a commitment not to

37. Mudallali and Duarte Lopes, *supra* note 9.
38. *Id.*
39. Doran, et al., Summary of the First Substantive Session of the Ad Hoc Open-Ended Working Group Towards a Global Pact for the Environment: 14-18 January 2019. 2019.

undermine existing relevant legal instruments and frameworks and relevant global, regional, and sectoral bodies.[40]

The second section includes thirteen substantive recommendations, as follows: (a) reaffirm the role of UNEP and UNEA; (b) catalyze efforts to further the implementation of international environmental law and environment-related instruments, including through accelerating the mobilization of the necessary means of implementation consistent with the AAAA and the 2030 Agenda; (c) promote further discussion of principles of international environmental law, recognizing the ongoing work by the ILC; (d) an invitation to the scientific community and scientific, technical and technological bodies of MEAs to work on crosscutting issues and information sharing (e) an invitation to the governing bodies of MEAs to promote policy coherence and consider challenges in implementation; (f) foster increased cooperation and coordination among the governing bodies of MEAs; (g) promote increased efforts to streamline the reporting and/or monitoring processes of MEAs and scientific bodies, as well as an invitation to increased sharing of information between them, and for joint reporting, as an when appropriate; (h) encouraging Member States to ratify MEAs and implement them; (i) encourage Member States to ratify MEAs if they haven't already done so, and effectively implement them; (j) encourage Member States to strengthen regulatory frameworks at the national level, as well as the capacity of the judiciary to apply international environmental law; (k) promote active and meaningful stakeholder engagement in the different fora related to the implementation of international environmental law and environment-related instruments; (l) explore further ways for Member States to support and make full use of the Montevideo Programme V to foster the environmental rule of law and advance the implementation of environmental law; (m) encourage UNEP to develop UN system-wide strategies on how they could best support Member States in the integration and implementation of international environmental law.[41]

By the proposed draft elements circulated by the Co-Chairs, the Group would recommend the UNGA to (i) consider adopting an international instrument at a high-level UN conference, with a view to strengthening the implementation of international environmental law; (ii) establish a preparatory committee prior to that conference, to make substantive recommendations to the UNGA during the first half of 2020 on elements of an international instrument, including its nature, scope and parameters;

40. Mudallali and Duarte Lopes, *supra* note 28, Item I.
41. *Id.* Item II.

(iii) determine a specific timeline by which the negotiations would take place and reach a conclusion; and (iv) establish that the negotiations are to be open to all UN Member States, members of specialized agencies and parties to the multilateral environment agreements, with others invited as observers in accordance with the past practice of the UN.[42]

However, the agreed substantive recommendations were more limited. The OEWG recommended (a) circulating the recommendations to UN Member States, specialized agencies and governing bodies of MEAs; and (b) forwarding the recommendations to UNEA for its consideration. UNEA, in turn, shall prepare, at its fifth session in February 2021, a political declaration for a UN high-level meeting. The declaration shall be subject to voluntary funding and be adopted in the context of commemoration of the creation of UNEP by the 1972 Stockholm Conference. It shall be drafted with a view to strengthening the implementation of international environmental law, and international environmental governance in line with paragraph 88 of the "Future We Want."

President Macron had set an ambitious goal to have the text adopted by 2020, which will no longer be achieved.[43] On the first substantive session, the delegations observed that there was relatively little time to prepare recommendations for the UNGA by the end of the first half of 2019. They acknowledged that whatever package of recommendations emerged would probably, of necessity, fall short of what is objectively needed to completely overhaul the international environmental law regime, given the current climate for multilateralism and the risks that would accompany any attempt to force a new normative consensus.[44] The *Earth Negotiations Bulletin* analysis of the meeting highlights that "fear played a role and ultimately shaped the outcome: fear of losing sovereignty, fear of complicating existing MEA regimes, fear of opening up established principles and their varied/contested application, and, significantly for developing countries, a fear of committing to steps that they lack the capacity to implement."[45]

The OEWG ultimately agreed on a "weaker" recommendation for the UNGA with a longer deadline than originally envisioned and no mention of a binding agreement. However, it "keeps the doors open for the conversation initiated by the global pact proposal to survive and inform a wider global conversation and set of aspirations that may be unleashed by the landmark 50th anniversary of the UN Conference on the Human Environment" in

42. *Id.* Item III.
43. Léia Santacroce, *supra* note 5.
44. Doran, et al., *supra* note 19.
45. Wagner. 2019.

2022.[46] The new deadline is more reasonable and allows for an in-depth negotiation of potential solutions to the challenges observed. The discussion of principles was also not set aside. Recommendation 2(c) recognizes the role of the discussion on environmental principles for enhancing implementation of international environmental law, thus still leaving the door open for the potential adoption of a new instrument. However, the Nairobi sessions broadened the set of questions, possibly opening a door for a multi-pronged solution that may also include an agreement on principles. The next section analyzes the main legal issues raised by delegations and how these were ultimately addressed in the draft recommendations.

V. Analysis of Substantive Issues Discussed and How the Recommendations Came About

Delegates substantially disagreed on a series of question related to gaps in international environmental law during the Nairobi sessions. Questions arose as to what constituted a gap, whether there were any, the reason behind gaps, whether gaps were intentional, and what could ultimately be done to address them. There was, however, a general understanding that the state of international environmental law was lacking. If nothing else, the Global Pact initiated a conversation on what was missing in the field, and what steps we could take within the UN system to achieve some progress. Based on the UNSG's report and the IISD summaries of the discussions held during the Nairobi sessions, this section examines the main legal issues raised by delegations and if and how the final recommendations ultimately tackled them. This review provides a background for how the recommendations come in play. These are complemented, when appropriate, by academic arguments raised by scholars on the Global Pact itself, the UNSG report, and, in some cases, by the written comments submitted by delegates, available at UNEP's website.

This section is divided as follows. Section A addresses a preliminary discussion on what a gap is, which was ultimately the focus on the first substantive session in Nairobi and continued to be an issue until the last session. Section B discusses the issue of fragmentation of international environmental law. Section C examines matters of process, a point that was constantly reinforced during the Nairobi sessions, and ultimately influenced the set of recommendations agreed on. Section D assesses gaps in the governance structure of international environmental law. Section E surveys implementation, which

46. *Id.*

many delegations reinforced was the true gap in international environmental law. Section F approaches environment-related areas. Section G focuses on environmental principles.

A. *What Is a Gap?*

The UNGA bestowed upon the UNSG a mandate to identify and assess "possible gaps in international environmental law and environment-related instruments,"[47] without defining what "gaps" denoted in that context. The meaning of "gaps" was clarified in the UNSG Report as a preliminary matter. Drawing from a legal dictionary, "gap" is defined in the report as a lacuna, void, defect or deficiency.[48] The wording of the Resolution allows for a comprehensive interpretation of the gap analysis.[49] The goal of the first substantive session of the OEWG was to assess the UNSG's report and discuss the gaps identified. However, as abridged by the IISD, this session turned out to be a game of deconstruction of the meaning of gaps.[50] The conclusions of the UNSG's report raised more questions than answers. Before the substantive issues could be discussed, there were several preliminary questions to be addressed. What is a gap? How is it defined? Can the supposed gaps identified by the UNSG be defined as gaps, or are those a result of intended policy decisions by the international community?

According to French & Kotzé, the language of the Resolution is both "progressive and conceptually incoherent," as it connects the identification of gaps with "their implementation."[51] Indeed, the very notion of a "gap" raises fundamental linguistic and conceptual complexities.[52] This was proven right at the Nairobi sessions. Questioning the mandate incumbent upon the UNSG, Prof. Bodansky asks whether "gaps" can even be identified and assessed in a "technical and evidence-based" manner as requested by the UNGA.[53] The Nordic Council of Ministers differentiated between factual and normative gaps. The first category included substantive (lack of

---

47. UNGA resolution, at para. 1.
48. UN Secretary-General, Gaps in International Environmental Law and Environment-Related Instruments: Towards a Global Pact for the Environment, UN Doc. A/73/419, 6 (30 November 2018). *See* Bryan A. Garner, A Dictionary of Modern Legal Usage, 2d ed. 496 (Oxford Univ. Press, 2001).
49. Duncan French & Louis J. Kotzé, *"Towards a Global Pact for the Environment": International Environmental Law's Factual, Technical and (Unmentionable) Normative Gaps*, 28 Rev. Eur., Comp. & Int'l Envtl. L. (2019).
50. Doran, et al., *supra* note 39, at 12; 13.
51. French & Kotzé, *supra* note 49, at XX.
52. *Id.*
53. *See* Hernández, et al. 2018 (contribution by Daniel Bodansky).

coverage of the issue in question), legal (guidelines exist but are not legally binding), membership-related (some parties are excluded from all or certain commitments), or geographic (an instrument does not apply to all regions), institutional (no institution/organization/instrument exists or is tasked to carry out particular functions) or compliance/enforcement-related (there is an agreement, but the compliance mechanism is very soft) gaps.[54] On the other hand, a normative gap exists when there is no agreement that an issue should be addressed. For example, there may be agreement that no instrument exists for a particular issue (a substantive gap) but disagreement on whether an instrument is necessary. It is also important to consider whether a gap results from a deliberate design choice when negotiating a legal instrument.[55] Susan Biniaz further listed gaps related to means of implementation, including inadequate domestic action, resources (insufficient funding, capacity, etc.), and political will.[56]

The report addressed five substantive types of gaps: (i) the scope and status of the principles of international environmental law; (ii) gaps relating to the sectoral regulatory regimes; (iii) environment-related instruments; (iv) gaps relating to the governance structure of international environmental law; and (v) gaps concerning the implementation and effectiveness of international environmental law.[57] It embodied regulatory gaps (substantive/normative gaps, including procedural and institutional) and governance gaps (implementation gaps). It analyzed gaps (i) within an MEA with respect to its content or ability to fulfil its object and purpose; (ii) between legal frameworks (e.g., substantive or procedural overlaps, discrepancies or conflicts); or (iii) where there is no regulation at all (e.g., limitations in substantive, institutional or geographical coverage).[58]

A discussion on "gaps" was quickly initiated in Nairobi. For some delegations, "gaps" should be interpreted in a narrow sense and be limited to normative ones. This interpretation would disregard some of the gaps identified in the report as "challenges." These delegates argued that deficiencies in implementation and other challenges would complicate the work of the OEWG and should thus not be discussed at this point.[59] However, since means of implementation was consistently highlighted by delegates as a major concern, this interpretation did not receive much traction. For other

54. URHO, et al. 2019. P. 80.
55. *Id.* at 80.
56. Biniaz, REV. EUR., COMP. & INT'L ENVTL. L. (2019) 35.
57. UN Secretary-General, *supra* 48, at 6.
58. *Id.* at 6.
59. Doran, et al., *supra* note 39, at 9.

delegations, gaps should be considered in their broader meaning, including normative, institutional or implementation gaps.[60] By assessing both regulatory and governance gaps, the report adopted a broader interpretation of what constitutes a "gap." Prof. Voigt clarifies that by focusing on the effectiveness of international environmental law, the report allows for exploring a wider set of parameters than merely the absence of rules and law.[61]

According to Biniaz, the strongest case for a "gap" may be when an entire environmental topic has been unaddressed (or sorely under-addressed).[62] This would constitute, in the language used by French & Kotzé, as a factual gap. An example would be the debate on marine plastic.[63] However, even that conclusion may be controversial. As argued by Guyana, the mere absence of a rule or agreement on a particular issue does not necessarily constitute a gap.[64] Egypt distinguished between a "gap," a void or lacuna in the international legislation, and a "deficiency," an outcome of an existing process that reflects a country's priorities and compromises.[65] The latter are policy decisions.

In some cases, particularly where there is already an international agreement on a particular subject, a putative "gap" may reflect a design choice on the part of negotiators.[66] These are "intentional" (US), "conscious and deliberate" (Australia, Canada and Argentina) decisions, which result from "political compromises" (Japan) and constitute "necessary gaps" (Guyana). When conceivable gaps occur within MEAs, these are described as "design elements" (US) and should be addressed in discussions under MEAs (Colombia) instead of by the OEWG.[67] These might have been motivated by considerations of substance, politics and/or participation. The choices might have involved, for example, one or more non-legally binding provisions, exceptions to a general rule, provisions that allow a party to opt out of a particular commitment, grace periods or the absence of compliance/enforcement procedures.[68] Some gaps reflect a necessary compromise among States (Brazil, the Russian Federation, Egypt, Mexico, Norway).[69] Many States are likely to consider any particular absence or omission part of the delicate balance that led to an acceptable agreement, whether these refer to the exclusion of a few countries from a commitment, accommodating special circumstances in an

60. Mudallali and Duarte Lopes, *supra* note 9, at 2.
61. Voigt, Rev. Eur., Comp. & Int'l Envtl. L. (2019). P. 16.
62. Biniaz, Rev. Eur., Comp. & Int'l Envtl. L. (2019). 34.
63. French & Kotzé, Rev. Eur., Comp. & Int'l Envtl. L. (2019).
64. Doran, et al., *supra* note 39, at 4.
65. *Id.*
66. Biniaz, Rev. Eur., Comp. & Int'l Envtl. L. (2019) 34.
67. Doran, et al., *supra* note 39 at 3; 4.
68. Biniaz, Rev. Eur., Comp. & Int'l Envtl. L. (2019) 34.
69. Mudallali and Duarte Lopes, *supra* note 9, at 2.

agreement, a light compliance regime or a non-legally binding approach to a particular instrument or provision.[70] As a matter of policy, this "gap" may lack a legal solution.[71]

Since it may be based on policy decisions, ascertaining factual gaps is a subjective exercise. Prof. Bodansky clarifies that legal gaps (or *non liquets*) exist, if at all, only in very rare cases where the law does not decide an issue one way or the other—where an action is neither permitted nor prohibited. Whether any such gaps exist in international environmental law is doubtful, since ordinarily the absence of a legal rule regulating an issue (say, plastics pollution or protection of a species) does not create a gap in the law; it simply means that, legally, states are free to act as they choose.[72] There is a discontinuity rather than a flaw to be filled. Through a subjective assessment, states make political and moral judgments about whether an agreement would serve a useful purpose.[73] If we accept that current MEAs are concrete evidence and manifestations of States' normative ambitions, it is clear that States have been decidedly unambitious in what they believe *should* exist as global environmental protection norms.[74]

The UNGA resolution seems to use the term "gap" as a flaw in the international environmental law field.[75] This understanding received a lot of resistance from states. Some delegates argued that there are no gaps in international environmental law. Others agreed with the gaps identified in the UNSG's report, but didn't agree with how they are formulated. Finally, there were those who said there are gaps, but not the ones in the UNSG's report.[76] To level the playing field at discussions, several delegations pointed out that before delving into the task of assessing and addressing gaps, a common understanding of the definition of a gap was necessary.[77] Those who held the "no gaps" view tended to support their positions with one of two broad, connected rationales: (i) fragmentation in international environmental law is the result of the very nature of the field, and indeed is desirable since different

70. Biniaz, Rev. Eur., Comp. & Int'l Envt'l L. (2019) 34-35.
71. French & Kotzé, Rev. Eur., Comp. & Int'l Envtl. L. (2019).
72. *See* Hernández, et al. 2018 (contribution by Daniel Bodansky).
73. *See id.*
74. French & Kotzé, Rev. Eur., Comp. & Int'l Envtl. L. (2019).
75. *See* Hernández, et al. 2018 (contribution by Daniel Bodansky).
76. Doran, et al., *supra* note 39, at 13.
77. Alessandra Lehmen, Towards a Global Pact for the Environment—Civil Society Inputs With Regard to Legal Considerations Raised at the First Substantive Session, International Center for Comparative Environmental Law (2019), *available at* https://cidce.org/towards-a-global-pact-for-the-environment-civil-society-inputs-with-regard-to-legal-considerations-raised-at-the-first-substantive-session/?utm_sour%E2%80%A6. Doran, et al., Summary of the First Substantive Session of the Ad Hoc Open-Ended Working Group Towards a Global Pact for the Environment: 14-18 January 2019. 2019. P. 10 (Japan).

MEAs are required to address different needs; and (ii) gaps in existing MEAs are the result of deliberate design by their respective parties.[78]

The lack of consensus or what is a possible gap was constantly recalled by delegates who opposed the process.[79] Several delegates argued that the report had exceeded its mandate.[80] This discussion was also used in an attempt to postpone a discussion on possible options to address said gaps until the OEWG decided whether gaps exist and what they are.[81] Summarizing the first session, Co-Chair Duarte Lopes called for a clear definition of a gap, with some preference for a focus on normative gaps, and a clearer identification of challenges and the need to distinguish between normative, institutional, and implementation gaps.[82] Additionally, several delegations reinforced that the identification of gaps should be made through a science-based process, with the notion that gaps should be understood broadly.

At the second session, delegates agreed on some of the elements of the "draft recommendations" to be suggested to the UNGA, which included a broad understanding of gaps in international environmental law, and whether these are lacunae, deficiencies, or challenges.[83] Co-Chair Mudallali recalled the discussions of the first session and noted that there would be no attempt to pre-empt discussions on an understanding of gaps.[84] They then moved forward to the discussion of potential options to address gaps through guiding questions circulated to delegates. Co-Chair Duarte Lopes emphasized, however, that by asking these questions the Co-Chairs do not mean to suggest that there is an agreement on the existence of gaps, the nature of those gaps, and on the need or opportunity to address them.[85] This reminder was essential, since several countries continued to try to lead the discussion back to the meaning of gaps.[86]

---

78. Doran, et al., *supra* note 39, at 13.
79. *Id.* at 10 (Russia, the US, and Saudi Arabia at the first session).
80. *Id.* at 4; 8; 10. US, Saudi Arabia, Belize, Canada.
81. *Id.* at 10. US, Argentina, Australia, and Canada.
82. *Id.* at 11.
83. Doran, et al., *supra* note 19, at 1.
84. *Id.* at 2.
85. *Id.* at 3.
86. *Id.* at 3. (US, arguing that options to address said gaps would depend on the precise identification of gaps, in an attempt to lead the discussion back to the focus of the first session. The US called on delegations to "slow down," focus on gaps, and consider options at the third substantive session once views had coalesced.) Australia, Ecuador, India, the Philippines, and Kenya said Member States should first arrive at a shared view of what constitutes a gap. New Zealand stated that while it is essential to settle on what is or is not a gap before discussing possible options, both may have to be examined together considering that there is no agreement on this question.

The broader question on the definition of gaps was addressed when discussing Question 1 of the second substantive session.[87] Argentina stressed that there are no gaps in international environmental law, since all situations relating to environmental issues can be resolved by implementing existing law.[88] Saudi Arabia, with the US, Egypt, Japan, and Brazil, underlined the absence of consensus on gaps.[89] Recalling the argument of "intentional gaps," Colombia noted that apparent gaps can appear in international environmental law under a number of circumstances, including where states have decided not to address certain issues.[90] The US called for the OEWG to conclude that it does not view design elements in existing MEAs as gaps.[91] The Federal States of Micronesia said that gaps should not be interpreted narrowly, but should include challenges, inconsistencies, and shortcomings in international environmental law.[92] Brazil, with Ecuador, noted consensus that gaps exist in the broad sense of the translation of existing legal norms into reality, and supported talking about "challenges" rather than "gaps," stressing that these exist regarding implementation and means of implementation.[93] Turkey noted that a *de jure* gap on paper may not be a *de facto* gap, and vice versa, and noted the importance of sovereign state decisions. He urged a focus on challenges.[94] Alternatively, other delegations underlined that previous decisions made by States should not prevent ambitious and innovative solutions today. Calling for a broader understanding of "gaps" as defined by the UNSG, ICEL notes:

> "Thus, the process should continue to encompass a review of deficiencies of normative nature, institutional or as pertaining to implementation, in international environmental law and environment-related instruments, as appropriate, to address, in a comprehensive and coherent manner, the challenges posed by environmental degradation in the context of sustainable development. Furthermore, this process is "open to participation by all States Members of the United Nations and all members of the specialized agencies," as well as "to relevant nongovernmental organizations in consultative status with the Economic and Social Council and those accredited to relevant confer-

87. *Id.* at 4. Question 1: What options can be considered to address the possible gaps or challenges related to principles of international environmental law mentioned by delegations without duplicating nor undermining existing law and ongoing efforts/processes? What would be the objective of such options? What methodology should be used to develop them?
88. *Id.* at 3.
89. *Id.* at 4.
90. *Id.* at 4.
91. *Id.* at 6.
92. *Id.* at 4.
93. *Id.* at 4.
94. *Id.* at 6.

ences and summits" related to sustainable development. In sum, the mandate of Resolution 72/277 is a focused, but comprehensive and inclusive, review of the relevant "gaps" in the field. ICEL notes that the global consensus in favor of advancing the UN Sustainable Development Goals (SDGs) offers the appropriate context for analysis of "gaps." Issues concerning "gaps" should be resolved in favor of the SDGs."[95]

At the end of the second session, Co-Chair Duarte Lopes proceeded to offer reflections from the Co-Chairs on the process, the current session, and the way forward, noting the discussion on definition of gaps in international environmental law and related instruments, which gaps should be considered, and options to address them.[96] When summarizing the session, the Secretariat included some conclusions on gaps: namely, a broad understanding of gaps as lacunae, deficiencies, or challenges, confirming the definition of the UNSG's report; the importance of identifying gaps through a science-based approach; a view that some gaps in environmental instruments are voluntarily designed and are often the result of delicately balanced compromises in difficult negotiations; and support for innovative solutions.[97] Also, an understanding of gaps in implementation ranging from a lack of capacity-building and financial and technological resources to an absence of the prioritization of political decision-making and political will, with weak monitoring; the importance of strengthening means of implementation, with a main focus on international cooperation, including provision for necessary funding, capacity-building, and the transfer of technology; and the link between political will and implementation.[98]

The IISD assertedly analyzed:

"In contrast to the broad focus on options, some early interventions sought to limit talks within the scope of the discussion held during the January session on "gaps" in the context of the UNSG's report, which some described as an "interminable" debate. The risk of the OEWG process disappearing amidst endless gaps and definitions was highlighted at a pre-session briefing organized by the French Government. Suggestions in plenary that the OEWG could not move forward in its discussion of options until it had reached agreement on the question of gaps were respectfully taken on board and simultaneously circumvented. This "throwback" to the first substantive session led some

95. International Council of Environmental Law (ICEL), Note on Options to Address Gaps Under Resolution 72/277 (10 May 2018) "Towards a Global Pact for the Environment," submitted for consideration in the 2019 Nairobi Consultations (Feb. 19, 2019), *available at* https://wedocs.unep.org/bitstream/handle/20.500.11822/27609/ICEL_Report.pdf?sequence=1&isAllowed=y.
96. Doran, et al., *supra* note 19, at 7.
97. *Id.* at 8.
98. *Id.* at 9.

> delegates to express frustration that the process was "going in circles." Others considered that while there may not be consensus on gaps, there was general agreement in the room that "challenges" existed. Most urged that a lack of consensus on gaps should not preclude the OEWG from moving forward. Considering the range of options that were in fact proposed, it could be said that this sentiment carried the day to some extent."[99]

Even on the final day of the OEWG at the third session, at least one delegate repeated the claim that negotiators were struggling with the meaning of "gaps."[100] Ecuador, Nicaragua, Saudi Arabia and Egypt used the lack of consensus on gaps as an argument to avoid developing recommendations.[101] Providing another response to this challenge, Japan and Canada proposed putting forward a menu of workable solutions.[102] The word "gap" was ultimately not included in the final recommendations agreed by the working group.[103]

B. *Fragmentation of International Environmental Law*

The UNSG's report traced several inefficiencies in international environmental law to a general lack of coherence and synergy among a large body of sectoral regulatory frameworks.[104] Fragmentation is inevitable given the "piecemeal, incremental and reactive nature of international environmental law-making."[105] The nature of environmental law-making resulted in sectoral regimes and a fragmented legal framework for environmental protection.[106] Different environmental problems require tailored-made solutions, drafted specifically for a set of issues, contexts, or geographical regions. The issue-by-issue governance approach has resulted in treaties well-tailored to address individual challenges, forming the scaffolding of today's international environmental legal architecture.[107]

Some scholars have welcomed the system for its ability to enable creative and innovative case-appropriate solutions.[108] ICEL rejects the notion

99. *Id.* at 10.
100. Doran, et al., *supra* note 39, at 10.
101. *Id.* at 4-5.
102. *Id.* at 4-5.
103. *See* Recommendations, as agreed by the working group (22 May 2019).
104. UN Secretary-General, *supra* 48, at 42.
105. *Id.* at 43.
106. *Id.* at 4, 42.
107. Navajas & Lobel, Fordham Envtl. L. Rev. 35 (2018).
108. *Id.*

of a dysfunctional fragmentation and recognizes the sectoral approach as a strength of the environmental legal system.[109] ICEL summarized the debate:

> "On the one hand, there is a recognition that fragmentation reflects the scope and inherent nature of international environmental law. On the other hand, it is also recognized that fragmentation becomes problematic when it creates a duplication of processes, lack of legal clarity and predictability, and that addressing fragmentation would facilitate the effective implementation of environmental law as well as the 2030 Agenda."[110]

The first round of discussions in Nairobi significantly addressed this issue, with some delegations welcoming fragmentation. Russia emphasized that fragmentation is necessary to achieve consensus on environmental matters.[111] Smaller and issue-specific agreements are usually faster to negotiate and enter into force, especially if those involve fewer countries.[112] Mexico and Brazil noted that it reflects a diversity of environmental problems and associated solutions.[113] For some delegations, fragmentation should be considered an asset, as it manifests the non-hierarchical character of international environmental law and its need to adapt to provide specific answers to specific situations.[114] Because of regionalization, and the pressure from neighboring countries to fulfill commitments, States are more likely to comply with international law.[115] Tailored-made solutions to environmental problems can ultimately lead to a higher level of performance.[116] Overall, the current MEA system has produced several positive results, including less polluted regional seas, the depletion of the ozone layer and reduction of acid rain, and a better scientific understanding of climate change.[117]

---

109. WCEL et al, Note on the United Nations Secretary-General's Report, "Gaps in International Environmental Law and Environment-Related Instruments: Towards a Global Pact for the Environment" (Dec. 10, 2018) 7. *See, i.e.*, International Law Commission, 59th Sess., "Fragmentation of International Law: Difficulties Arising From the Diversification and Expansion of International Law," UN Doc. A/CN.4/L.682 (13 April 2006) 11; Andreas Fischer-Lescano and Gunther Teubner, *Regime-Collisions: The Vain Search for Legal Unity in the Fragmentation of Global Law* (2004) 25(4) Mich. J. Int'l L. 999 (2004); Martti Koskenniemi and Päivi Leino, *Fragmentation of International Law? Postmodern Anxieties* 15(03) Leiden J. Int'l L. 553 (2002).
110. ICEL, *supra* note 95.
111. Doran, et al., *supra* note 39, at 3.
112. Frank Biermann et al., *The Fragmentation of Global Governance Architectures: A Framework for Analysis* (2009) 9(4) Global Envtl. Pol. 25. Alexandra Khrebtukova, *A Call to Freedom: Towards a Philosophy of International Law in an Era of Fragmentation*, 4 J. Int'l L. & Int'l Rel. 51, 51 (2008).
113. IISD (n. 111).
114. Mudallali and Duarte Lopes, *supra* note 9, at 2.
115. Gerhard Hafner, *Pros and Cons Ensuing From Fragmentation of International Law* 25 Mich. J. Int'l L. 849, 851 (2004).
116. Norichika Kanie, *Governance With Multilateral Environmental Agreements: A Healthy or Ill-Equipped Fragmentation?*, *in* Global Environmental Governance: Perspectives on the Current Debate 73-74 (Walter Hoffmann & Lydia Swart eds., 2007).
117. *Ibid.* 71, 73.

Nonetheless, it leads to a significant gap in international environmental law. Prof. Maxine Burkett argues that this compartmentalization has real-world impact, rendering environmental law and policy irrelevant to areas such as commercial law, corporate law and intellectual property.[118] Serbia stressed the need to take seriously the UNSG's conclusion that international environmental law is fragmented, incoherent, and piecemeal.[119] Some delegations underlined that fragmentation becomes problematic when it creates a lack of legal clarity and predictability, and that addressing fragmentation would facilitate implementation.[120] The many advantages brought by fragmentation do not necessarily mean that the perceived weaknesses should be left unaddressed. Given the role of environmental principles as building blocks, serving to supplement or complement more specific rules, aiding interpretation, filling gaps, and ultimately unifying the sectoral approach of international environmental law, the UNGA has recommended the adoption of an overarching legal framework of environmental principles.[121] It noted that a comprehensive and unifying international instrument clarifying all the principles of environmental law would contribute to making them more effective and strengthen their implementation.[122]

Several delegations stressed that international environmental law is a part of international law and that rules of international law can be used to fill the gaps. The role of customary international law, non-binding instruments and regional/national agreements were not sufficiently stressed in the Report and should be given more importance.[123] Some delegations highlighted that the existence of gaps prevented the implementation of international environmental law obligations, while other disagreed with this approach.[124] Taking an intermediate position, China pondered that fragmentation can be, depending on the issue area, a positive or a negative aspect of international environmental law; soft law may sometimes be a better tool to respond to the urgent nature of environmental issues; and more studies on the codification of principles are needed.[125] Similarly, Co-Chair Duarte Lopes, during an oral summary in the first session, noted how some view this as an asset and a reflection of the diversity of international environmental law, its non-hierarchical character, and ability to adapt and provide specialized answers to cer-

118. Hernández, et al. 2018 (contribution from Prof. Maxine Burkett).
119. Doran, et al., *supra* note 39, at 5.
120. Mudallali and Duarte Lopes, *supra* note 9, at 2.
121. UN Secretary-General, *supra* 48, at 4.
122. *Id.* at 6-5; 43.
123. Mudallali and Duarte Lopes, *supra* note 9, at 2.
124. *Id.*
125. Doran, et al., *supra* note 39, at 4.

tain issues. He acknowledged the view that some gaps can be intentional and a reflection of compromise among states parties, while for others fragmentation is regarded as problematic when it reflects a lack of legal clarity.[126] The issue was only briefly mentioned during the second[127] and third sessions.[128]

C. *Matters of Process*

The Nairobi sessions showed a lot of apprehension from countries regarding the effect of the consultative process on existing MEAs. States called for an open, inclusive, transparent, constructive, and meaningful Member State-led process. At the end of the second session, the Co-Chairs acknowledged a general agreement on a transparent discussion and the importance of consensus, the need to reach pragmatic outcomes that add value while avoiding duplication, and wide support for the view that the OEWG's work should not undermine or weaken existing instruments.[129] The need to reach an agreement based on consensus was one of the highest priorities of the Co-Chairs. Indeed, acknowledging that the agreement reached at the end of the third session was weak, Co-Chair Duarte Lopes said that it was nevertheless based on consensus, and thus represented a first step in a continuing process.[130] The conventional approach of having to build a working consensus for environmental agreements, sometimes in the context of strong or even hostile opposition, has shaped international environmental law.[131]

There was a general unanimity on guaranteeing that the process and the ongoing debate should not undermine existing instruments, bodies and processes.[132] Several countries reinforced the need to consider existing MEAs, so as to respect current processes, strengthen existing obligations, avoid weakening prevailing environmental law, principles and standards[133] or overlapping or duplicating existing international instruments.[134] Monaco advised against

126. *Id.* at 11.
127. Doran, et al., *supra* note 19, at 3. (Venezuela, arguing that fragmentation does not justify a legally binding instrument).
128. *Id.* at 4; 5. (Argentina, clarifying that international environmental law is inherently fragmented, a product of decentralization, spontaneity, and non-hierarchical pluralism; Chile, arguing that gaps and fragmentation in some areas of international law should not be a concern).
129. *Id.* at 8.
130. Doran, et al., *supra* note 39, at 1; 3; 8; 9; 10.
131. *Id.* at 11.
132. Mudallali and Duarte Lopes, *supra* note 9.
133. Doran, et al., *supra* note 39, at 2; 3; 4. Doran, et al., *supra* note 19, at 3; 6 (Australia, Bangladesh, Bolivia, Canada, Cuba, India, Romania, for the European Union (EU), and South Africa).
134. Doran, et al., *supra* note 39, at 3; 4; 9 (Australia, Bahrain, China, Colombia, Iraq). Doran, et al., *supra* note 19, at 3; 6 (Australia). Doran, et al., Summary of the Third Substantive Session of the Ad Hoc Open-Ended Working Group Towards a Global Pact for the Environment: 20-22 May 2019. *Global*

renegotiating existing MEAs, while Brazil noted that a hasty overhaul of the system could erase important concepts and principles. Delegations also highlighted the importance of basing the process on existing relevant political declarations, including the Stockholm Declaration, the Rio Declaration on environment and development, the Rio+20 Declaration, the 2030 Agenda, and the Addis Ababa Action Agenda.[135] ICEL noted the consensus on two substantive issues related to process:

> "Notably, two paramount consensus issues have emerged, and two other central issues identified, as a result of the first substantive session. First, consensus 2 that the ongoing consultations should not undermine existing instruments, bodies and processes. Second, agreement on basing the process on existing relevant political declarations—including the Stockholm Declaration, the Rio Declaration, the Rio+20 Declaration, and the Sendai Framework on Disaster Risk Reduction 2015-2030—and on existing relevant UNGA resolutions—such as the 2030 Sustainable Development Agenda and the Addis Ababa Action Agenda."[136]

Still, countries acknowledged the existing system needs a reboot, either through the clarification of ambiguities and strengthening of existing principles (El Salvador) or by improving cohesiveness at the global level (Colombia). China called for the progressive development of principles. Guyana also underscored that the OEWG process should bring added value in terms of cohesion, coherence, synergies, and effectiveness. Colombia explicitly stressed the need to bolster cooperation and coordination among MEAs. ICEL further notes:

> "A possible way to avoid duplication and backsliding is an explicit recognition that existing sector-specific agreements present lex specialis and therefore have priority and should not be undermined. Any codification is without prejudice to the specific expression of principles already established in international treaty law. A multifaceted response is called for and ICEL encourages the several conferences of the parties under international agreements, as well as the UNGA, to address the gaps identified where they have authority to do so."[137]

In the final recommendations submitted to the UNGA, the OEWG included as objectives for guiding the recommendations to (b) uphold respective obligations and commitments under international environmen-

---

Pact for the Environment. Vol. 35 No. 3, *available at* http://enb.iisd.org/download/pdf/enb3503e.pdf. 5 (Chile).

135. Mudallali and Duarte Lopes, *supra* note 9.

136. ICEL, *supra* note 95, at 2.

137. *Id.* at 4.

tal law of States members of the United Nations and members of specialized agencies; (c) contribute to the strengthening of implementation of international environmental law and environment-related instruments; (d) support the full implementation of the 2030 Agenda for Sustainable Development, as well as the outcome of the UN Conference on Environment and Development (Rio+20), including its paragraphs 88 and 89; (e) not undermine existing relevant legal instruments and frameworks and relevant global, regional and sectoral bodies.[138]

D. *International Environmental Governance*

The report called attention to the institutional fragmentation which characterizes international environmental law, with a heterogenous set of actors in a system of multi-actor governance with international institutions, treaty bodies, non-governmental organizations, the scientific community and the private sector.[139] The UN system, comprised of UNEP and several UN programmes and funds, and treaty bodies established by MEAs have yet to properly coordinate for coherent implementation. Institutional fragmentation and a lack of coordination are key challenges in international environmental governance.[140] The UNSG called for enhanced coordination in international environmental law, between MEAs, and with environment-related areas.[141]

Several Member States raised concerns about the institutional aspects of international environmental law, with Japan noting this was a good opportunity to reflect on how the international community has addressed pressing environmental issues through MEAs.[142] Lack of coherence and cooperation between different instruments contribute to creating challenges in implementation and fail to address the natural dependence of ecosystems. There was a general understanding that the OEWG could support the strengthening of the governance structure of international environmental law, while preserving the independence of each MEAs and respecting ongoing processes. The strengthening of synergies and promotion of better coordination and cooperation between MEAs, bodies and processes, building on ongoing initiatives, was stressed by many delegations. In this regard, many supported the idea that the OEWG considers the possibility of developing further work on the proposals made in the paragraph 83 of the Report.[143] Others noted

138. See Recommendations, as agreed by the working group (22 May 2019).
139. UN Secretary-General, *supra* 48, at 33.
140. *Id.* at 34.
141. *Id.* at 34-35.
142. Doran, et al., *supra* note 19.
143. Mudallali and Duarte Lopes, *supra* note 9.

that so far initiatives aimed at improving cooperation and coordination had not provided all the results expected. Some delegates further argued that this discussion should occur within respective MEAs, not by the OEWG.

Several nations underscored the role of UNEP as the global authority on environment in the UN system,[144] noticing the need to strengthen it as part of improving coordination in international environmental law.[145] Many delegations have called for supporting UNEP and strengthening the capacities of national systems under the Montevideo Programme (Programme of Development and the Periodic review of Environmental Law). Likewise, the role of UNEA as the main environmental body in the UN system was noted, especially in addressing governance gaps.[146] Brazil highlighted the need to address insufficient coordination in the UN system.[147] Other delegations underlined the need for the full implementation of paragraph 88 of the Rio+20 Declaration. There was a broad understanding regarding the importance of non-State actors' participation in governance, including major groups, indigenous people and local communities, youth, women, NGOs, and the business sector. Several delegations supported a more coherent and pro-active approach to the participation of stakeholders in the different MEAs. Other delegations highlighted that this participation should be carried out in accordance with international and national laws, reflecting the differences of each specific context.[148]

Institutional fragmentation and weak coordination between treaties can be addressed through various means, such as: (a) creating clusters and synergies between conventions; (b) mapping existing global and regional action plans and agreements to create an overview of coverage and identify interlinkages; (c) avoiding duplication of reporting and/or monitoring processes by using the same reporting channels and not creating additional burdens ("integrated reporting"); (d) sharing lessons learned and best practices; (e) developing implementation guidelines for multilateral environmental agreements; and (f) sharing information among the different scientific bodies that support the work of related multilateral environmental agreements.[149]

A few options in relation to these issues included strengthening UNEP and UNEA; a call by the General Assembly for increased cooperation and coordination among MEAs; a call by the General Assembly to all Member

144. *Id.*
145. Doran, et al., *supra* note 19.
146. Mudallali and Duarte Lopes, *supra* note 9.
147. Doran, et al., *supra* note 19.
148. Mudallali and Duarte Lopes, *supra* note 9.
149. UN Secretary-General, *supra* 48, at 35.

States that have not done so to ratify the MEAs and effectively implement them; the creation of working groups tasked with identifying possible synergies to be explored by different instruments and bodies; the creation of a specific forum where representatives of relevant instruments and bodies could meet and coordinate, while indicating that this could be done under UNEA; a call by the General Assembly for some mainstreaming of the environment within the UN system including through coordination mechanism such as the environment management group.

E. *Means of Implementation*

The UNSG's broad mandate included the assessment of implementation gaps,[150] which the report broadly called institutional gaps.[151] Although some countries objected to calling it a "gap," preferring the word "challenge,"[152] there is undoubtedly a missing link between the obligations States assume and their full implementation.[153] The fact that the Resolution expressly mentions 'implementation' firmly place these conversations within the ambit of the OEWG's inquiry. Lack of implementation was one of the main topics of discussion during the Nairobi sessions, and also significantly encompassed the core of the recommendations of the OEWG to the UNGA.

Implementation gaps include ineffectiveness in monitoring, reporting and verification, compliance and enforcement, the absence of liability rules, or the need for better harmonization, synergies and coordination with other MEAs. These arise for different reasons, ranging, for example, from capacity challenges, the need for facilitation and compliance, insufficient monitoring and law enforcement, to lack of political will.[154] Many delegations reaffirmed that means of implementations need to be strengthened, some noting that it should be the main focus of the working group, which should result in reinforcing international cooperation and effective means of implementation, including provision on the necessary funding, capacity-building and transfer of technology.[155]

150. Resolution.
151. UN Secretary-General, *supra* 48, at 6.
152. Oral summary second working group, p. 4.
153. Sue Biniaz specifically questioned the notion of a gap related to implementation, asking whether there is a gap when an agreement covers a subject, but the environment remains unsatisfactory addressed. Biniaz, Rev. Eur., Comp. & Int'l Envtl. L. (2019) 34-35.
154. Voigt, Rev. Eur., Comp. & Int'l Envtl. L. (2019) 23.
155. Oral summary second working group, p. 4.

The national implementation of international law represents one of the most significant challenges.[156] There is a broad understanding that national implementation is first and foremost the responsibility of States and that many countries face challenges to implement their obligations under different MEAs, taking into account national circumstances and priorities. The implementation deficit can be traced to knowledge gaps; a lack of adequate means of implementation, such as finance, capacity-building, knowledge sharing or technology transfer; lack of access to funding and environmentally-friendly technologies; the need for facilitation for compliance; a lack of coordination between relevant government departments as well as with other sectors; insufficient monitoring and law enforcement; weak compliance mechanism and weak monitoring; a lack of political will; and the inadequate engagement of different stakeholders, such as civil society and women's organizations.[157] Funding for implementation still remains insufficient, unpredictable and incoherent, and varies considerably among the different regimes. The lack of cooperation among governments, corporations and the financial community; and the inadequacy of systems for collecting, synthesizing and reporting back information and knowledge on such technologies are also highlighted as significant challenges in implementation.[158] Limited reporting for assessment of resources mobilized and compliance constraints the effective implementation of treaty provisions.[159]

The report assessed specific implementation challenges of different MEAs,[160] suggesting that the proliferation of instruments and the fragmentation in the regulatory regimes create the need for institutional coordination and cooperation, as well as the implementation of the various legal instruments in a mutually supportive manner.[161] It called for strengthening mechanisms to harness interlinkages and promote synergies for effective implementation of MEAs.[162] This could be done, for example, by clustering related MEAs.[163] It also suggested developing implementation guidelines for MEAs.[164] It was suggested that the Secretariats need to be provided with

156. UN Secretary-General, *supra* 48, at 36. *See also* UNEP, "Future Shape of International Law to Address Pollution of Global Significance Affecting the Earth's Ecosystems: Consolidated Report of Initial Consideration by Experts," 6 April 2018.
157. UN Secretary-General, *supra* 48, at 36. *See* David Victor, Kal Raustiala, and Eugene B. Skolnikoff, eds., *The Implementation and Effectiveness of International Environmental Commitments: Theory and Practice* (MIT Press, 1998). Doran, et al., *supra* note 19, at 3; 4.
158. UN Secretary-General, *supra* 48, at 36.
159. *Id.* at 37.
160. *See* Section III: Gaps Relating to Existing Regulatory Regimes.
161. UN Secretary-General, *supra* 48, at 30.
162. *Id.* at 34.
163. Synergies process launched by the Basel, Rotterdam and Stockholm Conventions.
164. UN Secretary-General, *supra* 48, at 35.

sufficient means to support developing countries to implement obligations. The importance of compliance was underlined, including through the development of compliance mechanisms. Some delegations were against having a global compliance mechanism, suggesting this should rather be addressed within the sphere of each specific MEA.[165]

Many delegations stressed the need to strengthen the means of implementation in international environmental law in line with Agenda 2030 and the Addis Ababa Action Agenda. There was a call for developed countries to increase their support to developing countries through increased financial resources, capacity-building and technology transfer, as well as for developing a tracking mechanism.[166] One of the objectives guiding the recommendations is to contribute to the strengthening of implementation of international environmental law and environment-related instruments;[167] and to d) support the full implementation of the 2030 Agenda for Sustainable Development, as well as the outcome of the UN Conference on Environment and Development (Rio+20), including its paragraphs 88 and 89.[168] A few delegations recommended to Member States to fully use the Montevideo Programme Programme of Development and the Periodic review of Environmental Law to foster the environmental rule of law and support the implementation of environmental law at all levels.[169]

Finally, gaps were identified in the dispute settlement, compliance and enforcement mechanisms, as well as in the assessment of liability and redress for transboundary environmental damage.[170] Regarding dispute settlements, several delegations emphasized the absence of an international environmental court. Some explained that the time was not ripe for such a court to be established.[171] Delegations also underlined the importance of strengthening the capacities of national judicial systems. On liability and redress for transboundary environmental damage, some delegations stressed that States have an obligation of conduct, not an obligation of results. Some delegations highlighted that there was not a predictable obligation for any transboundary environmental damages. While it was highlighted that the few regimes with rules on civil liability are very specific and not always coherent, many delega-

165. Oral summary second working group, p. 4.
166. Mudallali and Duarte Lopes, *supra* note 9, at 6.
167. Recommendations, item c.
168. Recommendations, item d.
169. Oral summary second working group, p. 4.
170. UN Secretary-General, *supra* 48, at 37-42.
171. Mudallali and Duarte Lopes, *supra* note 9, at 6.

tions underlined that it would not be appropriate for the ad-hoc open-ended working Group to make recommendations on liability.[172]

The OEWG's final recommendations to the UNGA include, among its substantive recommendations: an encouragement to all that have not done so to consider ratifying MEAs and to effectively implement them;[173] States members of the United Nations and all members of the specialized agencies to strengthen, where needed, environmental laws, policies and regulatory frameworks at the national level, as well as the capacities across all sectors for the effective implementation of international environmental law, including the administrative and justice sectors in accordance with national legal systems, while acknowledging the importance of international cooperation in supporting and complementing national actions;[174] encourages active and meaningful engagement of all relevant stakeholders at all levels in the different *fora* related to the implementation of international environment law and environment-related instruments;[175] explores further ways for States members of the United Nations and all members of the specialized agencies to support and make full use of the Fifth Programme for the Development and Periodic Review of Environmental Law (Montevideo Programme V) adopted by the fourth session of the United Nations Environment Assembly, in order to foster the environmental rule of law and advance the implementation of environmental law at all levels;[176] encourages the United Nations Environment Program, as Chair of the Environment Management Group (EMG) and in collaboration with the members of the Group, to continue to strengthen system-wide interagency coordination on environment and to call for active involvement and support of all EMG members for the implementation of system-wide strategies on the environment.[177] In line with this, the OEWG recommended that the General Assembly forwards these recommendations to the UNEA for its consideration, and to prepare, at its fifth session in February 2021, a political declaration for a UN high level meeting, in the context of the commemoration of the creation of UNEP, with a view to strengthening the implementation of international environmental law

172. Mudallali and Duarte Lopes, *supra* note 9.
173. Recommendations, item h.
174. Recommendations, item j.
175. Recommendations, item k.
176. Recommendations, item l.
177. Recommendations, item m.

and international environmental governance in line with para. 88 of the "Future We Want."[178]

In line with the suggestions by delegates and the recommendations to the UNGA, Prof. Voigt suggests that one of the ways the Global Pact (or a global pact) could add value is by addressing implementation deficiencies. She argues:

> "Coherence and coordination at the international level have been identified as easing implementation challenges but are seldom seen as the only ways to achieve effective implementation. A Pact could aim at bringing together state and non-state actors in a global compact to raise the necessary means for the effective implementation of environmental agreements. This could lead to cooperation on increased capacity-building across State borders and across the public/private divide. It could bring private companies and corporations onto the scene and provide a space for interaction on addressing financial, capacity and technology gaps."[179] "In this sense, a Pact could address implementation challenges, coordination deficits between MEAs (and between MEAs and other international treaties) or bring together actors from the public and private sector in the global concern for environmental protection."[180]

---

178. "88. We are committed to strengthening the role of the United Nations Environment Programme as the leading global environmental authority that sets the global environmental agenda, promotes the coherent implementation of the environmental dimension of sustainable development within the United Nations system and serves as an authoritative advocate for the global environment. We reaffirm General Assembly resolution 2997 (XXVII) of 15 December 1972 establishing the United Nations Environment Programme and other relevant resolutions that reinforce its mandate, as well as the Nairobi Declaration on the Role and Mandate of the United Nations Environment Programme of 7 February 199730 and the Malmö Ministerial Declaration of 31 May 2000. In this regard, we invite the Assembly, at its sixty-seventh session, to adopt a resolution strengthening and upgrading the United Nations Environment Programme in the following manner: (a) Establish universal membership in the Governing Council of the United Nations Environment Programme, as well as other measures to strengthen its governance as well as its responsiveness and accountability to Member States; (b) Have secure, stable, adequate and increased financial resources from the regular budget of the United Nations and voluntary contributions to fulfil its mandate; (c) Enhance the voice of the United Nations Environment Programme and its ability to fulfil its coordination mandate within the United Nations system by strengthening its engagement in key United Nations coordination bodies and empowering it to lead efforts to formulate United Nations system-wide strategies on the environment; (d) Promote a strong science-policy interface, building on existing international instruments, assessments, panels and information networks, including the Global Environment Outlook, as one of the processes aimed at bringing together information and assessment to support informed decision-making; (e) Disseminate and share evidence-based environmental information, and raise public awareness on critical, as well as emerging, environmental issues; (f) Provide capacity-building to countries, as well as support, and facilitate access to technology; (g) Progressively consolidate headquarters functions in Nairobi, as well as strengthen its regional presence, in order to assist countries, upon request, in the implementation of their national environmental policies, collaborating closely with other relevant entities of the United Nations system; (h) Ensure the active participation of all relevant stakeholders, drawing on best practices and models from relevant multilateral institutions and exploring new mechanisms to promote transparency and the effective engagement of civil society.
179. Voigt, Rev. Eur., Comp. & Int'l Envtl. L. 23 (2019).
180. *Id.* at 24.

During the closing plenary, non-governmental organizations (NGOs) described political will as the most important gap and accused those countries most responsible for the planet's ecological breakdown of attempting to "kill the process." Co-Chair Duarte Lopes captured the muted tone of the session when he responded by thanking the NGOs for helping to steer the ambition of the process, and acknowledging that the outcome was weak. Nevertheless, he said, it was based on consensus, and provides a first step in a continuing process.[181]

F. *Environment-Related Areas*

Although the UNGA called for the report on gaps to also cover environment-related instruments, several delegations raised concerns as to how the environmental aspects relate to processes in other areas. The term "environment-related instruments" is taken to include those international legal instruments that do not fall exclusively within the field of the environment or have as their primary objective the protection of the environment, such as those dealing with international trade, investment, intellectual property rights, human rights, peace and security, migration and disaster management.[182] Some delegations understood "environment-related instruments" as covering non-binding environmental instruments, and not as covering those international legal instruments that have an environmental dimension. However, some delegations called for the integrity of existing regimes, especially when related work is ongoing, and encouraged the relevant processes to consider the environment-related aspects of their work.[183]

There was a lot of criticism on this specific section of the report, which some deemed outdated, inaccurate or containing generalizations. For example, efforts from the World Intellectual Property Organization (WIPO) relating to the Convention on Biological Diversity (CBD) were not mentioned. Likewise, the assessments on rights of indigenous peoples and the jurisprudence on trade and investment were incomplete.[184] On trade instruments, some delegations underscored the need to find a balance between safeguarding trade interests and protecting the environment. On investment instruments, some delegations noted the growing tendency of taking into account environmental considerations in this sector, while others indicated that environmental clauses were still insufficiently included. On intellectual

181. Doran, et al. 2019.
182. UN Secretary-General, *supra* 48, at 6.
183. Doran, et al., *supra* note 19, at 9.
184. *Id.* at 7.

property rights, several delegations mentioned the ongoing work in this sector, while others stressed that more progress needed to be made. On human rights instruments, some delegations noted that many human rights cannot be fully enjoyed without the right to a clean and healthy environment. Some stressed that the human right sector was a distinct system not relevant in this context. In this regard, some delegations cautioned against the risk of politicization.[185] The IISD analyzed that the report's chapter on environment-related instruments sparked its own debate, leading one delegate to question whether it had "opened a can of worms."[186]

G. *Environmental Principles*

The report identified important inefficiencies in the role of environmental principles, in particular with respect to their content and legal status.[187] These result from general lack of coherence and synergy among a large body of sectoral regulatory frameworks. Fragmentation is inevitable given the "piecemeal, incremental and reactive nature of international environmental law-making."[188] While it is a frequent phenomenon in international law and multilateral decision-making, other fields rely on a binding framework instrument(s) with rules that provide coordination and coherence.[189] International environmental law still lacks such a framework.[190] To enhance the coherence and coordination of global environmental governance, the UNGA concluded that there is a need to further clarify the content and legal status of principles of environmental law in a "comprehensive and unifying law" that could provide for better harmonization, predictability and certainty.[191]

To a certain extent, the conclusion of the report might have given the impression to some states that it was already prejudging what the outcome of the OEWG had to be and, unsurprisingly, the report faced a critical reception.[192] In particular, several delegations (including Argentina, Iran and Morocco) expressed reservations about the need to adopt a new comprehensive legal instrument. As mentioned above, for some (and notably the European Union), a GPE is deemed necessary to "fill a gap" in IEL. However, not all states are of the view that the absence of an overarching treaty on

185. Mudallali and Duarte Lopes, *supra* note 9.
186. Doran, et al., *supra* note 19, at 13.
187. UN Secretary-General, *supra* 48, at 42.
188. *Id.* at 43.
189. *Id.* at 4. Examples include international human rights law, international trade law, and international law of the seas.
190. *Id.* at 5.
191. *Id.* at 43.
192. Doran, et al., *supra* note 19.

the environment constitutes a gap. For instance, for Argentina, "any gaps and shortcomings in IEL are in implementation, and relate to financing, capacity-building, and technology transfer, hinge on political will, and can be addressed through existing institutions."[193] From this perspective, the adoption of a GPE can of course not appear as a priority.[194]

Discussions on principles started at the organizational session. Several countries remarked on the need to reinforce existing principles and agreements. Brazil, China, Ecuador, India and Egypt highlighted the principles of the Rio Declaration as the basis for the engagement of developing countries, especially the principle of common but differentiated responsibilities (CBDR). Within this context, Brazil called for an agenda item on the Rio principles and their implementation.[195]

With regards to the methodology for developing such an exercise, several delegations highlighted the need to take into consideration principles of international environmental law already contemplated in existing instruments and political declarations as well as customary international law. In this regard, it was pointed out that there is a risk associated with reopening or redefining existing principles as this could possibly lead to a regression rather than a progression. There was a general warning about re-opening, re-negotiating, or weakening principles, noting that one principle can sometimes have different formulations across various instruments.[196] Several delegations stressed that this work should focus on the principles that gather international consensus. Other delegations indicated that such an exercise would be an opportunity to update existing principles and include emerging principles as international environmental law has considerably developed in the last decades.[197]

Some delegations identified gaps on principles, related to their interpretation, unequal implementation and lack of consistency. Other delegations did not identify such gaps. Some delegations noted that a few principles have matured to become customary international law while others constitute soft law. Further clarifications with regard to the scope of principles was needed. The value of codifying principles lies in supporting implementation, improving consistency and facilitating interpretation, including by developing a common understanding. Different views were expressed as to whether it should only encompass widely applicable and agreed upon principles or also

193. *Id.*
194. Saint-Geniès. 2019.
195. Lebada, Governments Commence Organizational Work on Global Pact for Environment 2018.
196. Doran, et al., *supra* note 39, at 8.
197. Doran, et al., *supra* note 19.

emerging ones. Some delegations noted that an instrument could also clarify emerging principles.

Many delegations underlined the importance of general principles as building blocks of international environmental law. Several delegations stressed the role of principles in promoting legal certainty, enhancing visibility of international environmental law, ensuring consistency of implementation, facilitating interpretation, as well as filling normative gaps.[198] A few underlying principles were particularly highlighted by countries as warranting special attention. Indonesia called for the inclusion of the leading principles of international environmental law in any new global pact. The Philippines cautioned that the UN already has an integrative framework for sustainable development, and that agreed principles and agreements should not be renegotiated. Nigeria proposed that new and omitted principles be consolidated in a pact, and emphasized the importance of climate justice and expanding the rights of those suffering from environmental harm.

Many delegations commented on the importance and content of several principles, including the principle of prevention, precaution, polluter-pays, common but differentiated responsibilities and respective capabilities, national sovereignty over natural resources, non-regression and progression, equity, access to environmental justice, and the right to a clean and healthy environment.[199] Several countries specifically emphasized the principles of sovereignty over national resources (Ethiopia, for the G-77/China, China, the Russian Federation, Saudi Arabia) and common but differentiated responsibilities (CBDR) (Ethiopia, for the G-77/China, Bolivia, Chile, Cuba, Egypt, Iraq). Bolivia called for recognition of the interdependence of ecological and social systems, and the legacy of colonialism, global debt, and questions of ecological injustice. Ecuador added that nature has a right to be respected and maintained. South Africa said the principles of equity and fair and equitable benefit sharing were not adequately addressed in the UNSG's report.[200]

Some delegations pointed out that the identification of principles of international environmental law is a delicate and controversial exercise, and that any action in that regard should wait for the outcome of the study launched by the International Law Commission (ILC) on the criteria to define general principles of law.[201] Some delegations suggested waiting for the ILC to conclude its work, while others indicated that this was not necessary as the ILC is not specifically addressing principles of international environmental law.

198. Mudallali and Duarte Lopes, *supra* note 9.
199. Doran, et al., *supra* note 19.
200. *Id.*
201. *Id.*

A few delegations added that a new instrument on principles would also apply whenever there is a vacuum of MEAs or regulations. Several delegations said that any further work on principles should be based on the Rio Declaration. The relevance of the principle of common but differentiated responsibilities and respective capabilities was noted a few times. Others reiterated the primacy of the principle of national sovereignty over natural resources.

A few options were mentioned in relation to this issue. One alternative would be to negotiate a new instrument. Different views were expressed on its nature and format: a legally-binding instrument, a high-level political declaration, a document agreed by the General Assembly. The nature could also be determined at a later stage, during the negotiation process launched for the purpose of negotiating a new instrument. Some delegations noted that negotiations don't need to be limited to principles but could also include other issues, such as means of implementation. Several delegations were against negotiating a new instrument, which was to some premature at this stage. Another option would be to hold further intergovernmental negotiations, either though the creation of a group of experts mandated by the General Assembly, through the UNEA, or refer to the ILC. A third option was to establish an International Court for the Environment, which several delegations objected.

The Nordic Council of Ministers noted that codifying principles of international environmental law requires a systemic analysis or the regional recognition of these principles.[202] Through a series of regional charts that group in one place most of the environmental law principles that governments have already accepted in their international agreements, the International Council of Environmental Law (ICEL) demonstrated the consensus on principles and objectives in international environmental law.[203] The "ICEL charts" set forth the correspondence between the Draft Global Pact and the UN Sustainable Development Goals, general principles of international soft law, multilateral environmental agreements, and various regional environmental agreements. They cover the African Union (AU), the Association of South East Asian States (ASEAN), the Caribbean Community (CARICOM), China, the Commonwealth Independent States (CIS), the League of Arab States (Arab League), the OAS, the Pacific Island Forum, South Asian Association for Regional Cooperation (SAARC) and South Asia Cooperative Environment Program (SACEP). Additionally, it includes charts focused on Multilateral

202. Urho, et al. 2019 82.
203. The charts can be accessed at https://libraryguides.law.pace.edu/icel.

Environmental Agreements, Soft Law Instruments and Sustainable Development Goals.

VI. Geopolitical Analysis

To help think about the pathway forward, this section provides an initial geopolitical analysis of the positions taken by delegates in Nairobi. It investigated each countries' positions as to a possible new framework agreement that codified principles, or, when applicable, to the Global Pact specifically. This section largely relies on the ENB summaries provided by the IISD[204] and the analysis of some official statements submitted by countries.[205] It does not particularly take into account the format such an agreement would take. In some cases, countries favored an agreement but had suggestions as to what it should include. Since the Global Pact was intended to be a working document, this is precisely the discussion it invited. These statements also set the stage to where they compromised.

This section groups countries in three categories: (A) countries directly against a new framework agreement, a Global Pact, or the codification of principles, (B) countries directly favoring it, and (C) countries within a gray area, in an undefined position. The third category also includes the countries which have not participated in the process so far (i.e. did not vote on the resolution, did not attend the organizational session in New York, nor any of the sessions in Nairobi). As the discussions develop, it is likely that some of these positions might change. However, it provides a blueprint of where we are right now.

Overall, the Nairobi negotiations revealed a major lack of consensus on the adoption of an agreement on principles. However, some remarks are warranted here. Since the sessions were not held at the UN headquarters, several countries interested in the process were not able to attend even though the OEWG received special funds to assist broad participation. In total, 35 countries did not participate in any stage of the negotiations. Several countries voted in favor of the resolution but did not attend the Nairobi sessions. The Global Pact was proposed just after the Paris Agreement was adopted, based on the argument that the political momentum favored such a new development. However, the Nairobi sessions showed that a few countries, including the United States, Japan, Brazil and Russia, showed a hard position against such an idea. The political context with respect to the global environment has

204. Doran, et al. 2019; Doran, et al., *supra* note 19; Doran, et al., *supra* note 39.
205. *See* https://globalpact.informea.org/homepage.

hardened. However, with a renewed support from the European Union, new coalitions can be built to attract broader support for ongoing negotiations.

A. *Countries Against a New Instrument*

Overall, 19 Member Countries directly opposed a new framework agreement, the codification of principles or a Global Pact specifically. These mainly related to a concern over the effects on existing agreements and an argument that existing instruments such as the Montevideo Program V, the Adis Ababba Action Agenda and the 2030 Agenda already fulfilled similar purposes. A few countries also referred to the ongoing work on principles by the International Law Commission. Argentina, Brazil, Japan, Philippines, Russia, Saudi Arabia, Syria, Turkey, United States, and Venezuela presented a strong opposition to the proposal. Bolivia, Cuba, Djibouti, Ecuador, Egypt, India, Iran, Korea, and Malaysia were slightly against it.

The United States opposed the process from its onset, calling for a vote on the resolution and opposing any reference to the Global Pact.[206] At the organizational session, the US argued that the resolution did not necessarily mandate the OEWG to make recommendations to the UNGA, in an effort to avoid any substantial document to result from the discussions.[207] In the first session, the US consistently questioned the UNSG's report, deeming it not objective and biased towards a Global Pact. It challenged the meaning of gaps and its analysis by the UNSG, repeatedly arguing that several gaps were intentional, and consisted of "design elements" in existing MEAs. During the three sessions, the country generally opposed any reference to principles of international environmental law. Additionally, the country resisted the idea of an overarching compliance mechanism and argued there is no universally recognized human right explicitly relating to the environment. The US claimed that national, rather than international, actions should improve implementation. The country relied on an extensive discussion on the problems and a potential solution to argue that there was no consensus, and an outcome would thus be hard to achieve. It opposed a legally binding instrument and argued that a non-binding instrument could undermine previous agreements. The US favored, however, a debate on improving coordination and enhanced cooperation among MEAs.

Japan did not vote on the resolution and opposed a new instrument. While the country expressed interest in considering the governance of inter-

206. Releases, General Assembly Decides to Establish Working Group Aimed at Identifying Gaps in International Environmental Law 2018.
207. Leone 2018.

national environmental law, it questioned the notion of gaps as included in the UNSG's report. Japan questioned the existence of a gap on principles and referred to the work of the ILC. It noted that it may be premature to codify certain principles that are neither already well established nor widely used in MEAs, and said it remains unclear how an overarching instrument compiling principles could address gaps and challenges in implementation of IEL. Japan suggested a menu of workable solutions given the lack of consensus on gaps and on a potential binding instrument.

Russia was against the resolution, censuring its drafting process. The country criticized the UNSG's report, especially as it lacked reference to sovereignty over natural resources. Russia reinforced the relevance of developing international environmental law based on consensus and welcomed fragmentation as a necessary feature to achieve it. It ultimately rejected a new framework for environmental law and questioned the significance of well-grounded non-binding agreements such as the 1992 Rio Declaration as a source of international law. Russia reinforced implementation as one of the main challenges of international environmental law and called for support for the Montevideo Programme V, but was wary of the impact of the development of sanctions. While Russia rejected any reference to further discussion on principles in the final recommendations, it suggested that UNEP should be requested to continue this debate.

While Brazil voted in favor of the resolution, it was quick to repudiate any proposal related to principles during the substantive sessions. It reinforced the role of the Rio Principles and challenged the methodology used by the UNSG to select the principles identified in the report. In particular, Brazil reinforced the principle of CBDR and the sovereignty of States. Significantly, it referred to the current investigation of the ILC on general principles of law as a prerequisite to any further examination of principles of international environmental law. It saw the diversification of international environmental law as a benefit and cautioned against "a hasty overhaul of the system." Paradoxically, Brazil noted the lack of consensus on a legally binding instrument while also expressing concern that a political declaration could have limited value. Brazil did not indicate an area which it believed warranted attention. It directed the discussions towards the lack of means of implementation, especially to strengthen finance, technology transfer, and capacity-building for developing countries. These are particularly important in support of the SDGs and MEAs. Brazil suggested the 2030 Agenda and UNEA could potentially act as platforms to bridge coordination gaps. Additionally, the

Addis Ababa Action Agenda (AAAA) could form the basis for means of implementation to underline the insufficiency of existing resources.

Argentina did not vote on the resolution but flagged its disapproval of the proposal since the beginning of the working group's discussions. It repeatedly asserted that there were no gaps in the substance of international environmental law, only in its implementation. These relate to financing, capacity-building, and technology transfer, hinge on political will, and can be addressed through existing processes and institutions such as the AAAA and the Montevideo Programme V. Specifically, the process should consider how to resolve the lack of means of implementation, how to improve coordination and synergy between international environmental organizations, and how not to undermine existing agreements and bodies. It recalled the absence of reference to sovereignty over natural resources in the UNSG's report and questioned the inclusion of the precautionary principle, arguing it remains controversial and could therefore not be considered customary law. The country was concerned about the duplication of efforts and stressed that a new instrument was not needed. Argentina argued that this process would only be credible if there were consensus on a decision. It rejected any reference to principles, directing the debate to the ongoing work conducted by the ILC.

Egypt did not vote on the resolution but was against any discussion on environmental principles. The country did not support a new mechanism, citing the lack of consensus on gaps and the risk of complicating existing international environmental law, arguing a one-size-fits-all approach was unrealistic. The country disagreed that a comprehensive and unifying instrument would strengthen implementation and underlined the risk of re-opening or redesigning existing principles. Egypt underscored that environmental principles evolved within sectoral regimes and may apply differently depending on the circumstances. An instrument unifying international environmental law may be useful for areas currently lacking regulation, but not for existing regimes. Egypt urged postponing the discussion on principles until the ILC has finished its work on general principles of law.

Turkey voted against the resolution, opposing a general top-down multilateral approach to address deficiencies in international environmental law. The country called for strengthening institutions, especially UNEP and UNEA, and using existing processes such as the Montevideo Programme V. Turkey also called for a focus on new issues such as marine litter. It rejected any reference to principles or environmental defenders. The Philippines voted against the resolution and positioned itself against a new framework, arguing that the 2030 Agenda already fulfilled a similar purpose and that States should not renegotiate consolidated agreements such as the Rio Declaration, and other principles included in the preamble of MEAs. Syria voted against the resolution, reinforcing the sovereignty of countries over natural resources and arguing one document would not achieve the international goal of protecting the environment. It also questioned the "concept of world environmental law," claiming it was still legally controversial. The country did not attend any of the sessions in Nairobi.

Saudi Arabia abstained from voting on the resolution. The country criticized the report for not being "technical and evidence-based," using the 1992 Rio Declaration as a source of international law, and for a "weak" analysis of gaps relating to existing regulatory regimes. It specifically noted the importance of the principle of national sovereignty over natural resources and common but differentiated responsibilities (CBDR) and argued that international environmental law principles are non-binding. It reinforced the need to strengthen implementation and explicitly called for additional financial resources and increased coordination between MEAs. It rejected any further discussion of principles of international environmental law or a new instrument altogether and identified the Montevideo Programme V as an avenue to increase implementation. Saudi Arabia said there was no consensus that "swift action is needed" to address environmental challenges. Iran abstained from voting on the resolution and cautioned against the creation of a comprehensive new instrument without recognizing root causes of gaps in international environmental law and called for creativity in reviving existing environmental instruments.

Djibouti did not vote on the resolution but was against the idea of a new instrument as it would create confusion. It saw fragmentation of international environmental law as the reason for its lack of efficiency and called for the harmonization of instruments and increased capacity-building for national implementation.[208] Ecuador did not vote on the resolution and was against "opening principles to discussion," questioning whether a new instrument would help improve the state of international environmental law. Rather, the country consistently referred to the need to improve means of implementation and capacity-building. Additionally, the country criticized the lack of reference to corporate responsibility for environmental damage, the right to development, the reduction of patterns of unsustainable consumption and

208. Commentaires de la République de Djibouti (OEWG's First Session), *available at* http://wedocs.unep.org/bitstream/handle/20.500.11822/27261/Commentaires%20de%20la%20R%c3%a9publique%20de%20Djibouti.pdf?sequence=100&isAllowed=y.

production, climate justice and the principle of national sovereignty over natural resources in the UNSG's report.

India voted in favor of the resolution. The country noted that technical and financial gaps also needed to be reflected in the OEWG's agenda. The country also reinforced the need to include the principle of CBDR and national sovereignty over natural resources in any discussion. India cautioned against undermining existing instruments and argued that many of the principles are subject-specific. The country cautioned that the non-paper from the Co-Chairs pushed institutionalization via a new instrument with no clarity on how this would address global challenges. It opposed further discussion on principles and rather focused on improving means of implementation.

Venezuela did not vote on the resolution but consistently positioned itself against the negotiation of a new instrument. The country cautioned about the risk of interfering with existing MEAs, leading to regression in terms of the validity and implications of international environmental law principles. Instead, the process should affirm existing principles and avoid re-interpretation. Bolivia did not vote on the resolution. The country was against further discussing principles and noted that the work of the ILC is distinct from the work on environmental principles. The country was cautious about undermining existing agreements. Bolivia called for increased commitment to means of implementation and strengthening the AAAA and the 2030 Agenda. It proposed that the process be taken to the UNGA or UNEA, with future consideration of a political declaration. Noting the rights of nature, Bolivia called for an interdisciplinary analysis of the normative evolution of the concept of the environment. The country also reinforced the role of indigenous groups, which was not adequately noted in the report.

Cuba did not vote on the resolution but voiced concerns about a potential new instrument. The country cautioned against undermining existing instruments and indicated that a single instrument dealing with all issues would not be the most consistent way to address a wide range of problems. Instead, Cuba underscored the need to strengthen existing agreements and called for more coordination across MEAs. The country reinforced the need to enhance means of implementation and opposed any reference to principles in the final recommendations. Malaysia abstained from voting on the resolution and reinforced the need to strengthen means of implementation, which the country called the most important gap in international environmental law. Malaysia opposed a global mechanism or instrument to cover existing MEAs. The Republic of Korea did not vote on the resolution and expressed concern about how the codification of principles could address gaps in international environmental.

B. *Countries Favoring a New Instrument*

The proposal of a Global Pact or, generally, the codification of principles received broad support of countries. In total, 59 countries wanted to continue a discussion on the codification of principles, including the EU's individual members. While the majority of EU countries have not showed a position in favor or against the Global Pact, these are included within the list of supporters.

The European Union voted in favor of the resolution and supported the process. The following five EU countries did not vote on the resolution and attended at least one session in Nairobi but made no statement for or against the codification of principles or a Global Pact: Austria, Hungary, the Netherlands, Poland, and Sweden. The following six EU countries voted in favor of the resolution but did not attend any of the sessions in Nairobi: Croatia, Cyprus, Latvia, Lithuania, Luxembourg, and Portugal. The following twelve EU countries voted in favor of the resolution and attended at least one session in Nairobi, but made no statement for or against the codification of principles or a Global Pact: Belgium, Czechia, Denmark, Estonia, Finland, Germany, Ireland, Italy, Malta, Romania, Slovakia, and the United Kingdom of Great Britain and Northern Ireland. France presented the proposed Global Pact and the resolution, but made no statement during the Nairobi sessions.

The EU noted that the report's list of principles is not exhaustive, these exist in different variations, and thus more work is needed. It saw potential for the OEWG to work on principles to strengthen environmental protection and suggested considering to what extent and how to address issues. It offered continuing support for a global pact initiative and strengthening IEL and environment-related instruments and disagreed with postponing any discussion of principles until the ILC had finished its work on general principles of law, describing the work of the ILC as responsive and reactive, while it is the role of states to take a lead in developing state practice. The EU said the OEWG's recommendations should include the adoption of an instrument within a certain timeline, where it could be either an instrument approved by the UNGA, a high-level declaration, a legally binding instrument, or some other option. The EU said any work on principles has to take into account their history and context and suggested that the OEWG process could acknowledge the relevance and importance of principles, but also express a commitment by states to be guided by or apply principles when they implement domestic policies. The EU proposed a legally binding instrument or a treaty containing: provisions safeguarding or enhancing environmental protection; and a list of, and other references to, IEL principles, together with other matters, to be possibly combined with a non-legally binding document adopted by 2020 or 2021. The EU stressed the importance of principles, calling for continuing dialogue.

Costa Rica voted in favor of the resolution and is in favor of the Global Pact. The country called for the international community to take advantage of this opportunity to reaffirm commitments to the environment and be ambitious. Arguing the Global Pact provided an opportunity to bolster multilateralism and the leading role of the UN system, the country called for an instrument in the form of a compilation of the main guiding principles of international environmental law, including a categorization of "lesser principles." It highlighted the right to a healthy and ecologically balanced environment. Costa Rica also noted deficiencies in implementation resulting from the proliferation of instruments and called for a centralizing process, hosted and managed by UNEP. The country suggested that there may be a need for the OEWG to have a multiplicity of outcomes.

Colombia voted in favor of the resolution and supported a new binding agreement on principles. The country highlighted the value of codifying existing principles and noted the need to recognize the evolution of principles as well as contributions from regions, such as the jurisprudence of the Inter-American Court of Human Rights. Colombia supported a new instrument to guide general principles that could serve a role in contributing to legal clarity, avoiding potential disputes, awareness raising, and dispute settlement and called for the inclusion of soft law in any compilation. However, Colombia warned that issues and challenges in international environmental law might not be resolved by a new treaty. The country called for further clarification of environmental principles through customary law, governance, and a possible declaration; negotiations that help identify options and consolidate and update principles agreed since the Rio Declaration and for deferring a decision on an international instrument, which would not necessarily be legally binding.

China voted in favor of the resolution and supported the development of a Global Pact. The country highlighted the potential of the Global Pact to strengthen global environmental governance and noted the OEWG should pursue progressive development of international environmental law. However, China highlighted the principles of CBDR and sovereignty over their natural resources as the basis for the engagement of developing countries. China underlined that different countries and scholars have different views on the "content and scope of application" of international environmental law principles and called for more research on the codification process. China also proposed an enhanced role for UNEP in the codification of principles.

Armenia did not vote on the resolution, but was open to a global pact, which it argued needed to be a dynamic document. Additionally, the country called for political will to support reforms in international environmental law. Benin voted in favor of the resolution and wanted to continue further discussion on principles of international environmental law. It called for a careful treatment of issues such as the precautionary principle and suggested focusing on coordination, synergies, and capacity-building. El Salvador did not vote on the resolution but called for strengthening existing principles in international environmental law and clarification of ambiguities. The country favored the Global Pact to strengthen existing principles and empower national implementation. El Salvador reinforced the principles of equity and sovereignty over national resources.[209] The country also underlined the importance of modes of implementation and proposed building on the AAAA. The Gambia did not vote on the resolution but was in favor of continuing the discussion on principles, supporting swift action on a global level for environmental protection. Guinea voted in favor of the resolution and supported bringing all principles into a single instrument.

Indonesia did not vote on the resolution but called for the inclusion of the leading principles of IEL in any new global pact, supporting continued discussion on the subject. The country also proposed to give special attention to the protection of environmental defenders. Uganda did not vote on the resolution but supported continued discussions on principles. The country noted that gaps had not been addressed by the OEWG, despite the opportunity to increase coherence and enhance implementation. Additionally, Uganda called for an implementation programme under UNEP with a longer-term horizon than that of the Montevideo Programme.

Belize did not vote on the resolution and expressed concern that the UNSG's report had gone beyond the mandate of the UNGA resolution, which required a factual, evidence-based report. Speaking for the Alliance of Small Island States (AOSIS), it stressed the need to stay true to the UNGA mandate, saying it remained open to convening an intergovernmental con-

---

209. Documento de Posición de El Salvador Sobre Viabilidad de un Pacto Global Sobre Medio Ambiente. El Salvador (Feb. 20, 2019-02-20 (OEWG's First Session), *available at* https://wedocs.unep.org/handle/20.500.11822/27606.

ference to adopt an instrument and called for the special circumstances of small island developing states to be recognized across all MEAs. Cambodia did not vote on the resolution but was committed to a potential Global Pact. Cameroon did not vote on the resolution. The country recognized the need to harmonize international environmental law but did not believe there was a need to unify it and questioned whether a global pact would resolve problems in implementation. Cameroon called for strengthening means of implementation and enforcement in international environmental law. It called on the OEWG to consider innovative and emerging principles. Cameroon suggested the recommendations of the OEWG should be a single integrated package addressing gaps and challenges, fragmentation of IEL, principles, and implementation. Noting a linkage between means of implementation and principles of international environmental law, the country requested retention of the paragraph on promoting further discussion on principles, calling the principles the "heart" of the global pact process. It additionally supported referring to the parameters for a final outcome of the global pact for the environment process.

Tunisia voted in favor of the resolution and supported further discussions on principles, called for the autonomy of MEAs, and noted the opportunity to improve implementation and overcome environmental challenges. Burkina Farso voted in favor of the resolution and noted that a global pact could help address gaps at the state, regional, and international levels and help bolster the binding nature of general principles of IEL, as well as the implementation role of judges. The country called for delegates to be "candid" when stating whether a pact is possible and underscored the fundamental challenge of implementation of existing agreements. Uruguay is in favor of the codification of principles. The country stressed that unifying the various principles does not contradict diverse MEAs that provide different solutions to specific issues. Uruguay called for the consolidation of existing principles, while tracking their development. Principles should be compiled without being codified, separately from the ILC, so that this compilation can also include new principles. Noting the Montevideo V Programme, the country clarified that it is complementary to the OEWG's work, which shows that new frameworks do not necessarily modify existing MEAs.

The Democratic Republic of Congo (DRC) voted in favor of the resolution and showed support for an overarching instrument, saying it could unify IEL, provide for visibility of its principles, and strengthen cooperation. The country asked for continuing a discussion on principles. However, the DRC also questioned whether a global pact could solve issues in implementation. The country noted the need to strengthen means of implementation available to developing countries. The DRC called for building on progress made in IEL, including the Montevideo Programme and UNEP's role in assisting implementation. Senegal voted in favor of the resolution and supported the idea of a Global Pact. The country called for a Global Pact that should also be a democratic institution for more equity between North and South, and incorporate a human rights and gender-based approach. Senegal highlighted the importance of capacity-building, technology transfer, and coordination of IEL. The country was disappointed with the final recommendations because no action was proposed on a Global Pact.

The Federal States of Micronesia voted in favor of the resolution and supported the idea of a Global Pact. The country highlighted the vulnerability of small island developing states and the need for a comprehensive approach to facilitate implementation. FSM noted a global pact could both call for greater IEL governance synergies between institutions and consolidate a number of principles. The country called for a consolidated approach to existing principles, while tracking their development and particularly objected referring to the discussion on principles by the ILC. The FSM highlighted that a formal instrument can be powerful, whether it is binding or not and called for an expert-led approach to the development of a global pact, including the use of surveys, and for an intergovernmental conference preceded by a one-year preparatory process. The country underlined two case studies demonstrating the need for clarity in, and compilation of, international environmental law principles, citing: a resolution on geoengineering withdrawn at UNEA-4, where the difficulties in garnering consensus demonstrated inconsistent interpretations of the precautionary principle, and the international community's delay in recognizing the right to a healthy environment as an important environmental principle. It noted that MEAs must be viewed as evolving responses to new challenges and said that the process offered a solution to international environmental law's main challenges, including lack of common principles, fragmentation, and the need for attention to MOI.

Guyana voted in favor of the resolution and said a Global Pact can add value in the area of governance. Guyana suggested two pathways for additional research to gain better insight into the need for a Global Pact. The country called for a summary of the gaps discussed with options for how each might be addressed, to help determine the necessity and shape of a Global Pact, as well as a report with a synthesis of how environmental law principles have been treated in domestic jurisprudence and legislation. Guyana urged strengthening means of implementation and cautioned against referring the work on principles to the ILC, suggesting that UNEP be requested to promote it instead. Mali did not vote on the resolution but mentioned its support for the proposal. The country said it was "high time" for a universal legal instrument for environmental law. Monaco voted in favor of the resolution but cautioned against undermining existing agreements. The country stressed the essential role of international legally binding instruments in environmental protection and highlighted the need for unity of international environmental law. Morocco voted in favor of the resolution and reinforced the need to strengthen means of implementation, noting a link to principles. The country supported further discussion on principles and a political declaration.

Mexico supported further discussion on principles and was favorable to a political declaration. The country said a pact should be flexible in its form and legal nature, harmonizing all principles of international environmental law, linking with the 2030 Agenda, and incorporating means of implementation and strengthening relevant UN bodies. Mexico called for clarity in international environmental law and a consolidated approach to existing principles, while tracking their development. UNEP could be responsible for further promoting a discussion on principles. The country called for further negotiations, noting the upcoming anniversary of the Earth Summit in 2022, and possible the adoption of a political declaration linked to the 2030 Agenda and the SDGs, taking account principles and implementation. Nigeria abstained from voting on the resolution. The country supported the codification of environmental principles but noted uncertainty on how it will close gaps.

St. Lucia did not vote on the resolution and attended the Nairobi sessions, making limited statements referring to the need to provide concrete recommendations and an analysis of international environmental law principles and related environmental instruments. While St. Lucia did not explicitly favor the Global Pact or the codification of principles, the country showed support for strengthening environmental principles in their submissions to the OEWG. Samoa did not vote on the resolution but was open to discussing the need for a Global Pact. The country called for greater synergy between regional and international agreements. Serbia did not vote on the resolution but was supportive of the initiative. However, the country noted it would be difficult to seek a global pact, and said the choice was to let the moment pass or risk "tampering" with the system to improve it. Serbia invited delegations to go beyond the UNSG's report to see if a pact could be achieved by examining what is needed for national implementation. Togo did not vote on the resolution and attended the Nairobi sessions, supporting a legally binding instrument and considering socio-economic issues in implementation.

Canada voted in favor of the resolution but was not entirely convinced that a single overarching framework would bring about overall effectiveness in international environmental law, cautioning that a new instrument could reduce resources for existing ones. The country said any discussion on principles is premature and cautioned against unwinding political compromises. Specifically, the country questioned the precise scope and content of environmental obligations, and whether codifying the principle of non-regression would create a risk that states would take on weaker obligations to preserve flexibility in future negotiations. Canada noted that the main gap in international environmental law is in domestic implementation and invited delegations to go beyond the UNSG's report to see if a pact can be achieved by examining what is needed for national implementation. The country recommended considering multiple options for the process, and supported "further discussion" of principles, noting that many of these are already incorporated in MEAs. Finally, Canada expressed concerns about committing to a discussion where an outcome could be pre-judged but indicated support for clarificatory text on the event.

Switzerland did not vote on the resolution but was supportive of negotiating a new agreement. The country said, however, that a pact must not be restricted to codifying principles, nor should it be the sole solution for the gaps, which primarily require better governance structures. Cautioning that reformulating principles could result in regression in established principles of IEL, the country called for any codification to focus on new principles. Switzerland said ambiguity contributed to achieving consensus in MEAs and that, instead of overarching legal principles, bottom-up approaches should be privileged. The country outlined several options to address the possible gaps or challenges related to principles: an instrument; transferring and applying existing principles from one geographic region or level to other regions or levels; and targeting the specific deficit of each principle within its current setting, for instance in the MEA in which the principle is embedded.

Bangladesh voted in favor of the resolution and offered support for any instrument that will reduce gaps between MEAs. However, the country stressed that the principles of existing IEL are the result of prolonged negotiations and represent a delicate balance and suggested that it may be appropriate to consider special and differential treatment of principles in certain circumstances. Bangladesh also noted the consideration of a new instrument should await broad consensus that it will add value. Peru voted in favor of the resolution and underscored that principles such as environmental justice could be included, and that international environmental law is an evolving field responding to new circumstances, creating a regular need to review what has previously been agreed. It said a future instrument should incorporate a human rights and gender-based approach and called for further discussion on principles.

C. *Gray Area*

The majority of countries fall within a gray zone of an undefined position, either because their participation in Nairobi was limited, attending none or few sessions, or having made limited statements. In total, 82 countries are characterized as "undefined." Additionally, 35 countries have not participated in any part of the discussion so far (Afghanistan, Bahamas, Cabo Verde, Dominica, Dominican Republic, Fiji, Grenada, Guinea-Bissau, Haiti, Jamaica, Kazakhstan, Kiribati, Kyrgyzstan, Lao People's Democratic Republic, Lesotho, Lichtenstein, Marshall Islands, Mauritius, Mozambique, Namibia, Nauru, Oman, Palau, Papua New Guinea, Republic of Moldova, Saint Vincent and the Grenadines, San Marino, San Tomé and Príncipe, Soloman Islands, South Sudan, Trinidad and Tobago, Uzbekistan, Vanuatu, Yemen, Zimbabwe). As such, 117 can still be persuaded one way or another. However, it should be noted that several of these might vote as a group.

The following 22 countries did not vote on the resolution and attended at least one session in Nairobi, but made no statement for or against the codification of principles or a Global Pact: Antigua and Barbuda, Azerbaijan, Botswana, Comoros, Congo, Fiji, the Holy See, Iceland, Israel, Kuwait, Liberia, Mongolia, Myanmar, Nepal, Panama, Rwanda, Saint Kitts and Nevis, Sierra Leone, the State of Palestine, Sudan, Ukraine, Vietnam. Thirteen countries (Albania, Andorra, Angola, Bosnia and Herzegovina, Bulgaria, Central African Republic, Equatorial Guinea, Ghana, Libya, Montenegro, Seychelles, the former Yuguslav Republic of Macedonia, Turkmenistan) voted in favor of the resolution but did not attend any of the sessions in Nairobi. Some attended only the organizational session in New York, including Barbados, Brunei Darussalam, Tonga, Slovenia, and the United Arab Emirates. The following nine countries voted in favor of the resolution and attended at least one session in Nairobi but made no statement for or against the codification of principles or a Global Pact: Bhutan, Jordan, Lebanon, Madagascar, Niger, Qatar, Sri Lanka, Suriname, and Tuvalu. Two countries, Belarus and Tajikistan, abstained from voting on the resolution and did not attended any sessions. Nicaragua abstained from voting on the resolution and reinforced the need to strengthen means of implementation.

A few countries mildly favored further discussion on principles or the idea of a Global Pact. Côte d'Ivoire did not vote on the resolution and made limited remarks during the third session, asking for further discussion on principles and more regional discussion. Gabon voted in favor of the resolution and requested furthering the discussion on principles. Malawi did not vote on the resolution and called for strengthening means of implementation available to developing countries. The country supported a continued discussion on principles. Eswatini did not vote on the resolution and remained open to discussing a new instrument providing it was agreed by consensus by Member States.[210] Tanzania did not vote on the resolution and made limited statements during the sessions. The country reinforced modes of implementation but opposed adding reference to international environmental governance on strengthening implementation. Tanzania objected the specific mention of environmental defenders or indigenous peoples and local communities. Maldives did not vote on the resolution and made limited statements underlining the role of Montevideo Programme V and challenges in national implementation. Burundi did not vote on the resolution and attended the Nairobi sessions, but made limited statements. The country said consideration of a new instrument should await broad consensus that it will add value, linked the process to the SDGs, and called for more specificity on MEAs and cooperation.

Iraq did not vote on the resolution and was conscious about avoiding duplicating existing MEAs. The country stressed that a global pact should support the most vulnerable countries, include the principle of CBDR, achieve climate justice and respect national sovereignty. Algeria did not vote on the resolution but expressed full support of the OEWG's work. The country cautioned against re-negotiating international agreements and noted that some principles identified in the report do not enjoy universal support due to national policies. It reinforced the need for strengthened implementation. Pakistan did not vote on the resolution and attended one session in Nairobi but made a limited statement on the need to simplify international environmental law and increase environmental protection without detrimentally affecting developing countries.

210. Statement of the Kingdom of Eswatini to the Co-Chairs Non-Paper Draft Recommendations (OEWG Third Session), *available at* https://wedocs.unep.org/bitstream/handle/20.500.11822/28338/Eswatini_Statement.pdf?sequence=1&isAllowed=y.

New Zealand did not vote on the resolution and questioned how an overarching one-size-fits-all framework could improve the situation in areas such as marine pollution. The country endorsed the benefits of coordination and synergies and welcomed the positive results international environmental law had already achieved. Honduras did not vote on the resolution and made limited statements during the sessions, stressing the principle of CBDR should be included in any potential instrument. Bahrain did not vote on the resolution. The country suggesting clarifying principles and objectives such as sustainable development but was concerned about the risk of new instruments on duplicating and repeating existing MEAs. Bahrain proposed language on modes of implementation as a prerequisite to upholding states' respective obligations and commitments. Australia did not vote on the resolution and was cautious about the process of issuing recommendations to the UNGA. The country was concerned about the effect of a potential new agreement on existing international environmental law and how it would relate to national laws. Australia also questioned how the Global Pact would address the gaps identified in the UNSG's Report. South Africa did not vote on the resolution and attended the Nairobi sessions, highlighting the need for means of implementation and strengthened multilateral approaches. South Africa supported the development of a non-legally binding instrument.

Eritrea did not vote on the resolution. Speaking for the African Group, the country cautioned against undermining existing agreements, called for strengthening UNEP's role, and underlined the role of the AAAA and the 2030 Agenda. Zambia did not vote on the resolution and made limited statements on the sessions. Speaking for the African Group, the country questioned several dimensions of the UNSG's report, including that it does not sufficiently account for the role of the Rio and Stockholm Declarations, and suggested that strengthening the role of UNEP could play a central role in improving coordination in international environmental law. Ethiopia did not vote on the resolution and did not express strong views for or against a new instrument. However, speaking for G-77/China, the country reinforced the need for increasing means of implementation and capacity-building and made sure to reinforce that the principles of sovereignty over national resources and common but differentiated responsibilities should be included in any potential agreement.

Singapore did not vote on the resolution and expressed concern about the risk of undermining existing international environmental law. The country questioned whether international environmental law principles should apply wholesale in areas such as trade, investment, intellectual property, and human rights. Singapore noted limited support among states for the adoption of a legally binding instrument, calling for a pragmatic approach to other possible options and the consideration of the principles in the specific context of MEAs, as well as different national circumstances in the principles' application. Singapore ultimately agreed that the OEWG should not recommend that UNGA adopt an instrument.

Chile voted in favor of the resolution and mildly favored a global pact during the first session. The country suggested analyzing which principles of international environmental law were generally agreed upon and going beyond the UNSG's report to see if a pact could be achieved by examining the needs for national implementation. However, Chile was concerned about undermining existing MEAs and invited an examination of the effects of a treaty on international environmental law. Additionally, it called for focusing the discussions during the second session on how to improve coordination and synergies between MEAs. It also presented a comprehensive view of the discussions, involving norms, institutions, and implementation. Chile did not object to language referring to the promotion of further discussion on principles during the third session but said a new instrument could be counterproductive and lead to duplication of efforts since there was no consensus on a new global platform to address gaps. Kenya voted in favor of the resolution and underlined the 1992 Rio Declaration as a source of core principles of IEL, together with the principles of non-regression and progression as set out in the Paris Agreement.

Chad voted in favor of the resolution. The country attended the Nairobi sessions but made limited comments stressing the importance of access to justice and capacity-building for national implementation, as well as "strengthening" UNEP's role. Georgia voted in favor of the resolution and reinforced the need to support developing countries in implementing international environmental law. Guatemala voted in favor of the resolution and attended two sessions, making limited statements calling for language on preventing environmental damage. Paraguay voted in favor of the resolution and attended one session, making a limited statement on the need to bolster already existing coordination mechanisms between the UN and MEAs.

Norway voted in favor of the resolution and expressed doubt as to the merits of a legally binding pact, suggesting that recommendations to the UNGA could address the need to strengthen international environmental law. Norway further noted that many principles are already established in customary international law, based on the Stockholm and Rio Declarations, and questioned how overarching codification could change and risk adversely affecting the application and interpretation of principles in individual MEAs.

Document 5: The Nairobi Outcome Statement (Recommendations, as Agreed by the Working Group) (May 2019)[1]

The ad hoc open-ended working group established by General Assembly Resolution 72/277 of 10 May 2018 entitled "Towards a Global Pact for the Environment" recommends to the General Assembly the following:

1. Objectives guiding the recommendations:

   a) reinforce the protection of the environment for present and future generations

   b) uphold respective obligations and commitments under international environmental law of States members of the United Nations and members of specialized agencies

   c) contribute to the strengthening of implementation of international environmental law and environment-related instruments

   d) support the full implementation of the 2030 Agenda for Sustainable Development, as well as the outcome of the UN Conference on Environment and Development (Rio+20), including its paragraphs 88 and 89

   e) not undermine existing relevant legal instruments and frameworks and relevant global, regional and sectoral bodies

2. Substantive recommendations:

   a) reaffirms the role of the United Nations Environment Programme (UNEP) as the leading global environmental authority that sets the global environmental agenda, promotes the coherent implementation of the environmental dimension of sustainable development within the United Nations system and serves as an authoritative advocate for the global environment, and the role of the United Nations Environment Assembly (UNEA)

   b) calls for renewed efforts at all levels to enhance the implementation of existing obligations and commitments under international environmental law, stressing the importance of enhanced ambition regarding means of implementation, including the provision and mobilization of all types and sources of means of implementation, consistent with the Addis Ababa Action Agenda and the 2030 Agenda for Sustainable Development

   c) recognizes the role of discussions on principles of international environmental law for enhancing the implementation of international environmental law, also noting the ongoing work in the International Law Commission on general principles of law

1. Adopted by the UNGA in September 2019, as detailed in the next chapter.

d) invites the scientific community to further their work on interconnected and crosscutting issues by sharing information among the leading scientific, technical and technological bodies that inform the work of Multilateral Environmental Agreements and environmental processes, as well encourages the scientific, technical and technological bodies to strengthen cooperation among themselves

e) invites the governing bodies of the Multilateral Environmental Agreements, while preserving their independence and respective mandates, to increase their efforts to promote policy coherence across environmental instruments at all relevant levels and to consider identifying and addressing implementation challenges in their regimes, with a view to strengthening implementation at the national and international level

f) invites the governing bodies and secretariats of Multilateral Environmental Agreements to enhance cooperation and collaboration among themselves within the scope of their respective mandates, as well as between them and UNEP and UNEA, building on work already done

g) encourages the governing bodies of Multilateral Environmental Agreements and scientific, technical and technological bodies to exchange information and experiences, including with a view to considering the streamlining of reporting and/or monitoring processes

h) encourages all that have not done so to consider ratifying Multilateral Environmental Agreements and to effectively implement them

i) encourages States members of the United Nations and all members of the specialized agencies to strengthen, where needed, environmental laws, policies and regulatory frameworks at the national level, as well as the capacities across all sectors for the effective implementation of international environmental law, including the administrative and justice sectors in accordance with national legal systems, while acknowledging the importance of international cooperation in supporting and complementing national actions

j) encourages States members of the United Nations and all members of the specialized agencies to mainstream environment into sectoral policies and programs at all levels, including into national development and sustainable development plans, to enhance the implementation of international environmental law and applicable environment-related instruments

k) encourages active and meaningful engagement of all relevant stakeholders at all levels in the different *fora* related to the implementation of international environment law and environment-related instruments

l) explores further ways for States members of the United Nations and all members of the specialized agencies to support and make full use of the Fifth Programme for the Development and Periodic Review of Environmental Law

(Montevideo Programme V) adopted by the fourth session of the United Nations Environment Assembly, in order to foster the environmental rule of law and advance the implementation of environmental law at all levels

m) encourages the United Nations Environment Program, as Chair of the Environment Management Group (EMG) and in collaboration with the members of the Group, to continue to strengthen system-wide inter-agency coordination on environment and to call for active involvement and support of all EMG members for the implementation of system-wide strategies on the environment

3. Consideration of further work:

The working group recommends that the General Assembly:

a) Circulates the above-mentioned recommendations and make them available to States members of the United Nations and members of Specialized Agencies and the Governing Bodies of Multilateral Environment Agreements for their consideration and action, as appropriate

b) Forwards these recommendations to the United Nations Environment Assembly for its consideration, and to prepare, at its fifth session in February 2021, a political declaration for a UN high level meeting subject to voluntary funding, in the context of the commemoration of the creation of UN Environment Programme by the United Nations Conference on the Human Environment held in Stockholm from 5-16 June 1972, with a view to strengthening the implementation of international environmental law, and international environmental governance in line with paragraph 88 of the "Future We Want".

Document 6: ICEL's Analysis of the Consensus Recommendations (June 2019)

INTERNATIONAL COUNCIL OF ENVIRONMENTAL LAW (ICEL) - JUNE 2019

ANALYSIS OF THE CONSENSUS RECOMMENDATIONS TO STRENGTHEN IMPLEMENTATION OF INTERNATIONAL ENVIRONMENTAL LAW UNDER UNGA RESOLUTION 72/277 "TOWARDS A GLOBAL PACT FOR THE ENVIRONMENT"

(as agreed by the Ad Hoc Open-Ended Working Group in Nairobi on 22 May 2019)

Executive Summary

ICEL submits this Note to provide an analysis of the Recommendations by the ad hoc open-ended working group, based on consultations held in Nairobi between January and May 2019. The ad hoc open-ended working group considered the Report of the UN Secretary General on "Gaps in international environmental law and environment-related instruments: towards a global pact for the environment" (A/73/419, 30 November 2018), pursuant to UNGA Resolution 72/277 (10 May 2018) "Towards a global pact for the environment." The Recommendations, adopted by consensus, for consideration by the General Assembly, are reproduced below.

Thereafter, this Note provides (1) brief observations on the constructive work of the consultations, under the able Co-Chairs; (2) comments on the Objectives, which state the principles that serve as foundations for the Recommendations; (3) analysis of the several substantive recommendations; and (4) observations on the further work that now will be the focus of the UN General Assembly.

The Recommendations, taken as a whole, constitute a significant milestone towards achieving an enhanced framework of cooperation among States — and of coordination within the UN System — to strengthen the implementation of environmental law and support the full implementation of the 2030 Agenda for Sustainable Development, the mandate under Resolution 72/277, within a precise timeframe in the period 2019-2022. ICEL finds that the consensus is a positive step forward toward providing institutional and policy steps that are essential for the realization of the Sustainable Development Goals.

On the issue of solidifying established principles of international environmental law for enhancing the implementation of international environmental law, while recognizing the role of discussions on principles, there is no clear path forward. The same is true for the preparations of the UN high level meeting for the 50th commemoration of the creation of the UN Environment Programme by the United Nations Conference on the Human Environment in 2022.

This Note sets forth an independent assessment by a working group of expert members of the International Council of Environmental Law (ICEL).[1] Since 1969, when it was established in New Delhi, ICEL has advanced knowledge on international environmental law and the legal foundations for sustainable development. As an international non-governmental organization accredited to the UN Economic and Social Council since 1973, ICEL has shared its expertise with ECOSOC, UN Members States, and international organizations. ICEL's members are senior environmental law experts drawn from all of the UN regions and all legal traditions: civil law, common law, socialist law, Islamic law, and customary law.

Note on the Recommendations of the Ad Hoc Open-Ended-Working Group Established by General Assembly Resolution 72/277, Adopted in Nairobi on May 22, 2019

(1) Welcoming the Nairobi 2019 Consensus Recommendations

This Note welcomes the Recommendations agreed by the ad hoc open-ended working group (OEWG) established by UNGA Resolution 72/277, "Towards a global pact for the environment,"[2] at the conclusion of three substantive meetings in Nairobi, Kenya, on 22 May 2019.[3] The Recommendations constitute a significant milestone towards achieving an enhanced framework of cooperation among States — and of coordination within the UN System — to strengthen the implementation of environmental law and support the full implementation of the 2030 Agenda for Sustainable Development within a precise timeframe in the period 2019-2022. ICEL finds that the consensus is a positive step forward toward providing institutional and policy steps that are essential for the realization of the Sustainable Development Goals (SDGs). It was important to reach a constructive outcome that can grow in ambition and commitment as all Member States, the entire UN system, and civil society contribute to their implementation.

The underlying concern stated in Resolution 72/277 is the "need to continue to address, in a comprehensive and coherent manner, the challenges posed by environmental degradation in the context of sustainable development." To be sure, the severity of the state of the environment caused by anthropogenic stress on the Earth's ecosystem, evidences the critical need for immediate action by all. Among the recent scientific assessments, the Global Environmental Outlook 6 indicates: *"sustainable development targets and internationally agreed goals are not expected to be achieved, including on climate change, biodiversity loss, water scarcity, excess nutrient*

---

1. ICEL was founded in New Delhi in 1969 and is constituted under Article 60 of the Swiss Civil Code (Canton of Geneva). It has been accredited to the UN Economic and Social Council (ECOSOC) since 1973, and maintains representatives in Bonn, Geneva, Nairobi, and New York. It is a Member of IUCN. Contact via ICEL Executive Governor at nrobinson@law.pace.edu.
2. A/RES/72/277, *available at* https://undocs.org/A/RES/72/277.
3. *See* Recommendations, *at* https://www.unenvironment.org/events/conference/towards-global-pact-environment.

run-off, land degradation and ocean acidification (well established).'[4] And the Global Assessment Report on Biodiversity and Ecosystem Services notes: "*Past and ongoing rapid declines in biodiversity, ecosystem functions and many of nature's contributions to people mean that most international societal and environmental goals, such as those embodied in the Aichi Biodiversity Targets and the 2030 Agenda for Sustainable Development, will not be achieved based on current trajectories. These declines will also undermine other goals, such as those specified in the Paris Agreement adopted under the United Nations Framework Convention on Climate Change and the 2050 Vision for Biodiversity.*"[5]

Therefore, the purpose of this Note is to analyze the significance of the Recommendations and how to advance them for prompt "*consideration and action*"[6] by all the Member States, Specialized Agencies, and the Governing Bodies of Multilateral Environment Agreements (MEAs), taking into account the first report ever issued by the U.N. Secretary-General concerning the field of international environmental law, A/73/419 (30 November 2018).[7] In addition, the Note offers suggestions on the way forward to prepare for the fifth session of the United Nations Environment Assembly (UNEA), in February 2021, and for a momentous UN high level meeting for the 50th commemoration of the creation of UN Environment Programme (UNEP) by the United Nations Conference on the Human Environment in 2022.

Significantly, the UN High-Level Political Forum on Sustainable Development (HLPF) — not mentioned in the Recommendations — launched by the General Assembly following the Rio+20 outcome document ("The Future We Want"), is the universal, intergovernmental forum in charge of reviewing the implementation of sustainable development commitments and providing guidance on the follow-up of the 2030 Agenda and the SDGs. The HLPF will meet twice in 2019. In July, under the auspices of ECOSOC, for the fourth time, at which point it would have completed a first-round review of all 17 SDGs and means of implementation. In September, for the first time, under the auspices of the General Assembly, at the level of Heads of State and Government, to discuss the overall status of implementation of the 2030 Agenda and to prepare a political declaration on the subject. Thus, the Recommendations are timely input for the HLPF, at both meetings in 2019.

---

4. *See* https://www.unenvironment.org/resources/global-environment-outlook-6, Summary for Policy-Makers at 4.1. See also ***Global Land Outlook*** produced by the UN Convention to Combat Desertification Secretariat in 2017: "Scientific knowledge on dryland production systems remains underdeveloped and is often side-lined in favor of management approaches that have been developed for humid lands. This is compounded by inadequate data on dryland environments and economies, which allow important decisions to be made in an information vacuum"; https://knowledge.unccd.int/publication/full-report, at 64; see also the first World Ocean Assessment: https://www.un.org/Depts/los/global_reporting/WOA_RegProcess.htm; "Knowledge Gaps" are identified at 42 to 47.
5. Global assessment report on biodiversity and ecosystem services of the Intergovernmental Science-Policy Platform on Biodiversity and Ecosystem Services (IPBES) (May 2019), *available at* https://www.ipbes.net/global-assessment-report-biodiversity-ecosystem-services.
6. Recommendations, 3(a) (emphasis supplied).
7. *See* UN Secretary-General's Report on "Gaps in International Environmental Law and Environment-Related instruments: Towards a Global Pact for the Environment" (A/73/419, 30 November 2018), *at* https://globalpact.informea.org/report.

ICEL commends the hard work of the Co-Chairs, and the support of the Secretariat, to arrive at meaningful substantive Recommendations to fulfill the mandate set forth in Resolution 72/277. The fruitful consultations have sufficiently identified challenges in relation to principles, governance and implementation, and possible actions by Member States, Governing Bodies of MEAs, and the entire UN System, to tackle these challenges in order to advance environmental law and SGD implementation. The Recommendations mostly deal with the "what" is needed, however, and do not sufficiently address the "how" or the "when" to review or follow-up on such actions and challenges.

ICEL respectfully offers two suggestions on the way forward to prepare for UNEA-5, in February 2021, and the UN high level meeting in the context of the 50th commemoration of the creation of the UNEP by the UN Conference on the Human Environment in 2022. First, it would be appropriate for the General Assembly and all the relevant organs and bodies of the UN System and governing bodies of MEAs, to develop follow-up processes on the Recommendations to have meaningful input for UNEA-5 and the HLPF. Since a multifaceted response is called for, ICEL would encourage developing concrete actions to address the Recommendations, as well as the means and actors with authority to act on the solutions.

Second, for an adequate preparatory process leading to the UN high level meeting, ICEL proposes that the General Assembly establish a preparatory committee for the 2022 anniversaries, with the mandate to draft decisions and a declaration that would contribute to implementation of the SDGs, taking into account the input from UNEA-5 on strengthening the implementation of international environmental law and international environmental governance. By 2022 we shall have seven years of experience in working to attain the SDGs by 2030, and the encouragement of a new Declaration would stimulate the additional cooperation needed to attain the SDGs.

The significance of the consensus-based Recommendations — although there was no agreement to kick-start an intergovernmental conference to adopt an international instrument to strengthen the implementation of international environmental law — is that they are the first step in a process that launched a commitment "to address, in a comprehensive and coherent manner, the challenges posed by environmental degradation in the context of sustainable development," the stated purpose in Resolution 72/277. Indeed, *"[s]ince the relevant environmental problems at stake are often of a global nature, the solution lies in collective action. The challenge is to encourage the participation of all relevant actors while at the same time ensuring that the commitments are ambitious enough to provide for an effective response to the problem, and to ensure that parties comply with their obligations,"* notes the Secretary-General's Report, referencing the work of Elinor Ostrom and Professor Scott Barret.[8]

8. *Id.* para. 23; *see* ELINOR OSTROM, GOVERNING THE COMMONS: THE EVOLUTION OF INSTITUTIONS FOR COLLECTIVE ACTION (Cambridge University Press, 1990); *see also* Elinor Ostrom, *Polycentric Systems for Coping With Collective Action and Global Environmental Change*, GLOBAL ENVTL. CHANGE, vol.

Remarkably, as mandated by Resolution 72/277, voluntary contributions, reaching approximately USD 2 million, funded the activities of the AOWG, and the special voluntary trust fund for the purpose of assisting developing countries—in particular, the least developed countries, landlocked developing countries and small island developing States—to attend the consultations. Despite this special voluntary trust fund, many Member States were unable to send delegations to Nairobi. Thus, it was important to reach a constructive outcome that can grow in ambition and gain the commitment of all Member States and the entire UN system. ICEL congratulates the donors that enabled the first intergovernmental review on the status of international environmental law and environmental governance needed to support the full implementation of international environmental law, environment-related instruments, the 2030 Agenda and the SDGs.

The Recommendations to the General Assembly include three sections. Section one, lays out the 5 objectives guiding the recommendations. Section two, with 13 substantive recommendations, can be divided in 6 subgroups: on the role of UNEP, on means of implementation, on principles of international environmental law, on strengthening the science-policy interface; on governance and effective MEAs, and on implementation challenges. Finally, section three, has 2 recommendations on the consideration of further work. The compromise text is based on the Co-Chairs' non-paper on draft elements of recommendations, dated 25 April 2019, input for the third substantive meeting, and three versions of draft recommendations by the Co-Chairs during the meeting May 20-22.[9]

(2) Comments on the Objectives Guiding the Recommendations

General Commentary: This section is highly commendable because five principles serve as foundations for the Recommendations and will guide and maintain an enhanced level of ambition as the Recommendations are carried-out by Member States, all within the UN System, and the Governing Bodies of MEAs. These five objectives are also essential to help galvanize active and meaningful engagement of all relevant stakeholders at all levels for the implementation of international environment law, environment-related instruments, and the 2030 Agenda for Sustainable Development.

20, No. 2 (October 2010); *see* Scott Barrett, *Environment and Statecraft: The Strategy of Environmental Treaty-Making* (Oxford University Press, 2003).

9. First version, Draft recommendations "zero draft" (dated May 20, 2019), presented during the beginning of the second day of consultations, with revisions to sections one and two of the non-paper, in response to suggestions from delegations during the first day. Section three of the "zero draft", on consideration of further work, was placed in brackets pending informal group consultations, co-facilitated by Elizabeth Taylor (Colombia's representative) and Solveig Crompton (Norway's representative). Second version, revised Draft recommendations (dated May 21, 2019), again with revisions to sections one and two, input for the final day of the meeting. Third version, revised Draft recommendations (dated May 22, 2019), included further revisions to sections one and two, and a rethought section three, upon which final consensus was reached, after certain amendments were negotiated at the closing plenary. *See* https://www.unenvironment.org/events/conference/towards-global-pact-environment.

a) reinforce the protection of the environment for present and future generations

Commentary: It is commendable that the Recommendations embrace intergenerational environmental protection as the first objective. Enshrined in the UN Charter's preamble, the welfare of both present and future generations, is also at the center of the UN's soon-to-be five decades long intergovernmental process to address environmental protection and sustainable development.[10] Principle 1 of the Stockholm Declaration of the UN Conference on the Human Environment in 1972, unequivocally expresses the common conviction that humankind "has the fundamental right to freedom, equality and adequate conditions of life, in an environment of a quality that permits a life of dignity and well-being, and ... *bears a solemn responsibility to protect and improve the environment for present and future generations.*"[11]

Intergenerational equity is also at the heart of the Brundtland Commission's formulation of sustainable development, arguably the most accepted definition: development that "meets the needs of the present without compromising the ability of future generations to meet their own needs".[12] And Principle 3 of the Rio Declaration on Environment and Development states that "[t]he right to development must be fulfilled so as to *equitably meet developmental and environmental needs of present and future generations.*"[13] As noted in the Draft International Covenant on Environment and Development by IUCN and ICEL, "[a]lthough it is difficult to predict with precision the aspirations of future generations, the basic human needs and values expressed in the two 1966 United Nations Covenants on Human Rights must be taken as the minimum requirements."[14]

Professor Edith Brown Weiss, devoted scholar of intergenerational equity, explains, "is based on the concept that each generation holds the Earth in common with other generations, past and future, with obligations to protect it for future generations and rights to benefit from it. It is based on a fundamental norm of fairness between generations in the conservation and use of the environment and its natural resources. *It provides a foundation for sustainable development, but it extends beyond it.*"[15] Further, "[i]ntergenerational equity has deep roots in diverse cultural and religious traditions, including the Judeo-Christian, Islamic, and Asian non-theistic traditions. It has roots in

10. *See* Edith Brown Weiss, Intergeneration Equity, *in Global Pact for the Environment, Legal Foundations* (herein "GPE Legal Foundations") (Cambridge University, C-EENRG Report 2019-1, March 2019), *available at* https://globalpactenvironment.org/uploads/Aguila-Vinuales-A-Global-Pact-for-the-Environment-Cambridge-Report-March-2019.pdf.
11. Principle 1 of the Declaration of the United Nations Conference on the Human Environment in 1972, *available at* http://www.un-documents.net/unchedec.htm.
12. Report of the WCED (Brundtland Commission), Our Common Future (1987), 51.
13. *See* http://www.un-documents.net/rio-dec.htm.
14. IUCN & ICEL, *Draft International Covenant on Environment and Development* (Fifth Edition, 2015), *available at* https://sustainabledevelopment.un.org/content/documents/2443Covenant_5th_edition.pdf.
15. *See* Edith Brown Weiss, Intergeneration Equity, *in GPE Legal Foundations, supra* note 10, at 51 (emphasis supplied).

Islamic law, civil law, common law, customary law in African and other communities, and Native American traditional law," points out Professor Brown Weiss.[16]

The Secretary-General's Report highlighted intergenerational equity as the fundamental goal of the process under Resolution 72/277, in the final conclusion: *We must collectively seize the opportunity to use international environmental law in new and dynamic ways to provide a strong and effective governance regime with a view to better safeguarding the environment for future generations.*[17] The Report does not specifically discuss the principle of intergenerational equity, however, although it is imbedded in the principle of sustainable development, addressed in the Report, which "is undeniably a cornerstone of international environmental law that has shaped the field since at least the 1980's."[18]

The Report moreover states that sustainable development is not simply a "soft law" principle, but that "[m]any international environmental law treaties make explicit or implicit references to the essential tenets of sustainable development," and that "is also referred to in other international agreements, such as trade and investment treaties and WTO agreements."[19] Furthermore, "international courts and tribunals have embraced sustainable development as a source of law and policy when addressing treaty implementation and the interpretation of norms."[20] As Professor Christina Voigt describes it, "sustainable development is a principle with normative content, which is defined by *the integration of present and future economic, social and environmental interests within limits set by certain essential ecological functions*."[21]

Intergenerational equity is also central to rights-based environmental protection, incorporated in at least 155 State Constitutions. This was rightly recognized in the 1993 landmark ruling by the Supreme Count of the Philippines in the case *Oposa Minors et al v. Factoran*, noting that "unless the rights to a balanced and healthful ecology and to health are mandated as state policies by the Constitution itself, thereby highlighting their continuing importance and imposing upon the state a solemn obligation to preserve the first and protect and advance the second, *the day would not be too far when all else would be lost not only for the present generation, but also for those to come — generations which stand to inherit nothing but parched earth incapable of sustaining life*."[22]

The Court also noted that intergenerational equity and the right to a balanced and healthful ecology are not "less important than any of the civil and political rights" and belong "to a different category of rights altogether for *it concerns nothing less than self-preservation and self-perpetuation ... the advancement of which may even be*

16. *Id.*
17. UN Secretary-General's Report (A/73/419), *supra* note 7, para. 113.
18. Virginie Barral and Pierre-Marie Dupuy, Sustainable Development and Integration, *in GPE Legal Foundations, supra* note 10, p. 44.
19. UN Secretary-General's Report (A/73/419), *supra* note 7, para. 20.
20. *Id.*
21. Cristina Voigt, *Sustainable Development as a Principle of International Law: Resolving Conflicts Between Climate Measures and WTO Law* (Martinus Nijhoff, 2009), p. 186.
22. Supreme Count of the Philippines in Oposa Minors et al. v. Factoran, G.R. No. 101083 July 30, 1993 (emphasis supplied).

said to predate all governments and constitutions. As a matter of fact, these basic rights need not even be written in the Constitution for they are assumed to exist from the inception of humankind."[23]

Finally, stressing intergeneration equity as the cornerstone objective guiding the Recommendations is meaningful because the principle of sustainable development "has been incorporated into the larger global agenda by the 2030 Agenda for Sustainable Development and the Sustainable Development Goals," [24] and the fourth objective guiding the recommendations, discussed below, is to "support the full implementation of the 2030 Agenda for Sustainable Development."

b) uphold respective obligations and commitments under international environmental law of States members of the United Nations and members of specialized agencies

and

c) contribute to the strengthening of implementation of international environmental law and environment-related instruments

Commentary: These two objectives are the essence of the mandate set forth in Resolution 72/277. Regarding b), it is worth noting the importance of including the commitments of member of UN specialized agencies, such as FAO, IMO, IAEA, ICAO and ILO, as the entire UN System must coherently address, and mutually support, the Recommendations.

Regarding c), it is worth noting the reference to "environment-related instruments". This expression "is taken to include those international legal instruments that do not fall exclusively within the field of the environment or have as their primary objective the protection of the environment. In this regard, it may be noted that environmental concerns have gradually penetrated other international regulatory frameworks, such as those dealing with international trade, investment, intellectual property rights, human rights, peace and security, migration and disaster management."[25] Therefore, the Recommendations embrace a holistic approach to pursue an effective legal framework to deliver on the sustainable development commitments and goals, discussed below.

d) support the full implementation of the 2030 Agenda for Sustainable Development, as well as the outcome of the UN Conference on

23. *Id. See also* Opinion and Order of November 10, 2016 by U.S. District Judge A. Aiken in *Juliana et al. v US et al.* – Case No. 6:15-cv-01517-TC: *"This action is of a different order than the typical environmental case," … "It alleges that the defendant's action and inactions … have so profoundly damaged the home planet that they threaten [the] plaintiffs' fundamental constitutional rights to life and liberty." "No doubt that the right to a climate system capable of sustaining human life is fundamental to a free and ordered society … a stable climate system is quite literally the foundation of society, without which there would be neither civilization nor progress".*

24. UN Secretary-General's Report (A/73/419), *supra* note 7, para. 20.

25. *Id.* para. 7.

Environment and Development (Rio+20), including its paragraphs 88 and 89

Commentary: The global consensus on the SDGs and the 2030 Agenda is a landmark achievement.[26] The SDGs make clear the gravity of today's environmental and social problems. Resolution 72/277 explicitly reaffirms the General Assembly's "commitment to working tirelessly for the full implementation of the Agenda by 2030." The UN Secretary-General's Report underscores that sustainable development principles have been incorporated into the larger global agenda by the 2030 Agenda for Sustainable Development.[27] However, the fragmented character of international environmental law is halting implementation and is likely to retard the attainment of all of the SDGs.

A major hurdle is that MEAs are not yet fully linked to all SDGs. For example, the principles and objectives found in the Convention on Biodiversity or the Ramsar Convention on Wetlands, are not tied to the terrestrial goals expressed in SDG 15. The UN Secretary-General's Report also stresses the importance of effective implementation of the legal framework established by the UN Convention on the Law of the Sea (UNCLOS) and its implementing agreements in order to achieve SDG 14 on oceans, seas and marine resources.[28] Whereas, governance, access to justice and information principles are central to all the SDGs, as set forth in SDG 16.[29] Clarification and reinforcement of international environmental law will promote the links between international and national environmental law and sustainable development, facilitate SDG integration, and contribute to a transformative realization of sustainability goals.

Arguably, the greatest hindrance to implementing environmental laws, both national and MEAS, as well as the 2030 Agenda, is the lack of shared commitment by States to making the environmental protection and the 2030 Agenda an over-arching priority. This has impeded sustainable development in the past and will also work to undermine the successful achievement of the SDGs. The Recommendations aim to address this central, circular, concern. First, calling for strengthening the capacity and synergies across the UN system to support the integration of the environment in the implementation of the 2030 Agenda. Second, seeking to promote the convergence of different strategies and to mainstream environment system-wide strategies into policies and programs at all levels. In addition, the Recommendations reference to the full implementation of UN Conference on Environment and Development (Rio+20), including its paragraphs 88 and 89. This is an acknowledgement that the commitments to enhance environmental governance must be fulfilled. These topics are further discussed in the commentary to substantive Recommendations below.

26. Macharia Kamau, Pamela Chasek, David C. O'Connor, Transforming Multilateral Diplomacy—The Inside Story of the Sustainable Development Goals (Routledge, 2018).

27. UN Secretary-General's Report (A/73/419), *supra* note 7, para. 20.

28. *Id.* para. 60.

29. *See* Marcos Orellana, *Governance and the Sustainable Development Goals: The Increasing Relevance of Access Rights in Principle 10 of the Rio Declaration*, Rev. Eur., Comp. & Int'l L., vol. 25, No. 1 (2016).

e) not undermine existing relevant legal instruments and frameworks and relevant global, regional and sectoral bodies

Commentary: Resolution 72/277 states that the process, and resulting implementation, "should not undermine existing relevant legal instruments and frameworks and relevant global, regional and sectoral bodies." This mandate for non-regression was echoed repeatedly by the delegations, many of which also called for progression. As noted in the Secretary-General's report, "[n]on -regression aims at ensuring that environmental protection is not weakened, while progression aims at the improvement of environmental legislation, including by increasing the level of protection, on the basis of the most recent scientific knowledge."[30] The concern over regression seems to have been overcome, but the issue of progression — linked to the level of ambition and challenges ahead — needs further consideration as the process launched by Resolution 72/277 continues in the coming years.

(3) Analysis of the Substantive recommendations

— On the role of UNEP:

a) reaffirms the role of the United Nations Environment Programme (UNEP) as the leading global environmental authority that sets the global environmental agenda, promotes the coherent implementation of the environmental dimension of sustainable development within the United Nations system and serves as an authoritative advocate for the global environment, and the role of the United Nations Environment Assembly (UNEA)

Commentary: The Recommendations reaffirm UNEP's and UNEA's established roles within the UN System. As the Secretary-General's Report notes: "[t]he role of UNEP as the leading global environmental authority that sets the global environmental agenda, promotes the coherent implementation of the environmental dimension of sustainable development within the United Nations system and serves as the authoritative advocate for the global environment was reaffirmed in Agenda 21, the Nairobi Declaration on the Role and Mandate of UNEP and the outcome document of the Rio+20 Conference, entitled "The future we want".[31]

Specifically, the Rio+20 outcome document, paragraph 88, invited the General Assembly, "to adopt a resolution *strengthening and upgrading* UNEP." This was accomplished by Resolution 67/213 in the manner set out in paragraph 88 of the Rio+20 outcome document. Resolution 67/213 also created UNEA, by establishing universal membership in the Governing Council of the UNEP, with the mandate "to expeditiously initiate the implementation of the provisions contained in paragraph 88 of the outcome document in their entirety."

30. UN Secretary-General's Report (A/73/419), *supra* note 7, para. 22.
31. *Id.* para. 78.

The language on UNEP is no different from paragraph 88 of the Rio+20 outcome document, while adding language on UNEA "as the highest decision-making body on the environment" faced stiff opposition with the main argument that there are decision-making bodies, such as Conferences of the Parties to MEAs, that do not come under UNEA. Proposed language on consolidating UNEP's headquarters in Nairobi also failed consensus. In sum, the Recommendations reiterate the roles of UNEP and UNEA, and call for the full implementation of paragraph 88, which remains far from satisfactory, particularly on following issues:

- **Funding**: Have secure, stable, adequate and increased financial resources from the regular budget of the United Nations and voluntary contributions to fulfil its mandate;
- **Empowerment**: Enhance the voice of UNEP and its ability to fulfil its coordination mandate within the United Nations system by strengthening UNEP engagement in key United Nations coordination bodies and empowering UNEP to lead efforts to formulate United Nations system-wide strategies on the environment;
- **Science**: Promote a strong science-policy interface, building on existing international instruments, assessments, panels and information networks, including the Global Environment Outlook, as one of the processes aimed at bringing together information and assessment to support informed decision-making;
- **Information**: Disseminate and share evidence-based environmental information and raise public awareness on critical as well as emerging environmental issues;
- **Capacity-building**: Provide capacity-building to countries, as well as support and facilitate access to technology;
- **Consolidation**: Progressively consolidate headquarters functions in Nairobi, as well as strengthen its regional presence, in order to assist countries, upon request, in the implementation of their national environmental policies, collaborating closely with other relevant entities of the United Nations system; and
- **Stakeholders:** Ensure the active participation of all relevant stakeholders drawing on best practices and models from relevant multilateral institutions and exploring new mechanisms to promote transparency and the effective engagement of civil society.

In particular, the proper funding is "critical for UNEP's visibility, credibility and ownership of the activities that contribute to the execution of its mandate,"[32] but was not specifically addressed in the Recommendations. As seen in the charts below,

32. Niko Urho, Maria Ivanova, Anna Dubrova, and Natalia Escobar-Pemberthy, *International Environmental Governance* (Nordic Council of Ministers), p. 40, *available at* https://www.norden.org/en/publication/international-environmental-governance.

UNEP's very modest funding has increased slightly, mostly as a result in earmarked contributions, while the UN regular budget allocation have also increased but remain at 4 percent of the overall income.[33]

Figure 1: UNEP's overall income between 2010-2011 and 2016-2017

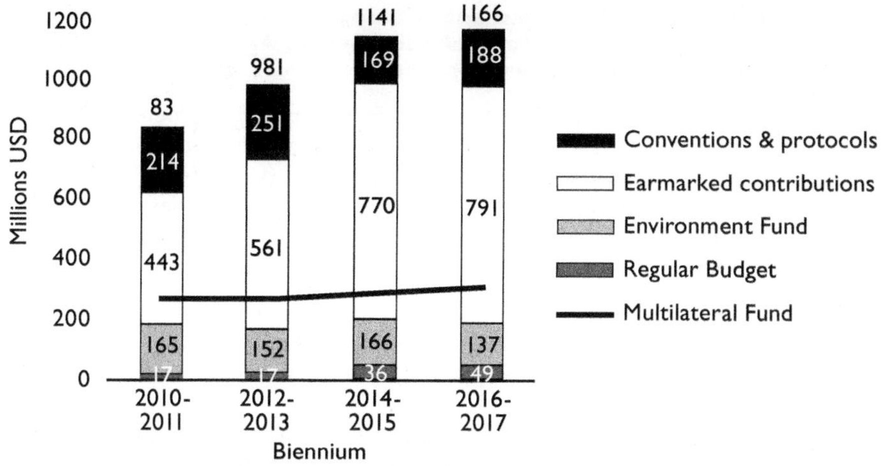

Source: Niko Urho, Maria Ivanova, Anna Dubrova, International Environmental Governance (Nordic Council of Ministers, 2019)

Figure 2: Share of UNEP's funding elements in 2010-2011 and 2016-2017

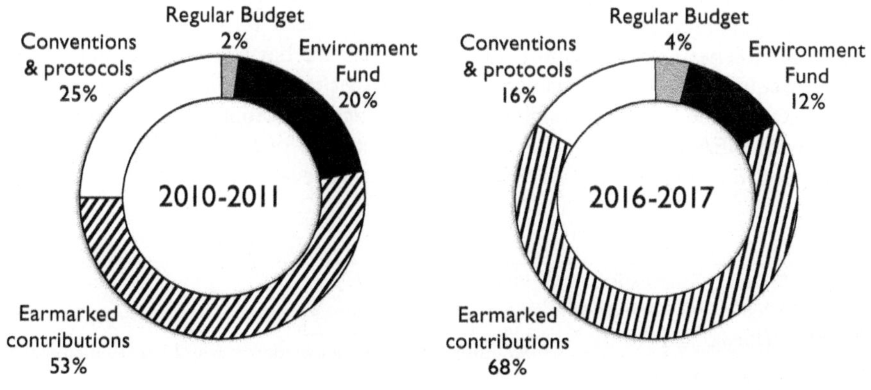

Source: Niko Urho, Maria Ivanova, Anna Dubrova, International Environmental Governance (Nordic

33. *International Environmental Governance, supra* note 32, pp. 33-40.

Council of Ministers, 2019)

— On Means of Implementation:

b) calls for renewed efforts at all levels to enhance the implementation of existing obligations and commitments under international environmental law, stressing the importance of enhanced ambition regarding means of implementation, including the provision and mobilization of all types and sources of means of implementation, consistent with the Addis Ababa Action Agenda and the 2030 Agenda for Sustainable Development

Commentary: The level of ambition regarding means of implementation was a fundamental topic in the Nairobi consultations. ICEL applauds that the Recommendations strongly emphasis the provision of, and access to, means of implementation—such as financial resources, environmentally sound technologies and technical and institutional capacities—as the critical variable in the effective implementation of commitments and compliance with international environmental law.[34]

On this topic, the barriers are well identified in the Secretary-General's Report, as follows: "*Generally, funding for implementation remains insufficient, unpredictable and incoherent, and varies considerably among the different regimes*. On the other hand, the barriers facing the effective transfer of environmentally sound technologies include the limited information and decision-support tools required for transfer; inadequate arrangements for the protection of patents and other intellectual property rights; the lack of cooperation among governments, corporations and the financial community with regard to investing in and making available environmentally sound technologies; and the inadequacy of systems for collecting, synthesizing and reporting back information and knowledge on such technologies."[35]

The Recommendations recognize that effective implementation of existing obligations and commitments under international environmental law requires efforts in education, technical assistance, and importantly, financial assistance.[36] Significantly, nearly all international environmental law regimes are but minimally funded today. While adequate financial mechanisms and the provision of technical and technological assistance and capacity-building are key to enable compliance and implementation with MEAs.[37] Indeed, effective implementation of MEAs requires strategic investment. Existing funding of MEAs needs to be re-evaluated and additional fund-

34. UN Secretary-General's Report (A/73/419), *supra* note 7, para. 87.
35. *Id.* para. 88 (emphasis supplied).
36. *See* UNEP, *Training Manual of International Environmental Law. 4. Compliance and Enforcement of Multilateral Environmental Agreements*, https://autlawiel.files.wordpress.com/2014/10/unep-tm-ch-4-compliance-and-enforcement-of-multilateral-environmental-agreements.pdf.
37. An example of a very effective funding mechanism, is the Multilateral Fund for the Implementation of the Montreal Protocol, with a total budget of US $540 million for the 2018-2020 triennium, plus additional voluntary contributions. *See* Multilateral Fund for the Implementation of the Montreal Protocol, http://www.multilateralfund.org/default.aspx.

ing provided. As long as each separate MEA has its own scarce funding stream, there will be "duplications and contradictions" within the system.[38]

States recognized the need for additional funding over three decades ago, in Agenda 21 (Chapter 33), particularly for the developing countries. The Recommendations reaffirm the Addis Ababa Action Agenda of the 3rd International Conference on Financing for Development, endorsed by the General Assembly on 27 July 2015, which is an integral part of the 2030 Agenda. The Addis Ababa Action Plan can be advanced by reference to strengthening implementation of international environmental law. Accelerated international cooperation is needed to attain both the Addis Ababa Action Agenda and the SDGs.

ICEL submits that enhanced ambition regarding means of implementation for sustainable development will require resources at a scale comparable to what States provide to their defense agencies. Climate change impacts will bring disruptions to all States. However, given the need to invest to build resilience and prepare, there is an unequal situation in the case of developing nations, especially small island States.[39] Developing nations have also played a leading role in the design and implementation of new environmental law as they have seen factual evidence of environmental harm.[40] Thus, enhanced ambition regarding means of implementation is warranted to react, respond, strengthen resilience, and deliver the 2030 Agenda for Sustainable Development.[41]

— On Principles of International Environmental Law:

c) **recognizes the role of discussions on principles of international environmental law for enhancing the implementation of international environmental law, also noting the ongoing work in the International Law Commission on general principles of law**

Commentary: The discussion on principles of international environmental law, mainly whether or not to codify such principles in an instrument, if appropriate, and, "if deemed necessary, the scope, parameters and feasibility of an international instrument," and whether to convene "an intergovernmental conference to adopt an international instrument," under the mandate of Resolution 72/277, were among the most controversial topics during the consultations.

Without clear consensus on the way forward in this respect, the consultations settled on "*recognizes*" the role of discussions on principles of international envi-

38. Adil Najam, Mihaela Papa, Nadaa Taiyab, "Global Environmental Governance. A Reform Agenda," IISD, Ministry of Foreign Affairs of Denmark, 2006, p. 53.
39. Lavanya Rajamani, The Changing Fortunes of Differential Treatment in the Evolution of International Environmental Law, *in International Affairs, 88.*3 (2012), 605-23, p. 623.
40. *See, e.g.*, Parvez Hassan, *Role of the South in the Development of International Environmental Law*, Chinese J. Envtl. L. 1 (2017) 133-57; and Adil Najam, "Developing Countries and Global Environmental Governance: From Contestation to Participation to Engagement," *in International Environmental Agreements: Politics, Law and Economics (*September 2005), Volume 5, Issue 3, pp. 303-21.
41. Nicholas Robinson, Principle of Resilience, *in GPE Legal Foundations, supra* note 10, p. 137.

ronmental law for enhancing the implementation of international environmental law. Thus, the compromise language recognizes the importance of the topic, which implies further discussion, but without specificity or clear path forward. Nonetheless, the synthesis of the status of the principles set forth in the Secretary-General's Report, and the ensuing consultations, provide guidance on convergence and divergence in views. The five convergence topics, borrowing from the Report, are:

i. Principles of international environmental law are an important building block and their usage is widespread. Some are included in non-binding instruments, including political instruments, while others are enshrined in issue-specific multilateral environmental agreements that are legally binding. When enshrined in such agreements, the scope of the principles is confined to that particular multilateral environmental agreement.[42]

ii. More generally, environmental principles also serve to supplement or complement more specific rules. The general character of the principles permits their application to the continuously evolving interrelationships between human activity and the environment.[43]

iii. Several international courts and tribunals have confirmed the existence of rules of customary international law relating to environmental protection, in particular the obligation to prevent environmental harm beyond national jurisdiction, the performance of due diligence, the duty to conduct an environmental impact assessment and the obligation of reparation for environmental damage.[44]

iv. There are important deficiencies with respect to principles of international environmental law, in particular with respect to their content and legal status. There are instances where there is no clarity as to the nature and content of a principle, or no judicial consensus as to its applicability, or no recognition in binding legal instruments, or all of the above. The degree of legal uncertainty surrounding many of these principles has a direct and indirect impact on the predictability and implementation of sectoral environmental regimes.[45]

v. There is a need to further clarify the principles of environmental law, without prejudice to the legal developments already achieved in the issue-specific contexts of various multilateral environmental agreements.[46]

On divergence, the two key issues are whether "[a] comprehensive and unifying international instrument clarifying all the principles of environmental law would contribute to making them more effective and strengthen their implementation" and whether "[a] comprehensive and unifying international instrument that gathers all the principles of environmental law

42. UN Secretary-General's Report (A/73/419), *supra* note 7, para. 9.
43. *Id.* para. 10.
44. *Id.* para. 101.
45. *Id.* para. 102.
46. *Id.*

could provide for better harmonization, predictability and certainty.'[47] It is manifest from the consultations that follow-up work on principles is warranted in order to advance in the implementation of international law. Particularly, the deliberations on principles did not fully evaluate which ones are widely accepted and which ones are emerging. Of the former, it would be appropriate to consider where more than one expression of the principle is found and provide for better harmonization, predictability and certainty in international environmental law. Some emerging principles may be important enough to acknowledge in a declaration as the progressive development of the law is necessary as real-world conditions change.

As noted in the Co-Chairs' summary of the second substantive session, many delegations understand "the added value of codifying or compiling principles to support implementation at all levels, improve consistency and facilitate interpretation, including by developing a common understanding," of the challenges and solutions posed by environmental degradation and sustainable development. As discussions on principles continue, ICEL observes that it would be effective and productive to employ the two-tier approach to consider widely applicable and agreed-upon principles, such as those based on the 1972 Stockholm Declaration, the World Charter for Nature and the 1992 Rio Declaration, as well as those embodied in the 2030 Agenda outcome document, and clarifying emerging ones, such as the non-regression principle.

Acknowledging broad consensus on guaranteeing that the consultations do not undermine existing instruments, bodies and processes, there is no risk associated with compiling and refining existing principles. In this respect, ICEL has provided Member States with the tools that enable overview of existing environmental law commitments, in cooperation with the Vance Center of the New York City Bar and the international law firm of White & Case. ICEL has assembled this information in a set of Charts ("ICEL Charts") available at https://libraryguides.law.pace.edu/icel.

The Charts identify general principles that have already been adopted within MEAs and regional agreements. They include: the African Union (AU), the Association of South East Asian States (ASEAN), the Caribbean Community (CARICOM), the Commonwealth of Independent States (CIS), the League of Arab States (Arab League), the Organization of American States (OAS), the South Asian Cooperative Agreement (SACEP) and the Pacific Islands Forum. ICEL has also assembled a Chart indicating the legal foundation provided by these agreed principles of international environmental law for each of the SDGs. The ICEL Charts reveal the consensus on principles and objectives in international environmental law.

Finally, ICEL salutes the reference to the work of the UN International Law Commission. ICEL follows closely the work of the International Law Commission on the progressive development of international law and its codification. Indeed, on May 30, 2019, ICEL held an informal discussion on the Recommendation with members of the ILC. The work of the ILC is different from the processes by which States

---

47. *Id.*

cooperate to define how to advance sustainable development in new ways, however. In any event, ultimately the ILC reports directly to the General Assembly, and some of ILC's work awaits consideration by the Assembly. Therefore, to continue the discussion on principles, *"also noting the ongoing work in the International Law Commission on general principles of law,"* provides an adequate and valuable guidance on the way forward.

— On Strengthening the Science-Policy Interface

d) invites the scientific community to further their work on interconnected and crosscutting issues by sharing information among the leading scientific, technical and technological bodies that inform the work of Multilateral Environmental Agreements and environmental processes, as well encourages the scientific, technical and technological bodies to strengthen cooperation among themselves

Commentary: This recommendation clearly ties in with Rio+20 outcome Paragraph 88 (d), which call on UNEP to "[p]romote a strong science-policy interface, building on existing international instruments, assessments, panels and information networks, including the Global Environment Outlook, as one of the processes aimed at bringing together information and assessment to support informed decision-making." Science-policy assessment processes include most importantly, aside from the GEO, the Global Sustainable Development Report, the Intergovernmental Panel on Climate Change, the Intergovernmental Science-Policy Platform on Biodiversity and Ecosystem Services, the International Resources Panel, the Global Land Outlook produced by the UN Convention to Combat Desertification Secretariat, and the World Ocean Assessment.[48] Such processes have become key mechanisms to input knowledge and advice to Member States, the UN System, and bodies of MEAs on global environmental issues.

UNEA has adopted resolutions on the science-policy interface that emphasize the role of such assessments, however, "[t]he extent to which UNEP is delivering on its science-policy mandate has been questioned, due to the lack of core funding."[49] The same would be true for specialized agencies and the entire UN System, particularly the HLPF on the follow-up of the 2030 Agenda with the Global Sustainable Development Report. Connecting science and policy through networks and platforms at all levels can be pursued by harnessing "big data" in open, transparent ways. As noted in a previous ICEL Notes, attention should be devoted to how such databases should link scientific and policy-related databases to improve interdisciplinary, integrated and cross-cutting approaches, and to harness big data initiatives, as well as supporting expert commissions in the relevant disciplines needed to strengthen the

48. *See* https://www.unenvironment.org/resources/global-environment-outlook-6, Summary for Policy-Makers; https://sustainabledevelopment.un.org/globalsdreport; https://www.ipcc.ch/; https://www.ipbes.net/global-assessment-report-biodiversity-ecosystem-services; https://knowledge.unccd.int/publication/full-report; https://www.un.org/Depts/los/global_reporting/WOA_RegProcess.htm; https://resourcepanel.org/.

49. *See International Environmental Governance, supra* note 32, p. 47.

implementation of international environmental law. These could include academies of science and other scientific bodies and other networks, IUCN's expert commissions, and regional bodies.

— On Governance and Effectiveness of MEAs:

e) invites the governing bodies of the Multilateral Environmental Agreements, while preserving their independence and respective mandates, to increase their efforts to promote policy coherence across environmental instruments at all relevant levels and to consider identifying and addressing implementation challenges in their regimes, with a view to strengthening implementation at the national and international level

f) invites the governing bodies and secretariats of Multilateral Environmental Agreements to enhance cooperation and collaboration among themselves within the scope of their respective mandates, as well as between them and UNEP and UNEA, building on work already done

g) encourages the governing bodies of Multilateral Environmental Agreements and scientific, technical and technological bodies to exchange information and experiences, including with a view to considering the streamlining of reporting and/or monitoring processes

h) encourages all that have not done so to consider ratifying Multilateral Environmental Agreements and to effectively implement them

Commentary: On the issue of governance and effective implementation of MEAs, the consultations quickly gained constructive consensus. To be sure, the severity of the state of the environment, evidences the critical need for coherence within the MEAs.[50] As noted in the Secretary-General's Report, "[t]he proliferation of multilateral environmental agreements and the resultant distinct and separate mandates ignore the unity, interconnectedness and interdependence of the Earth's ecosystem."[51] Further, the multiplicity of agreements has made it difficult for States to provide sufficient national civil servants and diplomats to participate in all the international regimes. It has also led to concerns about legal inconsistencies and institutional fragmentation[52] and a lack of legal certainty.

International environmental law has evolved rather quickly over the last four decades. There are more than 500 international environmental agreements[53] that directly or indirectly relate to the environment. This variety of normative instruments cover a diverse spectrum of issues, such as loss of biological diversity, atmo-

50. *See* Maria Ivanova, *Global Governance in the 21st Century: Rethinking the Environmental Pillar*, STAKEHOLDER F. (2011).
51. UN Secretary-General's Report (A/73/419), *supra* note 7, para. 80.
52. Joost Pauwelyn, *Bridging Fragmentation and Unity: International Law as a Universe of Inter-Connected Islands*, MICH. J. INT'L L. 25 (2003): 903.
53. Norichika Kanie, "Governance With Multilateral Environmental Agreements: A Healthy or Ill-Equipped Fragmentation?," *Green Planet Blues: Critical Perspectives on Global Environmental Politics* (2014): 137. UN Secretary-General's Report (A/73/419), *supra* note 7, para. 79.

spheric pollution, the deterioration of the oceans or the soil, or the problem of deforestation, among many others.[54] To this profusion of norms, a plethora of policymaking organs has to be added to complete the dominant heterogeneity. Indeed, the MEAs have created their own specific set of institutions (such as the Conference of the Parties, Secretariats, etc.) to ensure the proper functioning of the agreements.[55] Thus, there is "potential for overlap and conflict, institutional and policy incoherence and increased financial and administrative burdens on States parties."[56]

The difficulty lies in making significant process in the responses to these problems. While some efforts have been made to ensure mutual supportiveness among MEAs, "[m]ore efforts could be made to establish or strengthen mechanisms to harness interlinkages and promote synergies for more effective implementation,"[57] ICEL notes that the Recommendations, formulated as a weak "invitation" for the governing bodies of MEAs to "increase their efforts" do embrace suggestions to enhance synergies processes and clustering efforts of related MEAs — for example those dealing with atmosphere, or biodiversity, or chemicals and wastes— to improve policy coherence and ensure mutually supportive implementation.[58]

As noted the Secretary-General's Report, "[i]nstitutional fragmentation and weak coordination between treaties can be addressed through various means, such as: (a) creating clusters and synergies between conventions; (b) mapping existing global and regional action plans and agreements to create an overview of coverage and identify interlinkages; (c) avoiding duplication of reporting and/or monitoring processes by using the same reporting channels and not creating additional burdens ("integrated reporting"); (d) sharing lessons learned and best practices; (e) developing implementation guidelines for multilateral environmental agreements; and (f) sharing information among the different scientific bodies that support the work of related multilateral environmental agreements.[59] Further, enhanced coordination is necessary not only within the field of international environmental law, but also between MEAs and environment-related instruments."[60]

On the strengthening of governance of international environmental law, particularly to overcome lack of coherence and cooperation between the different MEAs, there is also a clear reference on the need for concrete recommendations by the General

---

54. Geoffrey Palmer, *New Ways to Make International Environmental Law*, 86 Am. J. Int'l L. 259, 263 (1992).
55. Indeed, international environmental institutions acquire their own character once they are established and start functioning. *See* Bharat Desai, *Institutionalizing International Environmental Law* (Transnational Publishers, 2004).
56. UN Secretary-General's Report (A/73/419), *supra* note 7, para. 80.
57. *Id.*
58. *Id.*
59. *Id.* para. 83 (noting that "Potential conflicts between treaty regimes can be managed by using legal means, including conflict clauses, mutual supportiveness or the application of the general rule of treaty interpretation contained in article 31, paragraph 3(c), of the Vienna Convention on the Law of Treaties.").
60. *Id.* para. 81.

Assembly for the full implementation of paragraph 89 of the Rio+20 outcome document. ICEL submits that such recommendations must underscore due care not to undermine specific regulatory regimes, avoid duplication, and respect the interdependence of each instrument and body. The OEWG has reaffirmed this notion and reiterated that any deficiencies identified under specific regimes are addressed in the context of each specific agreement, an explicit recognition that existing sector-specific agreements present specific law to be applied, *lex specialis*, and therefore have priority and should not be undermined.

— ***On Implementation challenges:***

i) **encourages States members of the United Nations and all members of the specialized agencies to strengthen, where needed, environmental laws, policies and regulatory frameworks at the national level, as well as the capacities across all sectors for the effective implementation of international environmental law, including the administrative and justice sectors in accordance with national legal systems, while acknowledging the importance of international cooperation in supporting and complementing national actions**

j) **encourages States members of the United Nations and all members of the specialized agencies to mainstream environment into sectoral policies and programs at all levels, including into national development and sustainable development plans, to enhance the implementation of international environmental law and applicable environment-related instruments**

k) **encourages active and meaningful engagement of all relevant stakeholders at all levels in the different fora related to the implementation of international environment law and environment-related instruments**

l) **explores further ways for States members of the United Nations and all members of the specialized agencies to support and make full use of the Fifth Programme for the Development and Periodic Review of Environmental Law (Montevideo Programme V) adopted by the fourth session of the United Nations Environment Assembly, in order to foster the environmental rule of law and advance the implementation of environmental law at all levels**

m) **encourages the United Nations Environment Program, as Chair of the Environment Management Group (EMG) and in collaboration with the members of the Group, to continue to strengthen system-wide inter-agency coordination on environment and to call for active involvement and support of all EMG members for the implementation of system-wide strategies on the environment**

Commentary: Strengthening the implementation of both international and domestic environmental law was identified as the fundamental element to guarantee the effective protection of the environment. National implementation is constrained in many countries mostly by lack of appropriate national legislation, financial resources, environmentally sound technologies and institutional capacities.[61] Implementation issues include "knowledge gaps; a lack of adequate means of implementation, such as finance, capacity-building or technology; the need for facilitation for compliance; a lack of coordination between relevant government departments as well as with other sectors; insufficient monitoring and law enforcement; a lack of political will; and the inadequate engagement of different stakeholders, such as civil society and women's organizations."[62]

Most of these issues, and possible responses, have been discussed above in relation to other Recommendations. As noted above, coherence, synergy and coordination of MEAs could improve implementation at the national and international levels. Despite the fact that some agreements are self-executing, States must also enact implementing regulations and have the capacity to ensure adequate compliance, monitoring, and reporting. Another significant challenge is that different ministries and agencies may be responsible for the implementation of different MEAs.

The recognition of the daunting implementation challenge is important but nothing new. In 1992, Agenda 21 (chapter 8, Integrating environment and development in decision-making) addressed the lack of implementation and poor compliance with regulations and MEAs[63] by strengthening domestic laws and institutions and building up national capacity.[64] Solutions require promoting coordination, cooperation, legal support, education and training in environmental law matters, respecting the national priorities and specific conditions of each nation.

The recommendation to mainstream environment into sectoral policies and programs at all levels, including into national development and sustainable development plans is notable but, to be effective, this effort would also require involvement and commitment of non-State actors. As noted in the Secretary-General's Report, "[n]ational implementation could be improved through the mainstreaming of environmental considerations into other sectors and the enhanced participation of non-State actors in decision-making and implementation."[65]

The recommendation on encouraging "active and meaningful engagement of all relevant stakeholders at all levels" is as clear recognition of the growing role of non-State's actors in the implementation of both environmental law and environment-related instruments. To be sure, non-State actors are increasingly participating in international environmental negotiations,[66] albeit often in an informal fashion, without clear rules regarding the scope of their involvement. Systems of international environmental law need to explore further how to observe Rio Declaration

61. UN Secretary-General's Report (A/73/419), *supra* note 7, para. 111.
62. *Id.* para. 86.
63. Agenda 21 (chapter 8). *See also* The Montevideo Program, https://www.unenvironment.org/explore-topics/environmental-governance/what-we-do/strengthening-institutions-0.
64. UNEP, Possible Elements for a Programme in the Area of Environmental Law for a Specific Period Beginning in 2020, UNEP/ENV.LAW/MTV.4/FP.3, Geneva, 12-14 September 2018.
65. *Id.*
66. Kal Raustiala, *The Participatory Revolution in International Environmental Law*, Harv. Envtl. L. Rev. 21 (1997): 537.

Principle 10, on "public participation in environment decision-making."[67] In a world of social media and information technologies and artificial intelligence, it is possible also to engage such actors to participate in debates and crafting solution about environmental challenges.

This recommendation does not make any specific indication on how to advance the role of non-State actors in environmental matters, however. In this respect, the Report of the Secretary-General provides helpful analysis:

> "Principle 10 of the Rio Declaration, Agenda 21 and the outcome document of the Rio+20 Conference, entitled "The future we want", have underlined the important role of non-State actors such as major groups, women, children and youth, indigenous peoples, non-governmental organizations, local authorities, workers and trade unions, business and industry, the scientific and technological community and farmers, as well as other stakeholders in the development and implementation of sustainable development policies. However, the scope and space for the participation of non-State actors in the international environmental legal process varies with the different treaty regimes. The preponderant mode of engagement of non-State actors is participation as observers in the negotiations that take place during the conferences of the parties to the multilateral environmental agreements, but *no clear and effective rules have been developed to facilitate their input regarding the negotiation process*. In specific instances, observers can participate in subsidiary bodies on an equal footing with parties, such as in partnerships structures. In regimes such as climate change and ozone, the scientific community has direct input into policy development through dedicated institutional mechanisms that provide independent and authoritative information upon which decisions can be based. *Very few regimes provide for public participation in the non-compliance procedures established to monitor, review and verify compliance with international obligations.*[68]

Thus, the rules and opportunities for meaningful and constructive engagement of non-State actors require urgent attention by all the relevant organs and bodies of the UN System, including the Specialized Agencies, UNEA, UNEP, and other pertinent programmes and funds, as well as the Governing Bodies of MEAs.

ICEL welcomes the recommendation that Member States and members of the specialized agencies support and make full use of the Montevideo Programme V adopted by UNEA-4[69] in order to foster the environmental rule of law, and advance

67. See, for example, "World Wide Views on Climate and Energy," 10,000 citizens, 97 Debates in 76 Countries (2015, Danish Board for Technology Foundation), organized through Missions Publiques, www.missionspubliques.com.
68. UN Secretary-General's Report (A/73/419), *supra* note 7, para. 84 (citing two models: The Convention on Access to Information, Public Participation in Decision-Making and Access to Justice in Environmental Matters (the Aarhus Convention) of 1998 provides the broadest latitude for public participation through procedural rights granted to non-State actors by States parties as well as the opportunity to participate in the Convention's non-compliance mechanism. A similar approach was adopted in the Regional Agreement on Access to Information, Public Participation and Justice in Environmental Matters in Latin America and the Caribbean (the Escazú Agreement) of 2018.).
69. *See* UNEP/EA.4/L.24.

the implementation of environmental law at all levels, which would strengthen national implementation of the SDGs. To that end, ICEL recommends streamlining global coordination, and fully finance, Montevideo V. While the Montevideo program is a global program for the development of environmental law in general under the auspices of UNEP, its mandate does not yet facilitate coordination of the national implementation efforts of the MEAS.

ICEL further recommends that, as part of streamlined global coordination of Montevideo V, serious consideration be given to strengthen efforts, and provide adequate funding, for consolidating and centralizing, as appropriate, the databases being created under the MEAs about national implementation of the SDGs and MEA undertakings. ICEL has cooperated in doing so for environmental laws around the world, through ECOLEX, an information service on environmental law operated jointly by FAO, IUCN and UNEP (see http//:ecolex.org), InforMEA, the information portal facilitated by UNEP to access MEAs (http://www.informea.org), which includes a portal on the process launched by Resolution 72/277 (https://globalpact.informea.org). Similar cooperative databases could be established across many international organizations that address aspects of implementing the SDGs.

The final substantive recommendation calling for UNEP, as Chair of the Environment Management Group (EMG) and in collaboration with the members of the Group, to continue to strengthen system-wide inter-agency coordination on environment, responds to concerns voiced by many that the EMG is "limited in effectiveness or scope."[70] Indeed, membership of the EMG consists of 51 specialized agencies, programmes and organs of the UN system, including the secretariats of MEAs, a colossal coordination task. There have been concerted efforts through the EMG, however, particularly "to build coherence among the biodiversity and chemicals regimes."[71] Thus, ICEL celebrates that the recommendation calls for active involvement and support of all EMG members for the implementation of system-wide strategies on the environment.

As noted above, on the role of UNEP, Paragraph 88 of the Rio+20 outcome document calls for enhancing "the voice of UNEP and its ability to fulfill its coordination mandate within the UN system by strengthening UNEP engagement in key UN coordination bodies and empowering UNEP to lead efforts to formulate UN system-wide strategies on the environment." Implementation of this paragraph has specifically focused on the EMG, "which is the primary coordination mechanism on environmental activities in the UN system established in 2001 pursuant to General Assembly Resolution 53/242 for the purpose of enhancing inter-agency coordination in the field of environment and human settlements."[72]

Four main weaknesses of the EMG have been identified: lack of high-level political engagement, the negative perception of the EMG as an instrument of UNEP's con-

70. UN Secretary-General's Report (A/73/419), *supra* note 7, para. 81. *See International Environmental Governance, supra* note 32, p. 41.
71. UN Secretary-General's Report (A/73/419), *supra* note 7, para. 81.
72. *See International Environmental Governance, supra* note 32, p. 41.

trol, human and financial resource constraints, and lack of clarity of purpose and outcomes.[73] In response, UNEP's governing council and later UNEA-1 requested consideration of additional measures to strengthen UNEP's voice and ability to fulfill its coordination mandate under the EMG. In this regard, both the Secretary-General and UNEP's executive director have been "invited" to take necessary steps to enhance UNEP's role in key UN coordination bodies and to identify possible measures to maximize the effectiveness and efficiency of the EMG. The EMG set up a task force consisting of members of UN agencies, which delivered a report for UNEA-2 in 2015 pointing out the need to update the terms of reference.

As a result of this effort, such terms have been revised to include the 2030 Agenda, and the EMG's working modalities have been clarified in its rules of procedure. However, "[d]espite action taken by the EMG to increase the effectiveness and efficiency of its work, its functions remain ultimately the same."[74] Therefore, ICEL would suggest a thorough review of environmental coordination under the Secretary-General, including a review EMG's mandate in relation to other UN environmental coordination bodies, such as UN-Water, to deliver a holistic approach to environmental issues and sustainable development.[75]

(4) Observations on the Consideration of Further Work

The working group recommends that the General Assembly:

a) **Circulates the above-mentioned recommendations and make them available to States members of the United Nations and members of Specialized Agencies and the Governing Bodies of Multilateral Environment Agreements for their consideration and action, as appropriate**

b) **Forwards these recommendations to the United Nations Environment Assembly for its consideration, and to prepare, at its fifth session in February 2021, a political declaration for a UN high level meeting subject to voluntary funding, in the context of the commemoration of the creation of UN Environment Programme by the United Nations Conference on the Human Environment held in Stockholm from 5-16 June 1972, with a view to strengthening the implementation of international environmental law, and international environmental governance in line with paragraph 88 of the "Future We Want."**

Commentary: To begin, a brief note on the genesis of the consensus Recommendations regarding consideration of further work to strengthen the implementation

73. *Id.* p. 42.
74. *Id.* (noting that "[u]ntil recently, the work of the EMG was thematically driven and happened mainly through issue management groups and task forces (EMG, 2015). These bodies have helped to enhance the coherent delivery of many thematic issues, including biodiversity, drylands, sound management of chemicals, and green economy (EMG, 2015). However, they have not enabled the creation of a genuinely system-wide approach to the delivery of the environmental dimension of sustainable development." *Id.* p. 43.
75. *Id.* p. 43.

of international environmental law and international environmental governance. The consensus text includes both a) proposal originated by the delegation of the United States of America to limit the outcome to solely circulating the recommendations to States and the secretariats of MEAs, and b) the Co-Chair's initial suggestion on follow-up work ("zero draft")[76], which was bracketed at the outset of the final round of consultations and referred to the informal group co-facilitated by the representatives of Colombia and Norway. Both proposals were considered during the final plenary.

Notably, subsection a) on circulating the Recommendations reads for "*consideration and action*" by all the Member States, and members of specialized agencies, and the governing bodies of MEAs. Regarding subsection b) on the follow-up process and outcome, "UN high level meeting" replaced "high level event", short of "high level United Nations conference", and retained "political declaration", short of "adoption of an international instrument". In addition, "taking into account" (the creation of UNEP and commemoration of the Stockholm Conference) changed to "in the context of", while "subject to voluntary funding" was added. Regrettably, the reference to a preparatory committee, prior to holding said meeting, was deleted leaving uncertainty on the preparatory work during 2020-2021.

The consensus text, while a significant first step in the UN process to strengthen the implementation of international environmental law and international environmental governance, raises important questions as to how to advance on the Recommendations, and on the process towards the UN high level meeting. Even so, the first step towards keeping the momentum is to advance the Recommendations for prompt "*consideration and action*" by all the Member States and all the relevant organs and bodies of the UN System — including specialized agencies, secretariat and the pertinent programmes and funds — and the governing bodies of MEAs. ICEL also suggests forwarding the Recommendations to the HLPF for consideration in the upcoming meetings in 2019, in July, under the auspices of ECOSOC, and in September, for the first time, under the auspices of the General Assembly.

ICEL respectfully offers two suggestions on the way forward to prepare for UNEA-5, in February 2021, and the UN high level meeting in the context of the 50th commemoration of the creation of the UNEP by the United Nations Conference on the Human Environment in 2022. First, it would be appropriate for the General Assembly and all the relevant organs and bodies of the UN System and governing bodies of MEAs, to develop follow-up processes on the Recommendations to have meaningful input for UNEA-5 and the HLPF. Since a multifaceted response is called for, ICEL would encourage developing concrete actions to address the Recommendations, as well as the means and actors with authority to act on the solutions.

Second, for an adequate preparatory process leading to the UN high level meeting to commemorate 5 decades of UN commitment to environmental stewardship and sustainable development, ICEL proposes that the General Assembly establish

76. *See* https://www.unenvironment.org/events/conference/towards-global-pact-environment.

a preparatory committee for the 2022 anniversaries, with the mandate to draft decisions and a declaration that would contribute to implementation of the SDGs, taking into account the input from UNEA-5 on strengthening the implementation of international environmental law and international environmental governance. By 2022 we shall have seven years of experience in working to attain the SDGs by 2030, and the encouragement of a new Declaration would stimulate the additional cooperation needed to attain the SDGs.

ICEL's recommendation for the establishment of the preparatory committee for the 2022 anniversaries is based on the fruitful intergovernmental processes leading to the Stockholm, Rio and Johannesburg Declarations. To prepare the Stockholm Conference on the Human Environment in 1972, a preparatory committee was charged with the preparation of draft decisions for the conference.[77] Similarly, UNGA Resolution 44/228, which decided to convene the Rio Conference on Environment and Development in 1992, established a preparatory committee to prepare draft decisions that held four session between 1990-1992.[78] And the UN Commission on Sustainable Development acted as the preparatory committee for the 2002 Johannesburg World Summit on Sustainable Development and held three session between 2001-2002.[79]

These two suggestions on follow-up work could provide the basis for a momentous UN High Level meeting and global declaration in 2022 for the 50th anniversary of the Stockholm Declaration and the creation of the UNEP, the 30th anniversary of the Declaration of Rio de Janeiro on Environment and Development, and the 20th anniversary of the Declaration of Johannesburg on Sustainable Development. Such a timeframe for a new global declaration would also be timely for the mid-term review of the SDGs and the 2030 Sustainable Development Agenda. ICEL is gratified to see how these declarations have advanced the framework for sustainable development in all nations.

While Member States took the transformative leap of adopting the SDGs and the 2030 Agenda, ICEL observes that the Stockholm, Rio, and Johannesburg Declarations, as well the World Charter for Nature (UNGA Res. 37/7), and other subsequent declarations and instruments in the context of sustainable development are not fully aligned with the new transformational and universal vision set forth in the 2030 Agenda. The General Assembly acknowledged that "*[t]he challenges and commitments identified at these major conferences and summits are interrelated and call for integrated solutions,*" and stated: "*To address them effectively, a new approach is needed.*" (A/RES/70/1, para. 13). A robust global declaration on the environment and sustainable development in 2022 would be a way to express that new approach.

77. Report on the Working Group on the Declaration of the Human Environment, Annex II, *available at* https://www.un.org/ga/search/view_doc.asp?symbol=A/CONF.48/14/REV.1.
78. Rio Declaration on Environment and Development, UN Audiovisual Library of International Law, *available at* http://legal.un.org/avl/pdf/ha/dunche/rio_ph_e.pdf.
79. Report of the Commission on Sustainable Development acting as the preparatory committee for the 2002 World Summit on Sustainable Development, *available at* https://www.un.org/ga/search/view_doc.asp?symbol=A/CONF.199/4&Lang=E.

ICEL was already 2 years old when the General Assembly convened the Stockholm Conference. Environmental Law was born in that year, laying the basis for the concept of sustainable development. Much has been achieved to fashion "the world we want," but even more remains to be done in order to implement nationally and regionally the UN's multilateral cooperation on sustainable development.

International Council of Environmental Law

Executive Governor, Professor Nicholas A. Robinson
UN Representative (New York): Dr. Victor M. Tafur
UN Representative (Geneva): Ms. Milena Bellini-Sheppard
UN Representative (Nairobi): Mr. Donald Kaniaru
UN Representative (Bonn): Mr. Reinhard Krapp
Representative for the Ocean: Ms. Hiroko Muraki Gottlieb
Representative for ASEAN: Professor Koh Kheng Lian

ICEL Secretariat
Director of the Secretariat: Professor Teresa Parejo
Instituto Pascual Madoz Del Territorio
Urbanismo y Medioambiente
Universidad Carlos III de Madrid
Campus de Getafe
C/ Madrid 126
28903 Madrid, SPAIN

This is ICEL's fifth submission for consideration in the process launched by Resolution 72/277, to follow-up on the initial Note of 10 December 2018 on the Report of the Secretary-General entitled "Gaps in international environmental law and environment-related instruments: towards a global pact for the environment" (A/73/419); a second Note on the agreed principles that provide a foundation for restating a common aspiration and global vision for sustaining Earth's shared biosphere, dated 10 January 2019; a third Note on options to address gaps under Resolution 72/277; and, a fourth Note on elements for consensus on draft recommendations, dated 12 April 2019. The ICEL Notes may be accessed on the website of the Law Library at the Elisabeth Haub School of Law, NY, at (https://libraryguides.law.pace.edu/icel), see also, http://icel.international.

Chapter 5: Phase V: Back to New York (July 2019 – Ongoing)

After the adoption of the consensus-based recommendations by the OEWG, the Co-Chairs returned to New York, bringing the process back to the UNGA. Chapter 5, entitled "Back to New York," focuses on the most recent developments of the fulfillment of the Resolution "Towards a Global Pact for the Environment." It notes the events since June 2019 until August 2019, when this was last updated. Section I covers an informal briefing from the Co-Chairs to the President of the General Assembly in July 2019. Section II briefly notes a UNEA-5 Bureau meeting, in which the recommendations of the OEWG were highlighted. Section III relates to the adoption of Resolution No. A/RES/73/333 by the UNGA, fully adopting the recommendations from the OEWG. Section IV presents a potential timeline for 2022.

The timeline below portrays Phase V.

Figure 5: Phase V Timeline "Back to New York" (July 2019 – Ongoing)

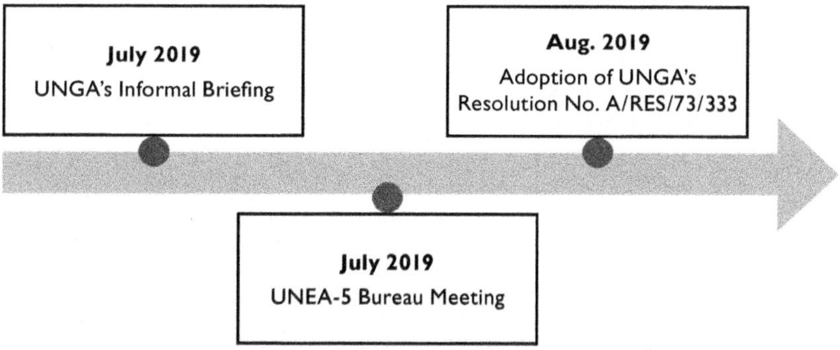

I. Informal Briefing of the UNGA

The Co-Chairs presented the recommendations to the President of the UNGA María Fernanda Espinosa during an informal meeting on July 9th,

2019.[1] Both the UNGA President and the Co-Chairs stressed the significance of having satisfied the mandate by consensus. During the briefing, the EU made the following key points: (i) the working group adhered to its mandate; welcomed the outcome and underscored that it was reached by consensus, calling it a "significant achievement" that "should not be underestimated," thus demonstrating that countries can work together for strengthening international cooperation aiming at environmental protection for common global interests; (ii) believed that it is very important to bring the Nairobi discussions to New York and share what was achieved; (iii) along with a group of countries, intended to table a short resolution for the GA to endorse what was achieved in Nairobi. It was estimated that a limited number of informal meetings would be sufficient to reach agreement before the end of July to adopt the resolution within the 73rd session of the GA. After the EU other delegations took the floor: Morocco (in support), France (in support), Russia (on how their comments were reflected in the report), and China (generally in support).[2]

II. UNEA-5 Bureau Meeting

The fifth session of the UN Environment Assembly (UNEA-5) is expected to take place during the last week of February 2021, in Nairobi, Kenya, as agreed during UNEA-3 in December 2017.[3] Ola Elvestuen, Norway's minister of climate and environment, was appointed president of UNEA-5. A Meeting of the Bureau of the 5th session of UNEA was held on July 3rd, 2019.[4] A Note to the Bureau entitled "Towards a Global Pact for the Environment" was forwarded prior to the meeting as a background document for Agenda Item 2: "A joint vision for the fifth Session of the UN Environment Assembly."[5] The note provided a one-page background on the process so far,

1. Report from ICEL representative Victor Tafur, e-mail from July 10, 2019. *See also* Amal Mudallali (@AmbMudallali). "The PGA @UN_PGA has been a great supporter of the environment and of the Global Pact and today under her leadership we briefed member states about the results of our work and fulfilling our mandate. Thank you PGA & the best of luck in seeing this process reach its conclusions." July 9, 2019. Tweet. UN Ga President (@UNGA). "Thank you, @LebanonUN & @ Portugal_UN, Co-Chairs of the Working Group, created by RES72/277, "Towards a Global Pact for the Environment" for the timely & important briefing. Find the actionable recommendations here (link: https://bit.ly/2YSjObG) bit.ly/2YSjObG #Environment4All #UN4ALL" July 9, 2019. Tweet.
2. Report from ICEL representative Victor Tafur, e-mail from July 10, 2019.
3. IISD, Fifth Session of the UN Environment Assembly (UNEA-5), *available at* http://sdg.iisd.org/events/fifth-session-of-the-un-environment-assembly-unea-5/.
4. UNEA Bureau Meetings, Meeting of the Bureau of the fifth session of the UN Environment Assembly (July 3, 2019), *available at* https://www.unenvironment.org/events/unea-bureau-meetings/meeting-bureau-fifth-session-un-environment-assembly.
5. United Nations Environment Programme, Meeting of the Bureau of the UN Environment Assembly, Note to Bureau of the UN Environment Assembly, "Towards a Global Pact for the Environment" (10

noting the recommendations of the working group to UNEA. In a background document related to finding a theme for UNEA-5, the challenges of implementation of MEAs and the UNGA resolution "Towards a Global Pact for the Environment" were highlighted.[6]

III. Adoption of Resolution No. A/RES/73/333

On August 30, 2019, the UN General Assembly adopted Resolution No. A/RES/73/333.[7] The UNGA welcomed the work of the OEWG established pursuant to General Assembly resolution 72/277, as well as its report, and endorsed all its recommendations, as well as its report.[8] The UNGA also authorized the Secretary-General to continue making use of the special voluntary trust fund in support of the process for implementation of the recommendations and for the facilitation of the participation of representatives from developing countries, in particular the least developed countries, landlocked developing countries and small island developing states for future meetings on the consideration of further work. The UNGA invited Member States, international financial institutions, donor agencies, intergovernmental organizations, non-governmental organizations and natural and juridical persons to make financial contributions to the voluntary trust fund.[9]

The resolution was facilitated by Finland, and cosponsored by the 28 EU member countries, plus EU candidate countries Albania, Montenegro, and North Macedonia, as well as potential candidate Bosnia and Herzegovina. Other sponsoring countries for tabling the resolution included Costa Rica, Lebanon, Micronesia, Palau and Uruguay. From the floor, Andorra, Colombia, Fiji, Georgia, Kenya, Lesotho, Monaco, Morocco, San Marina, Senegal and Ukraine also sponsored, totaling 48 countries. The resolution was adopted without a recorded vote.

Only 2 countries took the floor for explanation of the vote. The United States, to maintain prior statements made on the key UN documents mentioned in the considerations, such as, the 2030 Agenda for Sustainable Development and the outcome document of the United Nations Conference on

---

June 2019), https://wedocs.unep.org/bitstream/handle/20.500.11822/28461/GPE.Note%20to%20UN%20Environment%20Assembly%20Bureau%20%281%29.pdf?sequence=1&isAllowed=y.

6. United Nations Environment Programme, Meeting of the Bureau of the UN Environment Assembly, Finding the Right Theme for the 2020 UN Environment Assembly (17 June 2019), http://wedocs.unep.org/bitstream/handle/20.500.11822/28387/Note%20on%20theme%20for%20discussion%20by%20the%20Environment%20Assembly%20Bureau.pdf?sequence=15&isAllowed=y.
7. UNGA, Resolution No. A/RES/73/333 (adopted Aug. 30, 2019).
8. *Id.* para. 1.
9. *Id.* para. 2.

Sustainable Development, entitled "The Future We Want," and to note that the language on means on implementation should not be understood as any further financial commitment and that the governing bodies of the multilateral environmental agreements set the relevant specific policies. The other explanation was delivered by Norway, to support the recommendations, in particular as it pertains to the next UN Environment Assembly (UNEA-5), which it will preside in February 2021.

Indeed, the UN General Assembly resolution kicks off a new phase by forwarding these recommendations to the UNEA for its consideration, and to prepare, at its fifth session, in February 2021, a political declaration for a United Nations high-level meeting, subject to voluntary funding, in the context of the commemoration of the creation of the United Nations Environment Programme by the United Nations Conference on the Human Environment, held in Stockholm from 5 to 16 June 1972.

IV. Potential Timeline for 2022

With the renewed support from the European Union, the Global Pact received a renewed political encouragement. It is likely that the recommendations of the working group are adopted by the General Assembly, calling for a political declaration to be adopted by 2022, on the occasion of the 50th anniversary of the Stockholm Conference, and the 30th anniversary of the Rio Earth Summit. While there is yet no clarity on how to follow up on the recommendations and several pieces are yet to be filled, there is an opportunity to achieve progress in the development of international environmental law. The timeline below represents a potential roadmap to achieve this goal.

Figure 6: Roadmap for 2022

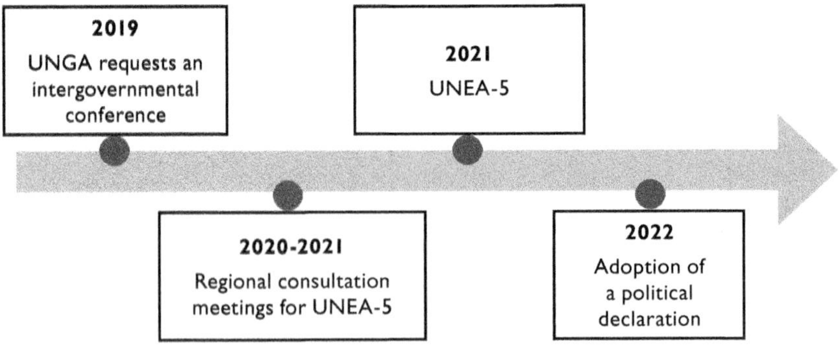

A. *Potential Steps Towards 2022*

The UNGA could ask the Secretary-General to prepare additional reports on more specific issues discussed during the Nairobi sessions, and reconvene the OEWG to discuss it. For example, during the first Nairobi session, Guyana suggested a summary of the gaps discussed with options for how each might be addressed, to help determine the necessity and shape of a Global Pact, as well as a report with a synthesis of how environmental law principles have been treated in domestic jurisprudence and legislation. ICEL suggested the recommendation of further intergovernmental negotiations on the progression of principles of international environmental law:

> "Such an exercise would be an opportunity to advance or update existing principles and include emerging principles in response to developments in the last decades, such as nonregression, progression, equity, resilience, and access to environmental justice. The work must include the possibility of developing an additional declaration or instrument on the right to a 4 clean and healthy environment. ICEL reiterates that the principle of sustainable development implies that "the right to development is to be balanced with and constrained by the right to a clean, safe, healthy and sustainable environment," xi embraced by at least 155 States. This would ensure that all UN Member States working towards the realization of the 2030 Sustainable Development Agenda apply this principle."[10]

B. *Stockholm +50 and Rio +30*

The Pact represents a new moment in the evolution of international environmental law in a time that marks the anniversary of significant documents. Since 1972, five "mega-conferences" were organized to discuss the current state of the environment.[11] Environmental "mega-conferences" address the overall trajectory of human development and its relationship to the environment as a whole and take a broader overview of complex environment and development issues over a longer time frame. They are preceded by years of preparations and negotiations, are large scale in every sense, attracting the

10. International Council of Environmental Law (ICEL), Note on Options to Address Gaps Under Resolution 72/277 (10 May 2018) "Towards a Global Pact for the Environment," submitted for consideration in the 2019 Nairobi Consultations (Feb. 19, 2019), *available at* https://wedocs.unep.org/bitstream/handle/20.500.11822/27609/ICEL_Report.pdf?sequence=1&isAllowed=y.
11. United Nations Conference on the Human Environment (UNHCE), Stockholm, 1972; United Nations Conference on Environment and Development—UNCED—or the "Earth Summit," Rio de Janeiro, 1992; Johannesburg World Summit on Sustainable Development (WSSD), "Earth Summit 2002," or Rio+10, Johannesburg, 2002; United Nations Conference on Sustainable Development (UNCSD) or "Rio+20," Rio de Janeiro, 2012.

participation of heads of state and thousands of individuals and groups, as well as capturing the attention of the world's media.[12] Each "mega" conference aims to discuss how much progress has been made since and plan further action for the future.

Seyfang outlines six core functions the environmental "mega conferences" seek to perform: setting global agendas; facilitating "joined-up thinking"; endorsing common principles; providing global leadership; building institutional capacity; and legitimizing global governance through inclusivity.[13] The anniversaries call for a new generation of fundamental principles, rights and duties related to the protection of the environment. There is an opportunity to organize another "mega-conference" to evaluate the state of the environment, renewing political commitments. States should take advantage of this opportunity and agree on concrete results to strengthen the environmental regime, rather than reducing a new summit to "political theatre" that only maintains the denial in the face of unprecedented environmental challenge.[14]

C. UNEA-5

As the world's highest-level decision-making body on the environment, UNEA addresses the critical environmental challenges facing the world today and reviews important and emerging environmental policy issues.[15] It functions as the world's "de facto Parliament for the Environment" by convening environment ministers on a biennial basis to set the global environmental agenda, contribute effectively to global solutions through the development of international environmental law and provide overarching policy guidance on emerging environmental challenges.[16]

The United Nations Environment Assembly (UNEA) creates and coordinates UN environmental activities and policies and develops international environmental law. With universal membership, UNEA is also the primary international body when it comes to discussing environmental issues, particularly those that require collective global action. UNEA was established in 2012 as part of the "strengthening and upgrading" of the United Nations

12. Gill Seyfang, *Environmental Mega-Conferences—From Stockholm to Johannesburg and Beyond*, 13 Global Environmental Change (2003) 224.
13. *Id.* at 223-24.
14. Carl Death, 2011, *Summit Theatre: Exemplary Governmentality and Environmental Diplomacy in Johannesburg and Copenhagen*, Envtl. Pol. 20 (1), 1-19. Peter Doran, 1993, *The Earth Summit (UNCED): Ecology as Spectacle*, Paradigms: Kent J. Int'l Rel., 7 (1), 55-65. Robert Falkner, 2012, *Global Environmentalism and the Greening of International Society*, Int'l Aff. 88 (3), 503-22.
15. http://web.unep.org/environmentassembly/un-environment-assembly-and-governing-council.
16. UNEP; Our Planet: The Magazine of the United Nations Environment Programme. ISSN: 1013–7394 (2014). UNEA-1, Decision 27/2.

Environment Programme after the United Nations Conference on Sustainable Development. While the UN Member States are the only voting members, the UNEA meetings, which occur every other year, include the voices of thousands of representatives of governments, international organizations and civil society groups.

UNEA sessions usually adopt many resolutions, which are proposed and negotiated by Member States. The draft resolutions and decisions adopted at each session are prepared during the meeting of the Open-Ended Committee of Permanent Representatives (OECPR),[17] which are held back-to-back with UNEA-5, and finalized by the Committee of the Whole. Though not legally binding, the resolutions identify key issues for the global environment and provide impetus for coordinated action. UNEA sessions also serve as forums for promoting the environmental dimension of the 2030 Agenda and providing input to annual sessions of the High-Level Political Forum on Sustainable Development (HLPF).

17. https://www.unenvironment.org/cpr/committee-permanent-representatives.

Document 7: Resolution No. A/RES/73/333 (August 2019)

Resolution adopted by the General Assembly on 30 August 2019

[*without reference to a Main Committee (A/73/L.108 and A/73/L.108/Add.1)*]

73/333. Follow-up to the report of the ad hoc open-ended working group established pursuant to General Assembly resolution 72/277

The General Assembly,

Recalling its resolution 72/277 of 10 May 2018, entitled "Towards a Global Pact

for the Environment",

Reaffirming the purposes and principles of the Charter of the United Nations,

Recalling the Declaration of the United Nations Conference on the Human

Environment,[1] the Rio Declaration on Environment and Development,[2] Agenda 21,[3] the Programme for the Further Implementation of Agenda 21,[4] the Johannesburg Declaration on Sustainable Development[5] and the Plan of Implementation of the World Summit on Sustainable Development (Johannesburg Plan of Implementation)[6] and the outcome document of the United Nations Conference on Sustainable Development, entitled "The future we want",[7] as well as the outcomes of all the major United Nations conferences and summits in the economic, social and environmental fields,

Recognizing existing obligations and commitments under international environmental law,

Reaffirming all the principles of the Rio Declaration,

Reaffirming also its resolution 70/1 of 25 September 2015, entitled "Transforming our world: the 2030 Agenda for Sustainable Development", in which it adopted a comprehensive, far-reaching and people-centred set of universal and transformative Sustainable Development Goals and targets, its commitment to working tirelessly for the full implementation of the Agenda by 2030, its recognition that eradicating

---

1. Report of the United Nations Conference on the Human Environment, Stockholm, 5-16 June 1972 (A/CONF.48/14/Rev.1), part one, chap. I.
2. *Ibid.*, annex II.
3. Report of the United Nations Conference on Environment and Development, Rio de Janeiro, 3-14 June 1992, vol. I, Resolutions Adopted by the Conference (United Nations publication, Sales No. E.93.I.8 and corrigendum), Resolution 1, annex I.
4. Resolution S-19/2, annex.
5. Report of the World Summit on Sustainable Development, Johannesburg, South Africa, 26 August-4 September 2002 (United Nations publication, Sales No. E.03.II.A.1 and corrigendum), chap. I, resolution 1, annex.
6. *Ibid.*, resolution 2, annex.
7. Resolution 66/288, annex.

poverty in all its forms and dimensions, including extreme poverty, is the greatest global challenge and an indispensable requirement for sustainable development, its commitment to achieving sustainable development in its three dimensions – economic, social and environmental – in a balanced and integrated manner, and to building upon the achievements of the Millennium Development Goals and seeking to address their unfinished business,

Stressing the need to continue to address, in a comprehensive and coherent manner, the challenges posed by environmental degradation in the context of sustainable development,

1. *Welcomes* the work of the ad hoc open-ended working group established pursuant to General Assembly resolution 72/277, as well as its report,[8] and endorses all its recommendations, as set out in the annex to the present resolution;

2. *Decides* that costs associated with the implementation of the present resolution and with the facilitation of the participation of representatives from developing countries, in particular the least developed countries, landlocked developing countries and small island developing States, in any future meeting related to the implementation of the recommendations on the consideration of further work as set forth in the annex, shall be met from voluntary contributions, requests the Secretary-General to continue to make use of the special voluntary trust fund established pursuant to paragraph 10 of resolution 72/277 for this purpose, and invites Member States, international financial institutions, donor agencies, intergovernmental organizations, non-governmental organizations and natural and juridical persons to make financial contributions to the voluntary trust fund.

103rd plenary meeting
30 August 2019

Annex

Recommendations of the ad hoc open-ended working group established pursuant to General Assembly resolution 72/277

Objectives guiding the recommendations

(1) Reinforce the protection of the environment for present and future generations;

(2) Uphold the respective obligations and commitments under international environmental law of States Members of the United Nations and members of specialized agencies;

(3) Contribute to the strengthening of the implementation of international environmental law and environment-related instruments;

8. A/AC.289/6/Rev.2.

(4) Support the full implementation of the 2030 Agenda for Sustainable Development,[9] as well as the outcome document of the United Nations Conference on Sustainable Development, entitled "The future we want",[10] including paragraphs 88 and 89 thereof;

(5) Not undermine existing relevant legal instruments and frameworks and relevant global, regional and sectoral bodies;

Substantive recommendations

(6) Reaffirm the role of the United Nations Environment Programme as the leading global environmental authority that sets the global environmental agenda, promotes the coherent implementation of the environmental dimension of sustainable development within the United Nations system and serves as an authoritative advocate for the global environment, and also reaffirm the role of the United Nations Environment Assembly;

(7) Call for renewed efforts at all levels to enhance the implementation of existing obligations and commitments under international environmental law, stressing the importance of enhanced ambition regarding means of implementation, including the provision and mobilization of all types and sources of means of implementation, consistent with the Addis Ababa Action Agenda of the Third International Conference on Financing for Development[11] and the 2030 Agenda for Sustainable Development;

(8) Recognize the role of discussions on principles of international environmental law in enhancing the implementation of international environmental law, also noting the ongoing work in the International Law Commission on general principles of law;

(9) Invite the scientific community to further its work on interconnected and cross-cutting issues by sharing information among the leading scientific, technical and technological bodies that inform the work of multilateral environmental agreements and environmental processes, and encourage the scientific, technical and technological bodies to strengthen cooperation among themselves;

(10) Invite the governing bodies of the multilateral environmental agreements, while preserving their independence and respective mandates, to increase their efforts to promote policy coherence across environmental instruments at all relevant levels and to consider identifying and addressing implementation challenges in their regimes, with a view to strengthening implementation at the national and international levels;

(11) Invite the governing bodies and secretariats of multilateral environmental agreements to enhance cooperation and collaboration among themselves within the scope of their respective mandates, as well as between themselves and the

9. Resolution 70/1.
10. Resolution 66/288, annex.
11. Resolution 69/313, annex.

United Nations Environment Programme and the United Nations Environment Assembly, building on work already done;

(12) Encourage the governing bodies of multilateral environmental agreements and scientific, technical and technological bodies to exchange information and experiences, including with a view to considering the streamlining of reporting and/or monitoring processes;

(13) Encourage all that have not yet done so to consider ratifying multilateral environmental agreements and to effectively implement them;

(14) Encourage States Members of the United Nations and all members of the specialized agencies to strengthen, where needed, environmental laws, policies and regulatory frameworks at the national level, as well as capacities across all sec tors for the effective implementation of international environmental law, including in the administrative and justice sectors in accordance with national legal systems, while acknowledging the importance of international cooperation in supporting and complementing national actions;

(15) Encourage States Members of the United Nations and all members of the specialized agencies to mainstream environment into sectoral policies and programmes at all levels, including into national development and sustainable development plans, to enhance the implementation of international environmental law and applicable environment-related instruments;

(16) Encourage the active and meaningful engagement of all relevant stakeholders at all levels in the different forums related to the implementation of international environment law and environment-related instruments;

(17) Encourage the exploration of further ways for States Members of the United Nations and all members of the specialized agencies to support and make full use of the fifth Programme for the Development and Periodic Review of Environmental Law (Montevideo Programme V), adopted at the fourth session of the United Nations Environment Assembly,[12] in order to foster environmental rule of law and advance the implementation of environmental law at all levels;

(18) Encourage the United Nations Environment Programme, as chair of the Environment Management Group, in collaboration with the other members of the Group, to continue to strengthen system-wide inter-agency coordination on the environment and to call for the active involvement and support of all members of the Group in the implementation of system-wide strategies on the environment.

Further work

(a) Circulate the above-mentioned recommendations and make them available to States Members of the United Nations, the members of specialized agencies and

12. *See* UNEP/EA.4/Res.20 and UNEP/EA.4/19, annex I.

the governing bodies of multilateral environment agreements for their consideration and action, as appropriate;

(b) Forward these recommendations to the United Nations Environment Assembly for its consideration, and to prepare, at its fifth session, in February 2021, a political declaration for a United Nations high-level meeting, subject to voluntary funding, in the context of the commemoration of the creation of the United Nations Environment Programme by the United Nations Conference on the Human Environment, held in Stockholm from 5 to 16 June 1972, with a view to strengthening the implementation of international environmental law and international environmental governance, in line with paragraph 88 of the outcome document of the United Nations Conference on Sustainable Development, entitled "The Future We Want."

Chapter 6: Conclusion: Prospects for 2020-2022

By the proposed draft elements circulated by the Co-Chairs, the Working Group recommended the UNGA to submit the recommendations to the United Nations Environment Assembly and for UNEA to consider preparing, at its fifth session in February 2021, a political declaration for a high-level UN conference, in the context of the commemoration of the creation of the UN Environment Programme by the United Nations Conference on the Human Environment held in Stockholm from 5-16 June 1972, with a view to strengthening the implementation of international environmental law, and international environmental governance in line with paragraph 88 of the "Future we Want." This chapter argues how a Global Pact could add value to the challenges identified in Nairobi, and why the discussion on principles remain relevant.

Faced with the environmental challenges of the Anthropocene and the ever-growing need for global action, cooperation between Member States needs to be enhanced and encouraged in order to bring new ways of promoting environmental management. The UNGA Resolution, the UNSG Report, and the Nairobi discussions have set the stage for this progression. It is now up to the UNGA and UNEA to move forward with this process, and to States to negotiate an agreement that truly promotes cooperation and enhanced action.

The debates in Nairobi broadened the set of issues originally championed by France to the UNGA. Through a re-examination of the defining gaps in international environmental law, the UNSG and delegates found gaps in areas such as the governance structure of international environmental law, the implementation of existing instruments and the coherence between MEAs. While many delegates disagreed on multiple issues, Member States generally acknowledged that the current state of international environmental law was lacking. The IISD summarized:

> "While the generative question of whether the world is ready for a legally binding global pact for the environment, as championed by France, remained on the table, the real impact of the French Government's initiative—for now—has been to unleash what is widely regarded as a necessary re-examination of the defining gap of our times, namely the gap between the stated promise and

ambition of the international environmental law regime and its impact or "fitness for purpose" at the dawn of the Anthropocene."[1]

Several delegations consistently asked about the added value of a Global Pact for the Environment during the Nairobi discussions. Prof. Voigt identifies five ways in which the Global Pact could add value to what already exists in international environmental law beyond the codification of principles.[2] She argues that while codification might add some value, there is a need to consider the dynamic role of principles, abstractness, indeterminacy and generality inherent in principles.[3] International environmental law could be more effective through a toolbox for its general improvement and the enhanced effectiveness of environmental protection. A "package" or "menu" of recommendations was suggested by a few delegations in Nairobi. The Global Pact could function as a 'compact' for bringing together the different tools and approaches to enhance coordination through procedural and substantive measures. This menu of options could include a tool to support better coordination and synergies between MEAs, addressing the problem of fragmentation and treaty congestion not only in international environmental law, but also in related areas.[4] A second option could be to combine in a framework agreement a common vision of international environmental law for the Anthropocene in an integrated, interdependent and holistic response to global environmental challenges.[5]

Third, a Global Pact could address implementation deficiencies through cooperation on increased capacity-building across State borders and the public/private divide. Prof. Voigt suggests a Pact could "aim at bringing together state and non-state actors in a global compact to raise the necessary means for the effective implementation of environmental agreements." It could bring private companies and corporations onto the scene and provide a space for

1. Doran, et al., Summary of the Second Substantive Session of the Ad Hoc Open-Ended Working Group Towards a Global Pact for the Environment, 2019.
2. Christina Voigt, *How a "Global Pact for the Environment" Could Add Value to International Environmental Law*, 28 Rev. Eur., Comp. & Int'l Envtl. L. 13 (2019).
3. *Id.* at 22.
4. *Id.* at 22. Procedurally, this could be done through various options, including: (i) creating clusters and synergies between conventions (e.g. as has been done for the Rotterdam, Basel and Stockholm Conventions) through back-to-back or joint meetings, joint budgeting, sharing of secretariats or collaboration of secretariats; (ii) mapping of existing global and regional action plans and agreements to create an overview of coverage and identify interlinkages; (iii) avoiding duplication of reporting and/or monitoring processes by developing common reporting channels without creating additional burdens ('integrated reporting'); (iv) developing implementation guidelines for MEAs; (v) further development of mutual supportiveness; or (vi) the establishment of joint clearing houses to share experiences, lessons learned and best practices across MEAs. Additionally, cooperation and coordination can be done through the identification of gaps and negotiation of possible amendments or decisions by the governing body, such as the Kigali Amendment to the Montreal Protocol on hydrofluorocarbons.
5. *Id.* at 23.

interaction on addressing financial, capacity and technology gaps.[6] Fourth, a Pact could mediate between international environmental law and related areas. A Pact could "assess and address, on a principled basis, how different objectives expressed in international treaties should apply and be weighed against each other, especially in cases of normative conflict."[7] Finally, another alternative would be for a Global Pact for the Environment to increase awareness of future environmental challenges or technologies which are not yet covered by international treaty law.[8]

While these options, along with the exercise done in Nairobi to identify further challenges and options to improve the effectiveness of international environmental law, provide a blueprint for the progressive development of international environmental law, it is important not to lose sight of the role of the codification of principles. Adopting environmental principles can address a broad range of issues, improving the effectiveness international environmental law overall. The Pact should be considered as a necessity, not a revolution. There is a need to strengthen international environmental law, solidify the human right to a healthy environment at the international level, and demand the adoption of the non-regression principle, connected to the intergenerational principle.

Principles function as "building blocks" for international environmental law. These "constitute both the backbone of the body of law governing international dealings and the potent cement that binds together the various and often disparate cogs and wheels of the normative framework of the international community."[9] While enshrined in multiple MEAs, principles have often developed in disparate ways and in instruments that may use different terms, with the result that even well accepted principles may be challenging for non-specialists to discern, inconsistencies in the law may develop, and questions may arise as to which are legally binding and which are interpretative principles.[10] Given the role of environmental principles as building blocks, serving to supplement or complement more specific rules, aiding interpretation, filling gaps, and ultimately unifying the sectoral approach of international environmental law, the UNSG has recommended the adoption of an overarching legal framework of environmental principles.[11]

6. *Id.* at 23.
7. *Id.* at 23.
8. *Id.* at 23.
9. *Id.* at 20.
10. Cymie R. Payne, A Global Pact for the Environment § 2019 (ASIL ed., American Society of International Law Vol. 22, Issue 12 ed. 2018).
11. UN Secretary-General, Gaps in International Environmental Law and Environment-Related Instruments: Towards a Global Pact for the Environment, UN Doc. A/73/419 (30 November 2018). 4.

The UNSG noted that a comprehensive and unifying international instrument clarifying all the principles of environmental law would contribute to making them more effective and strengthen their implementation.[12] A Pact could be a tool to collate and codify general environmental principles, to address their gaps and to encourage the emergence of new rights. ICEL notes the role of principles in promoting legal certainty and filling normative gaps.[13] Chabason & Hege argue that the added value of the Global Pact "should lie in the declaration of principles to facilitate the implementation of environmental law, at the global, regional and national levels."[14] Global environmental policy would thus be strengthened by a common universal text harmonising the key concepts and general principles of IEL. [15] Chabason & Hege further note

> "The definition of general principles of environmental law could be a unifying and codifying tool. These principles are currently spread between several international environmental conventions and declarations, with highly variable definitions and scope. National environmental laws reflect these differences more or less faithfully. A universal treaty, should that be the outcome of the negotiations, could lay out these general principles in a homogenous, coherent manner, and would thus facilitate the work of national legislators and judges, agencies responsible for environmental administration and regional and international courts." [16]

During the Nairobi sessions, it was generally acknowledged that better compliance with existing environmental norms was needed. As a treaty, the GPE would provide an authoritative reference, addressing this concern.[17] The main goal of the codification of principles is to achieve systemic integration in international environmental law. A Global Pact has the potential to clarify, consolidate, and legalize principles of international environmental law that now appear in hundreds of agreements and declarations. Perhaps more importantly, it also promises normative coherence for the international legal system as a whole.[18] If the Global Pact evolves into a treaty, it will clarify which principles are binding law and which are soft law. However,

12. *Id.* at 6-5; para. 43.
13. International Council of Environmental Law (ICEL), Note on Options to Address Gaps Under Resolution 72/277 (10 May 2018) "Towards a Global Pact for the Environment," submitted for consideration in the 2019 Nairobi Consultations (Feb. 19, 2019), ***available at*** https://wedocs.unep.org/bitstream/handle/20.500.11822/27609/ICEL_Report.pdf?sequence=1&isAllowed=y.
14. Chabason & Hege. 2019.
15. *Id.*
16. *Id.*
17. Payne, *supra* note 10.
18. Margaret Young, Global Pact for the Environment: Defragging International Law? § 2019 (EJIL ed., 2018).

Prof. Payne notes that the form of a treaty alone does not guarantee a norm is binding. She clarifies that some principles, even when enshrined in treaty form, reflect "soft law"—norms that are widely recognized but are not sufficiently precise or enforceable to be considered legally binding rules. Soft law principles are often used as interpretative guides.

> "This would require demonstrating that a new treaty or any new instrument is not just another layer to an already protean field, but an essential tool in ensuring coherence and simplifying interpretations that are obstacles to the effectiveness of existing texts. The world conferences of 1972, 1992, 2002 and 2012 strove to provide a comprehensive view of environmental challenges and highlighted certain key principles for the conduct of environmental action. However, the documents resulting from these events have only non-binding value (soft law) and often give rise to different interpretations by States and judges."[19]

A binding and widely ratified Global Pact for the Environment could provide clearer direction for treaty-interpreters to achieve systemic integration in public international law, due both to its ongoing crystallization of custom and to its potential status as a binding treaty. Questions that remain open or unadressed by international instruments, such as the issue of plastics in marine environments, could rely upon on a Global Pact.[20] While no binding agreement is negotiated, their broad regulation could rely on a general statement of binding principles.

> "This will imply making it clear that the effective application of existing texts will be facilitated by a binding framework text, since effectiveness is conditional upon opposability and justiciability, which are more difficult with soft law regulations. It should however be noted that in any case, effectiveness remains only potential or virtual, and could be a dead letter if it is not accompanied by guarantees of access to justice or information for citizens and civil society." [21]

Prof. Payne further argues, however, that principles have a normative effect despite its non-legally binding effect: "For example, practitioners report that the Ruggie principles have affected their clients' corporate social responsibility policies, even though they do not have the status of a treaty. The GPE, even if it does not become a treaty, could similarly carry significant nor-

19. Chabason & Hege. 2019.
20. Yann Aguila & Jorge E. Viñuales, *A Global Pact for the Environment: Conceptual Foundations*, 28 Rev. Eur., Comp. & Int'l Envtl. L. 3;5 (2019).
21. Chabason & Hege. 2019.

mative weight in state and nonstate practice."[22] Detailed application of the broad principles set forth in the GPE could then be provided through commentaries and model laws to assist with implementation and incorporation of the principles into domestic law.[23]

By establishing the right of every person to "live in an ecologically sound environment adequate for their health, well-being, dignity, culture and fulfilment", the Global Pact offers a new way for environmental protection to be achieved through adjudication by national and international courts and tribunals. The codification of the right to the environment further contributes to the justiciability of environmental principles. The UNSG's Report outlined several benefits of the global recognition of the human right to a healthy environment. First, recognition would "raise awareness of and reinforce the understanding that human rights norms require protection of the environment and that environmental protection depends on the exercise of human rights" and highlight that "environmental protection must be assigned the same level of importance as other interests that are fundamental to human dignity, equality and freedom."[24]

Second, it would crystallize and integrate the human rights norms relating to the environment, helping to ensure that they "continue to develop in a coherent, consistent and integrated manner."[25] Prof. Knox clarifies that the absence of a universally acknowledged right has not prevented the evolution of environmental human rights law, the presence of the right would provide a kind of capstone to that body of law, giving it a more unified and integrated presence.[26] Third, the recognition would place greater attention on those more vulnerable to the effects of environmental harm.[27] To further increase the protection, the Pact could strengthen individual or collective citizens' rights, including the protection of environmental rights defenders and whistleblowers, the rights of environmentally displaced persons, the victims of sudden- or slow-onset disasters. Issues related to environmental justice, the rights of indigenous peoples, access to justice and to administrative documents for citizens and NGOs, and the rights of stakeholder groups in international negotiations could also be covered by specific provisions.[28] Fourth, the recognition will raise "the profile and importance of environ-

22. Payne, *supra* note 10.
23. *Id.*
24. UNSG, *supra* note 11, at para. 39.
25. *Id.*
26. John H. Knox, *The Global Pact for the Environment: At the Crossroads of Human Rights and the Environment*, 28 Rev. Eur., Comp. & Int'l Envtl. L. (2019).
27. UNSG, *supra* note 11, at para. 45.
28. Chabason & Hege. 2019.

mental protection" and provide a basis for the enactment of stronger environmental laws, standards, regulations and policies," thus improving the overall effectiveness of international environmental law.[29] Prof. Knox argues that these benefits to not depend on the recognition of the Global Pact as a binding treaty.[30]

Additionally, a universal instrument on the general principles of environmental law would highlight innovative principles while helping to achieve the Sustainable Development Goals (SDGs), consistent with their universality and indivisibility.[31] The Global Pact provides a unique opportunity to develop a new approach to international standards and contribute to the implementation of the 2030 Agenda.[32] It could provide coordinating guidance for existing treaties, including on the guiding principles and concepts already contained in international instruments.[33] Finally, the role of the civil society needs to be reinforced. The Pact also imposes a duty to take care of the environment on "every person, natural or legal, public or private," thus broadening the range of actors responsible for the environment. It enforces the vital role of subnational entities, including cities and regions, and urges states to encourage their implementation of the Pact (Article 14).[34]

Given the advantages of the codification of principles, it is essential that the discussion continues. Moving forward, the focus should be on how, not if, to clarify the principles of international environmental law with normative value that facilitate consistency of interpretation and implementation in the context of sustainable development.[35]

> "On the methodology for consulting regarding codification of existing principles or the progressive development of emerging principles, one starting point can be with the principles of international environmental law already contemplated in existing instruments and political declarations as well as customary international law, including the principles of prevention, precaution, polluter-pays, common but differentiated responsibilities and respective capabilities, national sovereignty over natural resources, access to environmental information and environmental impact review. The work of the UN International Law Commission on such matters, as well as decisions of the International Court of Justice and relevant tribunals, can serve as basis to refining these principles. With broad consensus on guaranteeing that the ongoing consulta-

29. UNSG, *supra* note 11, at para. 40.
30. Knox, *supra* note 26, at 46.
31. Chabason & Hege. 2019.
32. *Id.*
33. Voigt, Rev. Eur., Comp. & Int'l Envtl. L. (2019), at 22-23.
34. Young. 2018.
35. ICEL, *supra* note 13.

tions do not undermine existing instruments, bodies and processes, there is a no risk associated with refining existing principles."[36]

Prof. Boer notes a series of questions that could stimulate debate, such as whether the current draft of the Pact is broad enough to specifically "address possible gaps in international environmental law and environment-related instruments," as instigated by the UNGA; if the current draft of the Pact includes all of the substantive provisions necessary to form an "umbrella" instrument to achieve its aims; or whether the current draft of the Pact should add more detailed environmental law principles.[37]

Following a rights-based approach, the Pact could identify new environmental rights, further emphasizing the link between human rights and the environment. New rights such as granting rights to nature, for example, could be adopted in the Pact, solidifying a trend followed recently by several countries. Recent developments in procedural rights should also be noted. As suggested by some delegates from Latin America, the discussions should consider the recently adopted Escazú Agreement on environment and human rights, signed on 4 March 2018 within the framework of the Economic Commission for Latin America and the Caribbean.[38] A human rights approach would help support stronger compliance mechanisms open to the public, as well as calls for new agreements on procedural access rights, such as the Aarhus Convention and the Escazú Agreement, and even for a global Principle 10 agreement.[39]

Concepts such as *buen vivir* ("living well" or "well-being") and ecological solidarity are worth discussing with a view to their possible inclusion in the Pact.[40] These facilitate the bringing together of environmental protection and an alternative development model that is more inclusive and mutually supportive.[41] The Pact could adopt a "holistic" concept of the environment advocated by climate justice, encompassing all relevant elements (biodiversity, land use, exploitation of natural resources, protection of the seas and oceans, but also the agricultural and food issue).[42] The Pact could a lso include recent doctrinal developments linked to Earth system governance, referring, for

36. ICEL, *supra* note 13.
37. Hernández, et al. 2018.
38. Escazú Agreement on Access to Information, Participation and Justice in Environmental Matters (adopted 4 March 2018, not yet in force).
39. Knox, Rev. Eur., Comp. & Int'l Envtl. L. (2019) 46.
40. Chabason & Hege. 2019.
41. Marta Torre-Schaub, Is the Global Pact for the Environment a Potential Lever for Climate Justice? IDDRI Blog Post, Mar. 7, 2019.
42. *Id.*

example, to planetary boundaries.[43] The Pact could include principles such as ecological solidarity, non-regression or international liability for environmental damage.[44] These are a few options on new developments in comparative environmental law, which could be included in a debate on the text of a political declaration. The next year invites such a debate with multiple options on which answers can properly address current and future challenges in environmental protection. It is essential that a new agreement presents a workable menu of answers providing emerging environmental principles to address the challenges of the Anthropocene.

43. Louis J. Kotzé & Duncan French, *A Critique of the Global Pact for the Environment: A Stillborn Initiative or the Foundation for Lex Anthropocenae?*, 18 Intl Envtl. Agreements: Pol., L. & Econ. 811 (2018).
44. Chabason & Hege. 2019.

Annex 1: Further Research: List of Websites

GPE—Legal Articles: https://globalpactenvironment.org/document/legal-articles/?lang=en

GPE—News: https://globalpactenvironment.org/news/?lang=en

GPE—Timeline: https://globalpactenvironment.org/the-pact/where-are-we-now/?lang=en

GPE Website: https://globalpactenvironment.org/?lang=en

IISD (Coverage of Negotiations): http://enb.iisd.org/enb/vol35/

Pace Law Global Pact Research Guide: https://libraryguides.law.pace.edu/icel

UNEA-5 Meetings: https://www.unenvironment.org/events/unea-bureau-meetings/meeting-bureau-fifth-session-un-environment-assembly

UN Environment GPE Conference (Nairobi Sessions): https://www.unenvironment.org/events/conference/towards-global-pact-environment

UNEP: https://globalpact.informea.org/about

Annex 2: Further Research: Academic Books and Articles on the Global Pact
(updated until September 2019)

Christina Voigt, *How a "Global Pact for the Environment" Could Add Value to International Environmental Law*, 28 Rev. Eur., Comp. & Int'l Envtl. L. 13 (2019).

Domenico Amirante, *The Global Pact for the Environment: A General Instrument to Face Climate Change*, Jindal Global L. Rev. (2019).

Duncan French & Louis J. Kotzé, *"Towards a Global Pact for the Environment": International Environmental Law's Factual, Technical and (Unmentionable) Normative Gaps*, 28 Rev. Eur., Comp. & Int'l Envtl. L. (2019).

Elena Loredana Pîrvu, *The New Global Pact for the Environment*, 15 Acta Universitatis Danubius Juridica 5 (2019).

Irina Moroianu Zlatescu, *Towards a Global Pact for the Environment*, Law Review: Judicial Doctrine & Case-Law 123 (2017).

Jasmin Raith, *The "Global Pact for the Environment"—A New Instrument to Protect the Planet?*, 15 J. Eur. Envtl. & Planning L. 3 (2018).

John H. Knox, *The Global Pact for the Environment: At the Crossroads of Human Rights and the Environment*, 28 Rev. Eur., Comp. & Int'l Envtl. L. (2019).

Louis J. Kotzé & Duncan French, *A Critique of the Global Pact for the Environment: A Stillborn Initiative or the Foundation for Lex Anthropocenae?*, 18 Int'l Envtl, Agreements: Pol., L. & Econ. 811 (2018).

Maria Magdalena Kenig-Witkowska, *The Draft Global Pact for the Environment*, *at* https://www.documents.clientearth.org/wp-content/uploads/library/2018-10-02-the-draft-global-pact-for-the-environment-ce-en.pdf.

Not All That Glitters Is Gold: An Analysis of the Global Pact for the Environment Project (2019).

Patrick Thieffry, *The Proposed Global Pact for the Environment and European Law*, 27 Eur. Energy & Envtl. L. Rev. 182 (2018).

Susan Biniaz, *The UNGA Resolution on a "Global Pact for the Environment": A Chance to Put the Horse Before the Cart*, 28 Rev. Eur., Comp. & Int'l Envtl. L. 33 (2019).

Teresa Parejo Navajas & Nathan Lobel, *Framing the Global Pact for the Environment: Why It Is Needed, What It Aims to Do, How It Proposes to Do It*, 30 Fordham Envtl. L. Rev. 32 (2018).

Teresa Parejo Navajas, *Primera Aproximación al Pacto Global del Medio Ambiente Por Qué Es una Buena Idea*, 40 REVISTA ARANZADI DE DERECHO AMBIENTAL 177 (2018).

Teresa Parejo-Navajas, *The Proposed Global Pact for the Environment: A Framework for Consistent Realisation of the Sustainable Development Goals*, 48 ENVTL. POL'Y & L. 256 (2018).

Yann Aguila, et al., PRINCIPIOS DE DERECHO AMBIENTAL Y AGENDA 2030 (Tirant Lo Blanch 2019).

Yann Aguila & Jorge E. Viñuales, *A Global Pact for the Environment: Conceptual Foundations*, 28 REV. EUR., COMP. & INT'L ENVTL. L. (2019).

Yann Aguila & Jorge E. Viñuales, A Global Pact for the Environment: Legal Foundations (C-EENRG C-EENRG Report 2019-1 ed. 2019).

Appendix: Bibliography

Adil Najam, *The Case Against a New International Environmental Organization*, 9 Global Governance 367 (2003).

Ana Maria Lebada, *Governments Commence Organizational Work on Global Pact for Environment,* 6 September 2018, IISD (2018), *available at* http://sdg.iisd.org/news/governments-commence-organizational-work-on-global-pact-for-environment/.

Christina Voigt, *How a "Global Pact for the Environment" Could Add Value to International Environmental Law*, 28 Rev. Eur., Comp. & Int'l Envtl. L. 13 (2019).

Elena Loredana Pîrvu, *The New Global Pact for the Environment*, 15 Acta Universitatis Danubius Juridica 5 (2019).

Faye Leone, *Governments Set Dates for Global Pact Discussions, Begin Debating Agenda*, IISD(2018), *available at* http://sdg.iisd.org/news/governments-set-dates-for-global-pact-discussions-begin-debating-agenda/.

Frank Biermann, A World Environment Organization: Solution or Threat for Effective International Environmental Governance? (Routledge Ebook Edition ed. 2005).

Frank Biermann, *The Case for a World Environment Organization*, 42 Environment 22 (2000).

Gerardo Ceballos, et al., *Accelerated Modern Human-Induced Species Losses: Entering the Sixth Mass Extinction*, 1 Sci. Advances (2015).

Gerardo Ceballos, et al., *Population Losses and the Sixth Mass Extinction*, 114 Proc. Nat'l Acad. Sci. U.S. Am. E6089 (2017).

Global Environment Outlook (GEO-6): Summary for Policymakers. pt. 26 (2019).

Increasing the Effectiveness of International Environmental Law: Duties of States, Rights of Individuals (2015).

Jan Zalasiewicz, et al., *The Working Group on the Anthropocene: Summary of Evidence and Interim Recommendations*, 19 Anthropocene 55 (2017).

Johan Rockström, et al., *A Safe Operating Space for Humanity*, 461 Nature (2009).

John Whalley & Ben Zissimos, *What Could a World Environmental Organization Do?*, 1 Global Environmental Politics 29 (2001).

Lijing Cheng, Kevin E. Trenberth, Peter Jacobs, Yongxin Zhang & John Fasullo, *Hurricane Harvey Links to Ocean Heat Content and Climate Change Adaptation*, Earth's Future 1 (2018).

Louis J. Kotzé, Global Environmental Constitutionalism in the Anthropocene (Hart Publishing Paperback Edition ed. 2016).

Maria Magdalena Kenig-Witkowska, *The Draft Global Pact for the Environment*, *at* https://www.documents.clientearth.org/wp-content/uploads/library/2018-10-02-the-draft-global-pact-for-the-environment-ce-en.pdf.

Marisol Anglés Hernández, et al., Global Perspectives on a Global Pact for the Environment § 2019 (Michael Burger, et al. eds., Sabin Center for Climate Change Law, Columbia University 2018).

Mike Hodson & Simon Marvin, *Urbanism in the Anthropocene: Ecological Urbanism or Premium Ecological Enclaves?*, 14 City 298 (2010).

Miroslav Lajcak, (All Permanent Representatives and Permanent Observers to the United Nations ed., The President of the General Assembly 2018).

Nathan Lobel, World Leaders Discuss a Global Pact for the Environment § 2019 (CCSI 2017).

Nicholas A. Robinson, *Fundamental Principles of Law for the Anthropocene?*, 44 Envtl. Pol'y & L. 13 (2014).

Nicholas A. Robinson, *IUCN's Proposed Covenant on Environment & Development*, 13 Pace Envtl. L. Rev. 133 (1995).

Nicholas A. Robinson, *Keynote: Sustaining Society in the Anthropocene Epoch*, 41 Denv. J. Int'l L. & Pol'y 467 (2013).

Niko Urho, et al., International Environmental Governance: Accomplishments and Way Forward (Nordic Council of Ministers 2019).

Not All That Glitters Is Gold: An Analysis of the Global Pact for the Environment Project (2019).

Paul J. Crutzen & Eugene F. Stoermer, *The "Anthropocene,"* 41 Global Change Newsletter 17 (2000).

Paul J. Crutzen, *Geology of Mankind*, 415 Nature 23 (2002).

Paul Voosen, *New Climate Models Forecast a Warming Surge*, 364 Science 222 (2019).

Peter Doran, et al., *Summary of the First Substantive Session of the Ad Hoc Open Ended Working Group Towards a Global Pact for the Environment: 14-18 January 2019,* Vol. 35, No. 1, International Institute for Sustainable Development (2019), *available at* http://enb.iisd.org/unep/globalpact/oewg1/.

Peter Doran, et al., *Summary of the Second Substantive Session of the Ad Hoc Open Ended Working Group Towards a Global Pact for the Environment,* Vol. 35, No. 2, International Institute for Sustainable Development (2019), *available at* http://enb.iisd.org/unep/globalpact/oewg2/.

Peter Doran, et al., *Summary of the Third Substantive Session of the Ad Hoc Open-ended Working Group Towards a Global Pact for the Environment: 20-22 May 2019,* Vol. 35, No. 3, International Institute for Sustainable Development (2019), *available at* http://enb.iisd.org/download/pdf/enb3503e.pdf.

Simon L. Lewis & Mark A. Maslin, *Defining the Anthropocene*, 519 Nature 171 (2015).

Susan Biniaz, *10 Questions to Ask About the Proposed "Global Pact for the Environment." at* http://columbiaclimatelaw.com/files/2017/08/Biniaz-2017-08-Global-Pact-for-the-Environment.pdf.

Susan Biniaz, *The UNGA Resolution on a "Global Pact for the Environment": A Chance to Put the Horse Before the Cart*, 28 Rev. Eur., Comp. & Int'l Envtl. L. 33 (2019).

Teresa Parejo Navajas & Nathan Lobel, *Framing the Global Pact for the Environment: Why It Is Needed, What It Aims to Do, How It Proposes to Do It*, 30 Fordham Envtl. L. Rev. 32 (2018).

United Nations Meetings Coverage and Press Releases, General Assembly Decides to Establish Working Group Aimed at Identifying Gaps in International Environmental Law § 2019 (United Nations UN Meeting coverage, GA 12015, 10 May 2018 ed. 2018).

United Nations Meetings Coverage and Press Releases, New Permanent Representative of Lebanon Presents Credentials (United Nations BIO/5055 ed. 2018).

United Nations Meetings Coverage and Press Releases, New Permanent Representative of Portugal Presents Credentials (United Nations BIO/5022 ed. 2017).

United Nations, The First Global Integrated Marine Assessment: World Ocean Assessment I (Cambridge University Press 2017).

UN, *Voting Record, Item 14 A/72/L.51 as Amended (Towards a Global Pact for the Environment)*, General Assembly 88th Plenary Meeting, UN (2018), *available at* http://papersmart.unmeetings.org/media2/18559921/vr-1.pdf.

What to Expect From a Global Pact for the Environment?, pt. 5 (2019).

White Paper: Toward a Global Pact for the Environment (2017).

Will Steffen, et al., *Planetary Boundaries: Guiding Human Development on a Changing Planet*, 347 Science (2015).

Will Steffen, et al., *The Anthropocene: Conceptual and Historical Perspectives*, 369 Phil. Transactions Royal Soc'y 842 (2011).

World Commission on Environmental Law, *Global Pact for the Environment Introduced to the World*, IUCN-WCEL(2017), *available at* https://www.iucn.org/commissions/world-commission-environmental-law/events-wcel/past-events/global-pact-environment-june-2017.

Yann Aguila, COP 21: "To Arms, Citizens, to Defend Your Rights!" § 2019 (HuffPost 2015).

Yann Aguila & Jorge E. Viñuales, *A Global Pact for the Environment: Conceptual Foundations*, 28 Rev. Eur., Comp. & Int'l Envtl. L. (2019).

Yann Aguila & Jorge E. Viñuales, *A Global Pact for the Environment: Conceptual Foundations*, *in* A Global Pact for the Environment—Legal Foundations (Yann Aguila & Jorge E. Viñuales eds., 2019).

Yann Aguila & Jorge E. Viñuales, A Global Pact for the Environment: Legal Foundations (C-EENRG C-EENRG Report 2019-1 ed. 2019).

Yann Aguila & Patricia Antunes Laydner, *Reforçar a Eficácia do Direito Ambiental do Meio Ambiente: Uma Proposta do Club de Juristes*, 82 Revista de Direito Ambiental (2016).